owl

IDEOLOGY AND
DESIRE IN
RENAISSANCE POETRY ❖

Ideology and Desire in Renaissance Poetry

The Subject of Donne ❖

Ronald Corthell

WAYNE STATE UNIVERSITY PRESS   DETROIT

Copyright © 1997 by Wayne State University Press,
Detroit, Michigan 48201. All rights are reserved.
No part of this book may be reproduced without formal permission.
Manufactured in the United States of America.
01 00 99 98 97   5 4 3 2 1

Library of Congress Cataloging-in-Publication Data

Corthell, Ronald, 1949–
      Ideology and desire in Renaissance poetry : the subject of Donne /
Ronald Corthell.
         p.   cm.
      Includes bibliographical references (p.   ) and index.
      ISBN 0-8143-2676-5 (alk. paper)
      1. Donne, John, 1572–1631—Criticism and interpretation.
2. Literature—History and criticism—Theory, etc.   3. Poetry—
Psychological aspects.   4. Literature—Philosophy.   5. Ideology in
literature.   6. Desire in literature.   7. Renaissance—England.
I. Title.
PR2248.C65   1997
821'.3—dc21   97-14777

For Laura

Contents

ACKNOWLEDGMENTS

I wish to thank a number of individuals and organizations for advice and support during the various stages of this project. David Novarr, late of Cornell University, introduced me to Donne's work early in my doctoral studies, and I wish I were able to discuss my ideas with him these many years later. I value the conversations, criticism, and support of the many Kent friends, colleagues, and students who have directly and indirectly influenced this book. In particular I want to thank Bob Bamberg, who established Kent State's Center for Literature and Psychoanalysis, a rich resource for me and other students of literature and culture over the past ten years. My indebtedness to the current director of the Center, Mark Bracher, is suggested in my many references to his publications, but I want here to express my thanks for his careful reading of drafts of this book and for his friendship and encouragement over the years. Doris Kadish led two lively and helpful reading groups while at Kent, lent an encouraging word to a very early sketch of my project, and spurred me on through her own scholarly productivity and good will.

I had the good fortune to participate in Stephen Greenblatt's National Endowment for the Humanities Summer Seminar on "Renaissance Self-Fashioning" and have greatly appreciated his continuing interest and support over the years since that experience. Like many Renaissance literary scholars, I am deeply indebted to Arthur Marotti, not only for his indispensable published work but also for his close and insightful reading of my manuscript and his support of new work in the field. Similarly, Arthur Kinney has aided me through his scholarly example and his advice on and editing of my own work. Paul Gehl more than held up his end of our long friendship and, in the midst of his own book-in-progress, let me camp out for a month in his study while I worked at the Newberry Library. David Loewenstein made me wince with a trenchant critique of an early version of chapter 2, and Marshall Alcorn provided a helpful reading of chapter 4 along with ideas for further work on the topic. I am greatly obliged to the two anonymous readers for the Wayne State University Press, who helped me see the strengths and weaknesses of my manuscript and offered valuable suggestions for its improvement.

I benefitted from the support of NEH not only for the summer seminar mentioned above but also for a summer stipend to pursue further research for chapters 1 and 3. A short-term fellowship at the Newberry's Center for Renaissance Studies enabled me to work with their deep recusant collection. I was also the beneficiary of semester and summer research awards from Kent State's Office of Research and Graduate Studies. I appreciate the interest and feedback at two of the John Donne Society's conferences and the 1994 "Contextualizing the Renaissance" conference at Binghamton University, where I presented early versions of chapters 2 and 4.

For permission to reprint material that originally appeared elsewhere, I thank the following publishers: University of Texas Press, for "Style and Self in Donne's Satires," *Texas Studies in Literature and Language* 24 (1982): 155–84; the English Department, North Carolina State University, for " 'Coscus onely breeds my just offence': A Note on Donne's 'Satire II' and the Inns of Court," *John Donne Journal* 6 (1987) 25–31; the Center for Medieval and Early Renaissance Studies, for "Donne's 'Disparitie': Inversion, Gender, and the Subject of Love in Some Songs and Sonnets," *Exemplaria* 1 (1989): 17–42; the Department of English, University of Massachusetts, for " 'The Secrecy of Man': Recusant Discourse and the Elizabethan Subject," *English Literary Renaissance* 19 (1989): 272–90; and Simon & Schuster, for "The Obscure Object of Desire: Donne's Anniversaries and the Cultural Production of Elizabeth Drury," in *Critical Essays on John Donne,* ed. Arthur F. Marotti (New York: G. K. Hall & Co., 1994), 123–40.

This book is dedicated to my wife, Laura Bartolo, who sustained me with advice, criticism, and encouragement throughout the long process of discovering what I wanted to say.

Introduction:
The Subject of Donne

In the introduction to their collection, *Soliciting Interpretation,* Elizabeth D. Harvey and Katherine Eisaman Maus noted that "recent changes in the methodology of reading Renaissance texts have important consequences not only for previously neglected or undervalued literature but for the texts that used to be absolutely central to the New Critical Project. . . . With the eclipse of formalism, some of these texts have suffered a relative neglect or marginalization—a displacement that has been particularly striking in the case of Donne."[1] My book does not aim to "rescue" Donne from the margins of literary history; rather, I want to approach the situation described by Harvey and Maus from something like the opposite direction. Donne has been done and undone. Should we be done with him? If Donne's poetry has indeed been marginalized, is the explanation suggested by Harvey and Maus sufficient to explain why? To rephrase these questions: In the present situation of English studies, which includes the interrogation of the canon, what would be the value of reading and teaching Donne?[2] This question is inseparable from the question of *how* to read and teach Donne after new historicism, and I want to place particular emphasis on the interdependence of motive and method when we read Renaissance texts. Questions of how and why we read these texts concern aspects of the relationship between literary texts and history while the methodological question has to do with the related and vexed issue of the relationship between literary texts and ideology in the Renaissance. On the other hand, the question of "Why Donne now?" has to do with the reader's own ideological position—with the ideology of literature. That is, the more or less professional issue raised by Harvey and Maus touches on a fundamental question concerning the value of literary studies. One benefit of the debate over new historicism has been to open a discussion of readers' investments

11

in the Renaissance and Renaissance literature, and I hope to contribute to that discussion in this book on the study of Donne's poetry.

My thinking about Donne is thus shaped by the context of recent theoretical debate over the relationship between literature and history. This debate underlies such diverse books on Donne as Arthur Marotti's *John Donne: Coterie Poet* and Thomas Docherty's *John Donne, Undone,* as well as Richard Strier's *Resistant Structures: Particularity, Radicalism, and Renaissance Texts,* which includes a central chapter on Donne directed at theoretical issues raised by scholars like Marotti and Docherty.[3] Both Marotti and Docherty write out of a desire to connect literature and history. Marotti proceeds on the assumption that we need to reconstruct as best we can the original conditions of literary production in order to understand the literary text. His work, which began independent of Renaissance new historicism, shares some features of that body of work while also revamping a biographical method of criticism in proffering a "complete" account of Donne the writer. Marotti's careerist Donne, masterfully fashioned out of R. C. Bald's biography, is firmly placed in the writing environment of the late sixteenth and early seventeenth centuries.

Docherty's historical aim looks at first to be similar to Marotti's. Docherty opens his book with the charge that "much of what passes for contemporary criticism of Donne contrives to ignore the historical culture which informed his writings, and the ideology which conditioned the act of writing or 'authority' itself." As it turns out, however, Docherty's historical project has little in common with Marotti's. He does not aspire to offer an account of Donne's entire career but, on the contrary, resists the urge to present a finished portrait. His understanding of historical context is perhaps best described as an attempt to problematize the history of ideas. Where Marotti aims at constructing more or less definitive social contexts for interpreting all of Donne's writing, Docherty speaks more broadly of "three main culturally significant and historically problematical areas which bear on Donne's writings: the scientific, which troubles secular historicity itself; the socio-cultural, in which woman raises certain defences in this male poet; and the aesthetic, in which mimetic writing itself becomes fraught with difficulty."[4] If Marotti aims at a demystification of Donne, Docherty attempts what might be called a remystification; he wants "to release Donne's texts into their full obscurity" in order to produce a reading "which stresses the very difficulty of 'meaning' or 'intending' for a writer such as Donne in the late European Renaissance."[5] This historical Donne resembles Stanley Fish's Donne—who resembles us. As Fish puts it, "Donne is sick and his poetry is sick; but he and it are sick in ways that are interestingly related to the contemporary critical scene."[6] Thus we have two quite distinct historicized versions of Donne. Both seem intent on producing a Donne as other: in Marotti's case this is a matter of embedding Donne's texts in an alien system of literary production; in Docherty the aim is to show Donne's failure to be himself, to be "Donne." For Marotti, being historical means showing that Donne is not like us; for Docherty, it means opening text and context—historicity itself—to poststructuralist analysis in order to show that Donne is not Donne.

Strier's book, which, along with Marotti's, figures prominently in my first chapter, is a lively and well-argued defense of close reading against the sorts of historical and theoretical frameworks—which Strier calls "schemes"—employed by Marotti and Docherty. Deeply suspicious of "any sort of approach to texts that knows in advance what they will or must be doing or saying, or, on the other hand, what they cannot possibly be doing or saying," Strier works hard to attend to what a text might be *saying* without prematurely deciding what that saying might *mean*.[7] Although he would "resist" a poststructuralist problematic, Strier is closer to Docherty's position than to Marotti's in the sense of being in favor of a release of Donne's texts into the difficulties of reading them. He especially fears totalizing systems of meaning as employed by both old and new historicists who, he argues, have occluded the radical "Jack" Donne so powerfully promoted by Strier's model critic, William Empson.[8]

Before staking out my own position in this debate I want to note that there are at least two levels to the argument about literature and history. I cannot claim to have kept them separate in what follows but it seems worth mentioning here that critics are debating 1) the issue of the relationship between the literary text and history, which includes "the times" during which a text was produced but also the history of its reception up to and including our own "times," and 2) the problem of a relationship between literary *study* and historical *study*. The ongoing critique of new historicism testifies, in fact, to the interrelationship of the two controversies; attacks on new historicist analyses of the relationships between literary works and other discourses of the period generally include a charge that the "history" is bad or that a historical method has been displaced by a poststructuralist text-mania.[9] In *Trials of Authorship*, for example, Jonathan Crewe has characterized new historicism as a romance that misrepresents the past in terms of the present. Alan Liu unmasks new historicism as "an ultimate formalism so 'powerful' that it colonizes the very world as its 'text' "; new historicism is not historical at all but a self-absorbed confession of an embarrassment by history.[10] In an historicist analysis of new historicism, Brook Thomas summarizes the dilemma of historical critics also formed by poststructuralism; new historicists, he writes, "claim authority for their reconstructions of literary history by appealing to historical evidence" while "they have to admit that their evidence is itself an inevitably partial construction of the past from a present perspective."[11] Thomas argues that this interpretive double bind is produced by "an ahistorical notion of disinterestedness"; we need to remind ourselves that disinterestedness is useful, that it is a variable, historically specific form of empowerment:

13

so long as we believe that we are empowered by knowledge of our situation in the world and so long as we believe that that situation has in part been determined by the past, the most empowering study of the past will be the one that comes as close as possible to telling how it really was. To state my point as a paradox: the present has an interest in maintaining a belief in disinterested inquiry into our past.[12]

I take Thomas's central point to be the location of the historical critic in contradiction; disinterest is always interested. Victoria Kahn has discussed the Renaissance roots of this conundrum, arguing that "a continuity of humanist reflection on 'knowledge and human interests' extends from the Renaissance to the present."[13] Kahn in fact provides a catalogue of familiar critical dilemmas in humanist concerns with the textuality of history, with "uncertainty about the criterion of ethical and judgment," with "conflicting conceptions of literature . . . as moral philosophy or aesthetic pleasure," to suggest that "many Renaissance texts can themselves be seen to reflect on the politics of Renaissance studies—the political dimension of literature, the political uses of literature, and—not least of all—the political interest of the image of literary autonomy." New historicist criticism thus "reproduces in a modern key the constitutive paradox of humanism, the interest in disinterestedness."[14]

I have quoted Thomas and Kahn at some length because they mark out the place of contradiction where I find Donne—beginning in the Satires and continuing through the struggles of the Holy Sonnets—and his readers— beginning with the likes of, say, Donne himself (who gave us "Jack Donne") or Thomas Carew and Isaac Walton, and continuing to present-day readers such as myself and the critics discussed in this book. What I argue in the following chapters is that Donne's textual practice in some of his poetry rehearses important aspects of the problematic relationship between literature and history outlined above by Thomas and Kahn. This textual practice, continued and developed by his readers and installed in the academic field of Renaissance literary studies, contributed to and continues to contribute to the creation of a literary ideology that has become an important way of thinking about the relationship between subjects and history.

In this study I understand ideology in a general, post-Althusserian sense as "a 'cement' that holds society together,"[15] an ensemble of social discourses and practices that call us into certain "subject-positions." I am sympathetic, however, to the arguments of cultural critics such as Richard Johnson who find such a broad definition to be lacking in critical power. Johnson contends that the ideological is what must be demonstrated not assumed in cultural analysis:

It may well be that all our knowledge of the world and all our conceptions of the self are "ideological," or more or less ideological, in that they are rendered partial by the operation of interests and of power. But this seems to me a proposition that has to be plausibly argued in particular cases rather than assumed at the beginning of every analysis.[16]

Johnson is right: the idea that everything is ideological does not get us very far. A related problem of theologizing tendencies in new historicist ideological critique is lampooned in Graham Bradshaw's title for the opening essay of *Misrepresentations:* "Is Shakespeare Evil?"[17] What needs to be resisted here is a monolithic, totalizing model of ideology.[18] The "social cement" analogy is somewhat unfortunate because it suggests a rigidity which seems inadequate to describe the various and complex ways ideology is experienced. A useful corrective is Terry Eagleton's understanding of ideology as "an inherently complex formation which, by inserting individuals into history in a variety of ways, allows of multiple kinds and degrees of access to that history."[19] This view is built on Althusser's concept of interpellation, but it allows for variation and failure in "particular cases." It conceives of ideology actively, as a *process* of "hailing" individuals to certain positions rather than as a fixed set of categories.[20]

This approach to ideology is aligned with recent thinking on the idea of the subject. Paul Smith has argued for "discerning the subject" by building upon Althusser's fundamental thesis "that subjectivity is constructed through ideological intervention and that 'subjects' are interpellated, called into position by specific social discourses."[21] For Smith, interpellation "is not complete and monolithic," as it appears to be in Althusser's formulation; "rather, interpellation also produces contradiction and negativity" (152). Smith's position is consistent with a number of recent developments in theory, such as the *Social Semiotics* of Robert Hodge and Gunther Kress. Hodge and Kress also emphasize contradiction in their orientation to semiotic systems as processes of constructing relations of power and solidarity in a social context. In readings of texts ranging from billboards to Cimabue Madonnas to Wonder Woman comics, they explore ideological forms as "the site of struggles and renegotiations of meanings."[22] This sense of struggle and renegotiation is also reflected in Stephen Greenblatt's emphasis on negotiation and circulation and Louis Montrose's treatment of subjectification as "an equivocal process."[23]

The point is to explore the particular valence of a literary work and an ideological formation. Eagleton has described this relation as a *production* of ideology. Revising classic Marxist aesthetics, he emphasizes "the closeness of relation between the 'ideological' and the 'aesthetic' " without reducing the relation to a homology:

> the problem-solving process of the text is never merely a matter of its reference outwards to certain pre-existent ideological cruxes. It is, rather, a matter of the "ideological" presenting itself in the form of the "aesthetic" and *vice versa*—of an "aesthetic" solution to ideological conflict producing in its turn an aesthetic problem which demands ideological resolution, and so on.[24]

15

Although Eagleton speaks of ideological and aesthetic *forms,* his approach would seem to escape the charge of ahistorical formalism that has been lodged against new historicism. In his formulation there is an "ideology of the text" such that it is really inappropriate to speak of the relations between text and ideology since the textual production of ideology "actively extends and elaborates" ideology[25]: "ideology is not the 'truth' of the text. . . . The 'truth' of the text is not an essence but a practice—the practice of its relation to ideology, and in terms of that to history."[26] Formal relationships are explored as "transactions which figure in the text as a process of more or less visible conflicts produced, resolved and thereby reproduced";[27] the goal, then, is not a poetics of culture but more like a rhetoric, a study of the process of producing ideological forms.[28]

A last and, as the book develops, increasingly decisive aspect of ideological analysis requires attending to the operations of desire in the process of interpellation. Donne is first and foremost canonized as a love poet, and an engagement with his work on ideology risks throwing out the baby with the bathwater if it does not consider the role of desire in ideology. The rich tradition of psychoanalytic discourse on the Renaissance and particularly Renaissance literature is a powerful corrective to new historicist privileging of the Symbolic order. It offers a way, as Slavoj Žižek writes, of "thinking out the link between Ideological State Apparatuses [say, the Elizabethan Court] and ideological interpellation: how does the Ideological State Apparatus . . . 'internalize' itself; how does it produce the effect of subjectivation, of recognition of one's ideological position?"[29] Žižek's answer is the paradox that interpellation succeeds by failing, that "this 'internalization' never fully succeeds, that there is always a residue, a leftover, a stain of traumatic irrationality and senselessness sticking to it, and that *this leftover, far from hindering the full submission of the subject to the ideological command, is the very condition of it.*"[30] Žižek's "residue," his "sublime object of ideology," is the mysterious "object-cause of desire" which is supposed to be hidden in the Other (here, ideology) and which catches the subject at a level deeper even than identification. In Žižek's counter-intuitive Lacanian formulation, ideology is a fantasy construction which, far from offering an escape from reality, serves as the path to the Real of desire, that stain or leftover which is not integrated.

This way of thinking about ideology from a Lacanian understanding of fantasy resonates in some respects with the emphasis in Eagleton and in some new historicist criticism on an extremely complex relationship between ideology and the literary text, even as it critiques such approaches. Žižek's theory and practice of ideological critique is the *terminus ad quem* of a conversation between psychoanalysis and new historicism carried on throughout the book, with the qualification that my purpose is also to read Žižek (as well as new historicists) in light of Donne as a *terminus a quo.* This colloquy facilitates a circulation of "interestedness" between Donne and his contexts, on the one hand, and the reader's contexts and Donne, on the other, a doubled focus on interpellations of Donne and readers of Donne that I am calling a "subject of Donne." In each chapter my aim is to explore the interrelationships of representation, identification, and desire in Donne's poetry and criticism of that poetry, but I also mean to suggest a shift in emphasis, invited by Donne's texts, from representation, to identification, to desire.

Whereas new historicists have tended to focus on a monolithic subject of power, I construe the "subject of Donne" to be multifarious in two closely related respects. First, I extend the notion of the subject of Donne to include the speaking subject of Donne's texts, the reading subject, and the academic "subject" known as Donne's poetry. The academic subject is key here, because I maintain that the study of Donne's poetry is, in actuality, a study of speaking and reading subjects dedicated to producing a form of literary subjectivity. Second, I regard the constitution of this subject (speaking, reading, academic) as a process of being called to various subject-positions. But as Smith and Žižek argue, this process of interpellation must also reckon with desire, which can produce contradiction and resistance—Žižek's "residue"—as well as containment and domination. This interplay of desire and ideology, I argue, constitutes a powerful form of literary subjectivity. Thus I treat Donne, in all senses outlined above, as the site of an ideological struggle to represent a Renaissance literary subjectivity that continues to influence the practice of teachers and scholars of Renaissance literature.

In writing about Donne's productions of ideology, then, I too am doing work on ideology, on the ideology of Donne. My approach to Donne's writings as sites of a process of subjectification attempts to acknowledge my own subject-position as a professional reader of Donne. Unlike John Carey or Marotti, I do not aim primarily at a reconstruction of Donne; what interests me are the ways we might construct Donne today and, more important, the stakes and consequences of such constructions.[31] Such considerations, it seems to me, are a part of any historical study. The newer historical readings of Donne tend to limit historical context to a reconstruction of the past, whereas I want to include as part of the historical meaning of Donne the act of reading him in an English literature class.

In this study I have tried to be cognizant of what Tony Bennett calls "reading formations," by which he means "a set of discursive and intertextual determinations which organise and animate the practice of reading, connecting texts and readers in specific relations to one another in constituting readers as reading subjects of particular types and texts as objects-to-be-read in particular ways."[32] Marotti has presented the most complete reconstruction to date of the conditions within which Donne's poems were produced. I do not believe, however, that these conditions provide us with a decisive structure of interpretation; as Bennett's definition of the reading formation suggests, such conditions are continually under construction themselves.[33]

Beneath the theory of coterie production and consumption of texts are some conventional assumptions about authorial intention and the original audience of a work. Marotti's reconstruction of the coterie conditions of production is really a reconstruction of Donne's intentions as perfectly harmonious with his reception by the original readers.[34] In a search for the original intent, Marotti revives Donne as the monarch of wit, master of meanings.

I see the speaking and reading subjects of Donne's poems as much less settled, in process. In poem after poem the reader is pushed and pulled between identification with a particular ideological formation and discomfort (Žižek's "leftover") with this identification. This oscillation between ideology and desire in a Donne poem is not a transcendence of ideology but, in Eagleton's phrase, a "practice of its relation to ideology," and hence, an action productive of another ideology, a literary ideology.

Thus I start by agreeing with Fish that it is a mistake "to put Donne in possession of his poetry and therefore of himself."[35] Donne, I believe, was deeply troubled about the possibility/impossibility of being someone, of being "Donne." The critical tradition has also oscillated between, to use new historicist terms, containment and subversion in its representations of Donne.[36] This division in Donne forms the substrate of Donne criticism: Donne the Petrarchist/Donne the anti-Petrarchist; Donne the monarchist/Donne the republican; Donne the Catholic/Donne the Protestant; Donne the winner/Donne the loser; or finally, Donne's own creation, Dr. Donne/Jack Donne. What interests me is why this subject of Donne might matter to me and my students. This is, I feel, a historical question, though not in the sense implied in Marotti's historicization of Donne.

I have tried to present Donne's writing as creative work on ideology that practices a variety of relationships to ideology and in turn produces a variety of "ideologies of the text." Donne activates and is activated by a considerable range of literary forms equivocally related to ideological conflicts, that is, forms which can be read as either resolutions or reproductions of ideological conflicts. These conflicts turn on some of the basic boundary disputes of the period, including self and other, the sacred and the secular, men and women, the private and the public, the human and the not-human. Donne's texts generally work at the site of these boundaries, opening and closing them in a process that involves the reader in ideological work on frequently interrelated questions of politics, gender, and religion.[37]

Donne's poetic work on ideology is worthy of special attention for two reasons. First, some of Donne's "solutions" to ideological conflict continue to form us as subjects of love and power. The interpellative power of his poems is particularly evident in their constructions of gender, privacy, and mutuality. The second reason is related to the first. Donne's creations of various subjects of love and power afford a perspective on some of the paradoxes of new historicism. What consequences might a rereading of Donne's texts have for new historicism? The various answers to this question must emerge in the individual readings that follow, but my hypothesis is that Donne can help us understand why we tend to construct "culture" as a poetic text.[38]

The first chapter, "Donne's New Historicism and the Practice of Satire," focusses on the subject of power, particularly as it has been analyzed by new historicist work on representation in Renaissance drama. The chapter begins by placing formal verse satire in a new historicist critical context, but it then inverts text and context to read new historicist texts in the context of Donne's subject of satire. My thesis in this chapter is that Donne's satirical rendition of late Elizabethan ideology, on the one hand, and new historicist representations of the same period, on the other, are early and late stages of a long historical process of working on the relationship between the literary text and ideology. In the Satires and in new historicist essays, the satirist and the critic produce a profoundly equivocal discourse on the subject. On the one hand, the subject is entirely contained by the ideological formations he satirizes/criticizes; on the other, satirist and critics want to reclaim a strength from their powerlessness. Like most Elizabethan verse satirists, Donne is obsessed with the problem of investing moral authority in a subject who speaks for a moral minority. Donne's Satires display the instability of the marginal subject of satire. Donne the satirist is repeatedly invaded by the other, subject of satire by object of satire. As a consequence, Donne's satirical production of ideology repeatedly slides into a satirical production of the subject of satire. In the act of defining the object of his attack Donne discovers his own desire in the object. The solution is not to do anything, or rather, the solution is to write, to textualize the problem. This textual practice, emerging in a context of early modern conflicts over authority and representation, contributes to the creation of a new, literary subject of history.

Two chapters on the "subject of love" follow. Donne's love poetry is his most nuanced body of work on the process of subjectification, but recent emphasis on the politics of love poetry has replaced an earlier, oversimplified view of Donne as the poet of mutual love with a new, but equally reductive portrait of a "cheerfully sexist" and "absolutist" lover.[39] Chapter 2 challenges this type of politicization of love poetry as symptomatic both of new historicism's exclusively theatrical model of power and of its conflation of desire and power. My aim is to complicate this understanding by treating the poems as struggles of a desiring subject of love to hold a position of male hegemony. In many of Donne's poems overtly concerned with sexual politics the subject of love and the subject of power work at cross purposes; although Donne's representations of women in these poems engage the reader in the ideological work of recuperating a masculinist position, the interpellation is seldom completely successful; the poems remain sites of gender struggle.[40] Chapter 3 examines Donne's poetry of "mutual love" in competing contexts of coterie poetics and Protestant marriage theory. Donne's version of "mutual love" shares some discursive origins with Protestant teaching on companionate marriage, but it finally offers a different resolution of contradictions from that provided by the Protestant ideology of marriage. In Donne's poems, I argue, the defense of mutual love is constructed as a defense of poetry; showing how these poems participate in a larger cultural production of privacy, I emphasize that Donne constructs the private life as a literary domain based on elitist and masculinist assumptions and that this construction has a continuing effect on the way literariness is conceptualized as an autonomous zone of privileged textuality.

This thesis of a literary ideology produced by Donne's writing is further tested in chapter 4 through a reading of the Anniversaries and the critical controversy that has attended the poems since their first publication in 1611–12. The Anniversaries gather together the themes of power, love, and gender explored in my earlier chapters. In foregrounding the problem of representing Elizabeth Drury, Donne, it seems to me, throws the whole cultural project of creating meaningful symbolic forms into relief. Not coincidentally, the Anniversaries have functioned as a prime site of critical debate about the Renaissance; this tradition of response to the poems is, to a large extent, the subject of my reading. I find the problem of the Anniversaries—its representation of Elizabeth Drury—reproduced in the rich and contentious critical history of the poems, which has used them to represent John Donne or specific developments in Renaissance intellectual and religious history. My reading attempts to balance a new historicist thematics of power and representation and a psychoanalytic focus on love and identification against a feminist critique of these perspectives based on the place of the daughter in Renaissance patriarchy. This chapter extends my discussion of Donne's contribution to the invention of literature by developing a gendered account of the link between literary/critical production and the production of the "Idea of a Woman" in the Anniversaries; it also points to the need for further study of the construction of daughters as cultural ideals in other works involving transactions between artists and patrons.

Chapter 5 deals with perhaps the central project of this literary ideology, the construction of inwardness; here I discuss Donne's Holy Sonnets in the light of competing accounts of subjectivity offered by new historicist and psychoanalytic critics. Although I argue from a historicist perspective that the powerful sense of subjectivity in these poems is the effect of ideological conflict not the cause, I also suggest, in line with Joel Fineman's psychoanalytic argument, that the subjectivity-effect so produced harmonizes in many respects with a psychoanalytic account of the structure of subjectivity.[41] Thus I mean to suggest a close connection between literariness and psychoanalysis. I press this argument at length in the last third of the chapter, where Žižek's Lacanian understanding of the ideological fantasy and recent psychoanalytic work on masochism and male subjectivity are read in the light of the famous Holy Sonnet "Batter my heart."

The new historicism has been described as a discourse of power and as an embarrassed discourse of powerlessness.[42] This contradiction is perhaps to be expected, given the New Historicist reliance on equivocal, paradoxical rhetoric. New historicist style is the style of Donne, as it was described by the New Critics. As mentioned earlier, one of my purposes has been to see what happens when Donne is introduced into the new construction of Renaissance culture instead of leaving him preserved in a wellwrought urn of earlier criticism. What I see happening is something like a return of the repressed. The critical tradition built around Donne's fetishized texts is still with us; as Liu and others are beginning to show, it continues as an interpellative force in much of Renaissance new historicism. Unlike Liu and others, however, I do not think this is necessarily bad news for new historicism in particular, or for literary criticism in general. The choice may not be so much one between formalism or non-formalism as between the possible uses of formalism. Will it be used to read culture as a vast poem or to explore the history of cultural forms, including the ongoing production and reception of forms by and in which we live? In this study I argue that Donne's writing is a formalist practice; by this I mean that Donne's poems work on ideological forms to produce solutions to extratextual problems. But I also think that we need to see writing about Donne in a similar light, as an intervention in a professional discourse that is also ideological.

Unlike Docherty, I do not dismiss earlier writing on Donne because I think of this writing as part of the Donne I am reading.[43] On the other hand, I want to read against or beside this Donne to gain a purchase on the ideological stakes of reading Donne in one way or another. This entails reading against some of the dominant reading formations that have contributed to Donne's installation in the canon in order to suggest how Donne's famous paradoxes and ironies and commentary on them work to control or contain a variety of threats to the speaking/reading subject. Recent criticism has emphasized Donne's strong identification with Jacobean absolutism. In another vein, Anthony Low has argued that Donne's love poems "reject tradition, authority, and other forms of discussion based on natural or social values, and instead begin with the absolute subject."[44] These two ways of conceiving the subject of Donne's poetry offer a choice between an Althusserian subject of power "subdu'd / To what it works in" and a creative subject of love capable of "transcending and eventually transforming" the conditions of its production.[45] Both views can be called absolutist, and I think we are coming to feel such a choice as a misunderstanding of the process of subjectification.

The following chapters are attempts at "discerning the subject" of Donne, challenging conclusions about either absolute subjection or transcendence.[46] Subjectivity is constructed "in strange way." Donne's poems offer neither an absolute subject nor a subject of history but an opportunity to participate in the work of creating ideological forms. This activity, which I take to be preeminently "authorized" by the literary ideology I inhabit, is a subject worth teaching.

ONE

Donne's New Historicism
and the Practice of Satire

MY READING OF Donne's Satires is constructed around the question of how
the writing of satires might fit into current poststructuralist and mainly new
historicist accounts of "subjectification" in late Elizabethan England. I understand subjectification as the "equivocal process" defined by Louis Montrose,
a process "on the one hand, shaping individuals as loci of consciousness
and initiators of action—endowing them with the capacity for agency; and,
on the other hand, positioning, motivating, and constraining them within—
subjecting them to—social networks and cultural codes that ultimately exceed
their comprehension or control."[1] Donne's Satires, I contend, are among
the fullest performances of this equivocal process in English Renaissance
literature; they produce a style of critique that rehearses the dilemma that has
come to characterize new historicism.

Donne's Satires work on a particular ideological crisis that, to borrow
John N. King's formulation, concerns "the relative merits of internal and
external authority."[2] Robert Weimann has recently discussed this question of
"bifold authority in Reformation discourse" as "a revolutionary potential for
redefining the relations between the authority of power and an alternative
source of authority that resides in conviction, knowledge, and the competent
uses of language. . . . Henceforth the authority derived from power and the
power of a new, subjective type of author-ity in the uses of discourse would
engage far more profoundly and frequently in conflict and contradiction."[3]
The Satires are a production of such conflicts and contradictions.[4] Donne tries
to center the satiric project in the satirist, but this subject of satire is divided by
competing models of authority; Donne's confidence in his verbal power exists
alongside the desire for an "authority derived from power." Thus Donne's
work on the ideological crisis of authority produces something like a de

Manian literary text, which "simultaneously asserts and denies the authority of its own rhetorical mode."[5] By questioning its own authority, however, Donne's text opens to critique the relations between power and authority in general and succeeds as a powerful representation of a moment of historical change.

The fashion for formal verse satire in the 1590s has not figured in new historicist representations of the English Renaissance. The theatrical construction of court culture by new historicists and new cultural critics might seem to offer little room for a Renaissance satyr, but a moment's reflection will suggest that this need not be so. The anthropological paradigm that informs much new historicist work would seem receptive to the self-conscious "primitivism" of much Renaissance verse satire.[6] In particular, the notorious Renaissance confusion of satires and satyrs would seem to offer an opening for new historicist work on satirists as a species of Renaissance wild men on the rampage in 1590s London. Verse satire can also claim the attention of new historicists for two very specific reasons. First, these writers overtly attacked social problems and abuses of power produced by the system described by the new cultural critics. The question thus arises as to whether verse satire functioned as a radical or oppositional discourse such as those described by Jonathan Dollimore in *Radical Tragedy.*[7] Second, and closely related to its critical aims, verse satire constituted an important literary form of self-fashioning in the 1590s. It could be used as a vehicle for launching a career, literary or nonliterary, and deserves consideration as a part of the signifying systems of patronage and literature as portrayed by Arthur Marotti and Richard Helgerson.[8]

Criticism of the 1940s and '50s on the genre and style of Elizabethan satire, best exemplified by the work of Arnold Stein and Alvin Kernan, captured this satiric project of self-presentation with the New-Critical category of the persona. The historical criticism of Donne's Satires that appeared in the 1970s and early '80s put earlier approaches to the test and succeeded in demonstrating Donne's violations of generic and stylistic canons of decorum for satire. At the same time, these and other critics treated the five poems as a sequence structured around narrative and thematic patterns of moral and religious awakening that were held to constitute a creative departure from classical and Renaissance precedent. Richard C. Newton's claim can serve as a summary of this liberal humanist criticism of the Satires: "Donne the satirist explores satire to the full, and by doing so becomes more than a satirist. . . . It is in the Satyres that the early Donne most completely encounters that doubting, questioning, and critical aspect of his character and makes it part of his wisdom as a poet and as a man."[9] My own readings are equivocally related to this tradition of criticism. I oppose the trend of some moral critics to detach the poems from discursive formations of the 1590s. At the same time, I want to extend the work of genre and stylistic critics by emphasizing the interrelationship of generic and stylistic categories and other late-Elizabethan ideological formations. Like all of the critics mentioned, I focus on the figure of the satirist, but the gist of my argument is that the subject of satire is divided and thus represents the problem, not the solution.

The uneasy relationship with earlier criticism is implied in my replacement of the concept of satiric persona with the concept of the "subject of satire." I prefer this concept to the earlier one because it suspends belief in Donne's mastery and thereby allows for the possibility of a Donne constructed by as well as ruling "The universall Monarchy of wit."[10] This sense that one is constructed by language, by the Lacanian Other, is, I argue, a major theme of the Satires.

I extend this understanding of subjectification by the Other to my own status as a reading subject. I want to acknowledge that in this and following chapters my own production of Donne is crossed by similar problems since it too is implicated in a process of subjectification—the production of Donne as a subject and of myself as a reading subject. As Alan Liu and others have recently argued, the *textual* construction of a subject—speaking or reading— has a way of containing us within representation.[11] A project of *reading* Donne against or even within his "times," like Donne's project of writing formal verse satires on the "times," runs the risk of *privileging* a certain kind of text instead of truly historicizing it, that is, connecting it to history. Donne's writing is centrally engaged by the problem of the relationship between literary text and history, and in this respect it anticipates some of the dilemmas of new historicism.

I realize that in making this claim I run the risk of collapsing differences between the Renaissance and the present. Liu has strongly critiqued this tendency in new historicism, calling it "our latest Romantic ideology unable to differentiate meaningfully between then and now, unable—at least at its present level of thought [1989]—to do more than be driven toward a refuge of intellect lost in history."[12] But this formulation misrepresents the problem of historicism, which is, as Dominic LaCapra argues, "how to understand and to negotiate varying degrees of proximity and distance in the relation to the 'other' that is both outside and inside ourselves."[13] Liu's own historicizing of new historicism, it seems to me, points to a link (though not an identity) between then and now. New historicism, he writes, is "our latest post-May 1970, post-May 1968, post-1917, . . . post-1789 (and so forth) imagination of an active role for intellect in the renascence of society." The last phrase suggests what is occluded by that parenthetic "and so forth": namely, that the "Romanticizing" of the Renaissance, at least as Liu has described it, began in the Renaissance. If one wants to find "a refuge of intellect lost in History," or a "mirror of desire" in which "the interpreter can *fantasize* about subverting dominance while dreaming away the total commitments of contestation," or, to select just one of many other of Liu's representations of postmodern anemia, a declaration of "self-effacement in the face of history,"[14] one could make a strong case for beginning in the Renaissance with such texts as *The Praise of Folly* or *Utopia*.

Or Donne's Satires. The Satires display an ongoing concern with their authority as discourses in the changing discursive economy of the times. I would suggest that Donne is working on two dimensions of the relationship between the literary and historical subject, the first being the extremely complicated relationship between the authority of his text and the authority of power and the second, less prominent but still important, being the relationship between the past and the present. Such an invention of early modern subjectivity is also the project of new historicism. Emerging both in Donne and in new historicist rhetoric are equivocal and processual representations of the relationship between text and power, literature and history, relationships that seem to underlie the matching "equivocal processes" of subjectification. What I am suggesting is an inversion of Liu's charge that new historicists have rewritten the Renaissance in their own image: the new historicist text is modeled after the equivocal Renaissance text. Liu is right to identify the formalism in new historicist writing, but this formalism is a legacy of the Renaissance "canonization" of texts, most famously enacted in Donne's poem of that title. In the end I hope also to suggest a somewhat equivocal relationship between Donne and new historicism by using new historicist texts to discuss Donne and Donne's texts to test new historicist representations of the Renaissance.

Arthur Marotti's *John Donne: Coterie Poet* is the most sustained and important effort to differentiate between then and now with respect to Donne's poetry. The reading of the Satires that follows acknowledges Marotti's importance at every turn but argues for a different way of understanding the relationship between text and context, a way that finally denies the last word on interpretation to the moment of production. Marotti argues that a study of Donne the satirist ought to begin with an understanding of the literary and social environment of the Inns of Court, where Donne began to write. This project is paralleled by another, usually overriding, concern with Donne's biography, specifically, the biography written by R. C. Bald. The subsumption of semiotic system to biographical master narrative produces a much-needed though limited interpretation of Donne's writings as "reflections" of his writing environments. Text reflects context. Marotti draws upon Gregory Bateson's highly pertinent ideas on "metacommunication," a form of discourse in which "the subject of discourse is the relationship between the speakers" and which constitutes "all exchanged cues and propositions about (a) codification and (b) the relationship between communicators."[15] The "metacommunicative power" of Donne's texts is increased, Marotti argues, by "[t]he basic fact that Donne's verse was originally coterie literature, . . . for author and reader had a social relationship apart from the text that could be evoked as a context of composition and of reception/interpretation" (20–21). In Marotti's application of this theory to Donne's texts both the relationship between the speakers and the codes are reified, represented as stable and coherent systems of relationship and signification reflected in Donne's texts. To put it another way, the coterie seems to exist independently of the metacommunicative texts, where we might expect to find that the texts have a more productive relationship to context. The result is that Donne's Satires and other texts assume a stability and finish as reflections of the fixed codes and relationships that work against the "interactive" relationship between text and context on which Marotti constructs his theory of the coterie.

Marotti goes on to argue that Donne set forth in his letters "a model of communication with his coterie reader that he sought, I believe, in most of his poetry," one characterized by the "negation or absence of discursive meaning. . . . Donne's dream of communication was one in which the reader or audience or congregation repeated, or mirrored in their responses, the thoughts and feelings of the author who made the text" (21–22).[16] The problem is that Marotti tends to write about Donne's relationship to the coterie according to this dream of transparency. Donne's intentions are generally assumed to be clear and to match the expectations of his audience. When Donne's intentions seem unclear, Marotti saves a coherent Donne by seeing deliberate manipulation of the coterie reader, "to clear the way, in his own and in his reader's minds, for higher understanding" (22). But this assurance breaks down too: "Donne thus seems to have created a kind of double relationship with his readers, alternately adversarial and intimate, sometimes to the point of being insulting and complimentary at the same time. Perhaps it was necessary for him to feel both distance and immediacy in the coterie circumstances in which he wrote" (23).

My readings portray a Donne who is usually constructing, but not always mastering, intentions, such as the intention to insult or compliment. A semiotic approach can help elucidate this "risk factor" of textual production, particularly in its analysis of the intricate relationship between context or system and text. As Gunther Kress and Robert Hodge have noted with respect to any semiotic system, "a system is constantly being reproduced and reconstituted in texts." In this process of reproduction, "the set of meanings is constantly deployed, and in being deployed is at risk of disruption."[17] This formulation shifts the emphasis from identification of codes to analysis of the ongoing process whereby codes are constructed, reinforced, or tested.

When an apparently simple satire like "Satire 1" ("Away thou fondling motley humorist") blurs "the boundary between self-satirization and satiric attack on the outside world," Marotti recuperates this apparent loss of identity by ascribing it to the ambivalence of the group Donne was addressing: "so too Donne and his readers were, no doubt, morally, intellectually, and emotionally ambivalent about their own attraction to the world outside their chambers" (40). Marotti's confidence is based upon Walton's biography: "Walton's description of Donne's life at Lincoln's Inn as arranged around a regimen of study from four o'clock to ten o'clock each morning, followed by less respectable activities in which he 'took great liberty,' seems to be reflected in the poet's splitting of himself in the first satire" (39). Instead of regarding the satires and other writings as reflections of Donne's lifestyle and the views of the coterie, I want to treat them as productions of a coterie or community, whether it be professional, political, religious, or literary. This process at once depends upon and interrogates what Marotti calls the metacommunicative level of discourse. Such an approach to Donne's satires and other poetry, I believe, is true to Marotti's strong central thesis concerning the interactive system of literary production in the Elizabethan and early Stuart period. It departs from Marotti by adopting, in place of the reflection theory of literature, a more activist position on the question of the literary text's cultural productivity.

Donne's satirical work on various systems of self-fashioning is a textual practice which creates a range of provisional, shifting relations between the subject and ideology. In a sense, Donne's practice promotes the sort of "close reading" advocated by Richard Strier in *Resistant Structures: Particularity, Radicalism, and Renaissance Texts* and enacted in his central essay on Satire 3.[18] I will consider Strier's reading of Satire 3 later in this chapter, but here at the outset I want to compare my approach to the Satires with Strier's general project, which is epitomized in his essay on Satire 3.

As noted in my Introduction, Strier argues for a reading practice suspicious of proleptic "schemes"—theories or historical assumptions that map out ahead of time what a text can or cannot be doing or saying.[19] In a series of readings of texts by a number of Renaissance writers, Strier repeatedly discovers, through his close reading, surprisingly "radical" thoughts which have generally been regarded as "impossible" for the period but which Strier then proceeds to recontextualize historically, by connecting these radical thoughts to Renaissance and Reformation contexts hitherto occluded by some theoretical or historical scheme. Strier anticipates "the *tu quoque*," stating, correctly in my view, that readers will have to decide on the basis of his readings whether he deserves this criticism. At the end of the first of two paragraphs devoted to this defense, Strier subtly introduces a new, highly charged term into the argument: "I have tried to make my orientations explicit, and though I do a good deal of polemicizing against various critical and historical schemes, I hope not to have put forth any *dogmas*" (my emphasis). In the second of these paragraphs Strier then refutes the idea that not having a dogma is itself a dogma, most effectively, I think, by noting that "the function of the promulgation of dogma was always to repress heresy, to shut down or narrow rather than to expand or encourage public discussion," while his purpose is clearly to promote debate.[20]

I think it is worth highlighting what Strier has accomplished in this passage and in his series of readings. It is, I maintain, very closely related to what Donne achieves in some of the Satires and many of his other poems. Both writers manage to privilege their particular textual practice—I would call it a literary practice—while still locating themselves very much "in the fray."[21] I contend that Strier's reading project is a consequence of a textual practice fully exemplified by Donne's practice of satire. Like Strier, Donne the satirist is uncomfortable with schemes, and, in the process of restlessly and brilliantly scrutinizing them, he sometimes turns up radical ideas. The recovery of Donne's "genuine" radicalism is Strier's version of Donne's seeking "true Religion."[22] Strier's goal is to complete Empson's project of " 'Rescuing Donne' from the hands of conservative or cynical scholars."[23] In what follows I resist the recuperation of a "genuine" Donne because I find Donne's subject of satire to be a divided, continually shifting subject, one always in process, always inventing new ways of textualizing history and a relation to history—in short, a literary subject. I hope this argument does not align me with the conservatives or the cynics.

Satire and Self-Fashioning

Satire 1, like Satires 2 and 4, works at establishing a subject position by producing an other even as it suggests that such self-definitions are unstable, if necessary, ideological projects.[24] Satire 1 opens with the reclusive scholarly satirist ordering his opposite, the "fondling motley humorist," "Away." The suggestion is that the scholar can be most truly himself only when "Consorted with these few bookes."[25] As most critics have noted, however, the use of a word such as "consorted," which here seems to mean "sorted with" (but in light of the activities of the humorist, could the sexual suggestion—not cited by OED before 1600—be possible? Donne seems to play with this meaning in l. 33), the coffinlike dimensions of the Inns of Court room, and the contradictory behavior of the scholar-satirist in following the humorist gently pull the satirist into the poem's circle of ridicule.[26] In the most extended scholarly reading of the poem, M. Thomas Hester challenges this standard view of the poem as an example of the "satirist satirized," finding the presentation of the satirist to be consistent with "ideals of Christian scholarship."[27] Hester correctly identifies elements of a Christian humanist ideology in the poem but, in my view, mistakenly reads the poem in terms of these ideals. I believe that what the poem reveals is the degree to which the fashioning of such ideals depends upon the production of an opposite. The satirist's position, even the position of Christian scholar, depends upon the presence ("sweare . . . Thou wilt not leave mee in the middle street"), not the absence ("Leave mee") of the humorist.

Thus the satirist performs a satirical version of the marriage ritual—"For better or worse take mee, or leave mee" (l. 25)—preparatory to setting out on his satirical rounds. The mock ceremonial satirizes the inconstancy of the humorist and parodies the homosociality of Marotti's coterie (this reaches a crisis when the humorist visits his whore near the end of the poem), but it also undercuts the moral autonomy that fires an effective satirist. This autonomy, as Hester has shown, seems inseparable from a Christian humanism implicit in the catalogue of books that opens the poem, a humanism that, throughout the Satires, is depicted as failing to live up to its ideal of reforming society. Apparently composed in a Lincoln's Inn efficiency apartment (on this, see Milgate, 118), Satire 1 begins by evoking the opening review of studies in *Dr. Faustus.* After the theologians and Aristotle, there is a comic falling off to the "jolly" ("overweeningly self-confident," according to Grierson and Milgate) "statesmen," "gathering Chroniclers" ("who merely gather information," again according to Milgate), and the "Giddie fantastique Poets of each land" (who take, deservedly according some humanists, last place). The inclusion of poetry and exclusion of law treatises would seem to "consort" the satirist with the "gentlemen" of the Inns who were interested in advancement by other means than the legal profession. This feature of the satirist takes on special significance in Satire 2. Here I want simply to emphasize the satiric potential of these poets; they are hardly "constant" company, and in any case one could argue that the satirist is one of them.[28] The scholar-satirist's commitment to learning, and the value of that learning, are in question from the start.

Even more important to the satire is the fact that these "scholarly" activities, with the possible exception of the writings of "giddie poets," are irrelevant to life on the street. Hester argues that the satirist is an Erasmian fool, "more concerned with the soul of himself and others than with what many would term rational behavior."[29] This identification, it seems to me, mistakes Donne's satirical production of Christian humanism for the real thing. In his preliminary scolding of the humorist, the Erasmian fool displays a detailed knowledge of the world he claims to abhor, a knowledge that clashes with such worn pieties as "At birth, and death, our bodies naked are" (l. 42). The clinching of this ironic portrait of satiric self-fashioning is the satirist's decision to leave with the humorist:

> But since thou like a contrite penitent,
> Charitably warn'd of thy sinnes, dost repent
> These vanities, and giddinesses, loe
> I shut my chamber doore, and "Come, lets goe." (ll. 49–52)

Milgate's quotation marks give us no help in assigning the last speech to the humorist or the satirist, but each possibility seems to work as well as the alternative. If the humorist is speaking, the scholar's smug assurance that he has gotten through to the "penitent" is sent up here. If the satirist calls for the departure, the decision to leave is indeed, as Hester suggests, irrational ("Since you've repented, let's check out the action," says the scholar), although nothing in the poem thus far, aside from the scholar's own self-justifying claim in line 50, suggests he is motivated by charity. In either case, motivation is at issue here: the scholar performs a satirical tour de force on the motivelessness of the humorist's desire to "go" ("But sooner may a cheape whore . . .") directly before finding himself—motiveless but still proud of "my conscience"—"in the street" (ll. 66, 67).[30] The unified subject of satire seems to drop out of sight at the moment of choice.

The scholar's Christian humanism enables him to assume a position of moral mastery with respect to his satiric butt; it does not help him make moral decisions, nor does it prove effectual in changing the humorist. But the moral superiority is supported, particularly in the second half of the poem out on the street, by weak witticisms not up to Donne's standards:

> Now leaps he upright, joggs me,'and cryes, "Do'you see
> Yonder well favour'd youth?" "Which?" "Oh,'tis hee
> That dances so divinely." "Oh," said I,
> "Stand still, must you dance here for company?"
> Hee droopt, wee went, till one (which did excell
> Th'Indians, in drinking his Tobacco well)
> Met us; they talk'd I whisper'd, "Let us goe,
> 'T may be you smell him not, truely I doe." (ll. 83–90)

> " . . . he hath travail'd." "Long?" "No, but to me"
> (Which understand none,) "he doth seeme to be
> Perfect French, and Italian." I reply'd,
> "So is the Poxe." (ll. 101–4)

These jokes score a few points against the humorist but they lack the moral punch we might expect after the buildup in the first half of the poem. Their chief function is to reinforce the scholar-satirist's superiority and detachment, not to exercise charity or to instruct the humorist. At the end of the satiric walkabout, the satirist's ineffectuality is reemphasized when his unfaithful mock marriage partner returns to his control, "hanging the head," only because of a physical beating by rival johns.

The center of this poem, and the community that would be constructed around it, fail to stabilize themselves. The Christian humanist is here produced as a hollow ego-ideal, a vapid Inns of Court wit who fashions himself against, and therefore is curiously bound to, Donne's man of the crowd. Consequently, the effect of the subject of satire on the world is as slight as that of the object of satire.

In Satire 2 this equivalence is broken in favor of the satiric butt, the lawyer Coscus, who succeeds at a self-aggrandizing textualization of history. The bond between the satirist and the satirized other is here more conflicted than that between scholar and humorist in Satire 1; as a result, the achievements of Coscus generate indignation, an anger that seems connected to a threat to the dignity of the satirist. The threat produces, however, not only a satiric counterattack on Coscus, who is identified with prostitutes, sodomists, and Satan himself, but also a subversive representation of the discourse of power; Coscus must "to every suitor lye in every thing, / Like a Kings favorite, yea like a King" (ll. 69–70).

This social critique of Satire 2 is part of the semiotics of the Inns of Court.[31] Membership at the Inns of Court had increased dramatically in the late 1590s, and partly as a result of this growth a debate ensued over their function in English society. The Inns, of course, had always served a dual purpose; as Sir John Fortescue noted in the fifteenth century, they were called Inns of Court "because the Students in them, did there, not only study the Laws, but use such other exercises as might make them the more serviceable to the King's Court."[32] During Donne's residency at the Inns, these two functions were causing an increasingly sharp division between the serious law students, on the one hand, and the students of civility, those "gentlemen" of the Inns addressed by Ben Jonson in the dedication of *Every Man Out of His Humor,* on the other. The "gentlemen" were especially anxious to cultivate courtly postures and activities that would set them apart from the lawyers and law students with whom they were associated and whose social status was still not high.[33] As a coterie of wits Donne and his circle were defining themselves by opposition to a professional group which Donne also represents as a threat to the traditional order of society.

If the activities of the young gentlemen of the Inns were antagonistic to the purposes of the legal professionals there, they were no less motivated by careerism. Marotti and Richard Helgerson have reminded us of the extraliterary ambitions of these Renaissance amateurs: The self-conscious adoption of the prodigal role always entailed a return to the world of responsibility, achievement, and power so bravely dismissed in Donne's love poems. The Inns served the gentlemen (sometimes, very young gentlemen—Donne was 19 when he entered Thavies Inn) as a kind of liminal community where they could make the passage from parental control to the larger social circle where they would assume their occupational identities. Their extravagant wit and manners were manipulations of the courtly codes, linguistic and behavioral, which they would have to master in order to enter the Elizabethan system of preferment and privilege. The social conflict at the Inns, then, can also be seen as a conflict between two systems of advancement: professionals like Coscus used the legal system, while the amateur gentlemen sought connections with the Court.[34]

Satire 2 participates in this social conflict at the Inns; the satirist works to gain the rhetorical upper hand over Coscus through the kinds of positioning noted above. Specifically, the poem is powered by the "tropes of courtesy" classified and analyzed by Frank Whigham.[35] It is not surprising that courtesy literature should contribute to the method of late Elizabethan satirists; it comprised the period's most extensive and coherent system of thinking about self-presentation, a preoccupation of sixteenth-century satirists noted by critics of the genre from Alvin Kernan with his notion of the satyr-persona to Hester and his Christian satirist. As Whigham points out, courtesy literature had an equivocal relationship to ideology; it was invented to maintain a status quo, but it could also be manipulated to undermine the established order. Furthermore, these two apparently opposed functions can slide together or escape the control of the user. Such instabilities and mixed motives of rhetoric produced the contradictions of courtly (and, I propose, satiric) self-presentation, described by Whigham as "weird phenomenological mixtures of arrogance and paranoia, each factor deriving from a desperate need for coherence, between the normative humanist expectations of the university and the murky resistant realities of court life as lived"[36]—between, that is, humanist theory and social practice. Satirists of the 1590s use the figures of courtly rhetoric both conservatively and subversively, sometimes slipping as suggested from one purpose to the other in the same poem. As a conservative device the satiric version of courtly rhetoric serves two purposes: it generates a protective definition of the true courtier-satirist, as opposed to the false courtiers, the satiric butts; and, as Whigham maintains, it also relieves strain "by postponing, accounting for, or mystifying the various levels of personal failure."[37] Donne's rhetoric is primarily conservative in Satire 2. In Satire 4, where a critical motive becomes most visible, it subverts the satirist's identity as well, disclosing his own entrapment in a false system of signification.

Donne's ironic ridicule of the poets at the beginning of Satire 2 traces a classic maneuver of courtly self-promotion.[38] Devaluing the work of poets to a level of insignificance, Donne deflects the reader's attention from the poetic game of advancement to Coscus's practice of law "for meere gaine" (l. 63).[39] Speaking for the coterie evoked by the nameless "Sir" addressed in line 1, Donne is particularly indignant at "the insolence / Of Coscus" who "was (alas) of late / But a scarce Poet" (ll. 39–40, 43–44). Coscus's abandonment of poetry for the law is an important element in Donne's satire, which turns on the problem of writing and its relationship to life: "When sicke with Poetrie, 'and possest with muse / Thou wast, and mad, I hop'd" (ll. 61–62). Why did the satirist hope? Perhaps the satirist had assumed that Coscus would follow the career path described by Helgerson and return from the prodigal episode of poetic madness to the prosaic world of work. In any case, Coscus's defection from the ranks of the poets is aggravated by his pathetic attempts to continue as a poet writing in a strained "metaphysical" style that woos "in language of the Pleas, and Bench" (l. 48). The love poets pitied by Donne rely upon the magical, incantatory power of language, "but witchcrafts charms / Bring not now their old fears, nor their old harmes" (ll. 17–18). Opposed to this mystification of poetic language is Coscus's affected metaphysical style, which reduces poetry to the level of a legal "motion" (l. 49).

But Coscus's legal writings, more than his legalese poems, are the objects of Donne's satire. Unlike the powerless rhymes of prodigal Petrarchists, the writs of Coscus are changing English society by redistributing the land. They imitate both their author's voraciousness and the objects of his desire: "In parchments then, large as his fields, hee drawes / Assurances, bigge, as gloss'd civill lawes" (ll. 87–88). The flaws in Coscus's texts, unlike those in the works of the poets, are intentional: "But when he sells or changes land, he'impairs / His writings, and (unwatch'd) leaves out, *ses heires*" (ll. 97–98). Coscus now writes with power.

The figure of ironic deprecation is part of a larger courtly strategy of privileging amateurism and recreation over professionalism and industry. The satirist's disinterested amateur stance is implicit in his patronizing attitude toward the professional playwright who is forced "to live by 'his labor'd sceanes" (l. 14) and the poets who "write to Lords, rewards to get" (l. 21), but it is chiefly discovered in his attack on the earnest careerism of Coscus. Coscus was formerly "sicke with Poetrie" and "mad," but his new poems confuse *otium* and *negotium*. His practice of law is marked by dull persistence; we observe him, "like a wedge in a blocke, wring to the barre" (l. 71). His industry and thrift help him to capitalize on the prodigality of rich young men such as he could have easily noted at the Inns of Court:

> spying heires melting with luxurie,
> Satan will not joy at their sinnes, as hee.
> For as a thrifty wench scrapes kitching-stuffe,
> And barrelling the droppings, and the snuffe,
> Of wasting candles, which in thirty yeare
> (Relique-like kept) perchance buyes wedding geare;
> Peecemeale he gets lands (ll. 79–85)

The busy lawyer "spends as much time / Wringing each Acre, as men pulling prime" (ll. 85–86); his profitable legal chicanery renders harmless by contrast the wasteful card playing of courtiers (who, of course, fancied the game of primero).

Donne sharpens his attack on Coscus, then, by contrasting the lawyer's self-interested diligence to the prodigality and versifying fashionable in the circle of gentlemen with whom Donne associated at the Inns of Court. It is important to notice how much Donne's charge that Coscus is the chief of sinners depends on this rhetorical strategy. The sins of Coscus are serious but not extraordinary: his lying is merely symptomatic of a systemic rot; and his technique of omitting key words from legal documents, "As slily'as any

Commenter goes by, / Hard words" (ll. 99–100), could have been learned from reading biblical commentaries. It is Coscus's success, his power, that breeds the "just offence" of the satirist, who aligns himself with figures of powerlessness and dispossession—poets, papists, "ruin'd Abbeyes," bilkcd heirs, old landlords. By another familiar gesture of courtly self-definition, Coscus's success, attributed to his moral failure, is contrasted with the satirist's self-acknowledged disconnectedness, which silently testifies to his moral superiority (and, of course, better qualifies him to exercise the power that has been usurped by Coscus). Against the new order being constructed through Coscus's legal texts, the satirist opposes a naturalized traditional order that is a commonplace of sixteenth-century satire:[40]

> Where are those spred woods which cloth'd hertofore
> Those bought lands? not built, nor burnt within dore.
> Where's th'old landlords troops, and almes? (ll. 103–5)

Dispossession and absence, then, mark the old, true nobility with which the satirist identifies himself. His confession of powerlessness in the closing lines underscores this identification of the poet and a lost, natural aristocracy even as it executes a courtly maneuver of denying the seriousness of what has been said: "but my words none drawes / Within the vast reach of th'huge statute laws" (ll. 111–12).

Donne's characterization of Coscus as singularly hateful reproduces a typical early modern attitude toward lawyers and the law. Lawyers have, of course, traditionally served as the butts of satire, but Renaissance attacks on them displayed a new anxiety. As William Bouwsma argued in "Lawyers and Early Modern Culture," "lawyers represented the omnipresent danger inherent in the increasingly mysterious machinery for social organization, before which the individual felt more and more helpless." To men like Donne, who felt acutely the effects of being knocked loose of traditional moorings, the lawyer took on special importance in his role as a shaper of the emerging order that was replacing the old agrarian society; he was, in Bouwsma's words, "an obvious scapegoat for the general guilt of a world in transition, made anxious not only by the immediate insecurities of life in society but also by the abandonment of old ways and values."[41]

In Satire 2 these social changes are related by analogy to the Reformation. The opening comparison of the "poore, disarm'd" poets to "Papists, not worth hate" (l. 10), marks the attack on poetry as a Puritan discourse; as Milgate points out, the case against poetry set out in lines 5–10 parrots "the common Puritan charge that poetry, the nurse of idleness and effeminacy, takes men from fruitful labour and is the enemy of the military virtues" (129). More suggestive still is an analogy inspired by Coscus's wooing "in language of the Pleas and Bench" (l. 48):

> words, words, which would teare
> The tender labyrinth of a soft maids eare,
> More, more, then ten Sclavonians scolding, more
> Then when winds in our ruin'd Abbeyes rore. (ll. 57–60)

After something like a Polish joke, the evocation of the ruined abbeys is particularly striking. It suggests a link between Coscus and a historical process that began with the dissolution of the monasteries so that his compassing of "all our land" becomes a stage in that long sequence of events. The reference to a displaced monastic order is picked up later in the poem, when Donne compares the prolix Coscus to Luther after he renounced his monastic vows: Coscus

> spares no length; as in those first dayes
> When Luther was profest, he did desire
> Short *Pater nosters,* saying as a Fryer
> Each day his beads, but having left those lawes,
> Addes to Christs prayer, the Power and glory clause. (ll. 92–96)

As Milgate comments, "the analogy is very loose when it concerns the point of 'writing at greater length' " (137), but this aspect of the comparison is overridden by the articulation with other analogies distributed throughout the poem, all of which urge a connection between Coscus's legal rewriting of the social order and shifting religious doctrines and practices, which are also, as suggested earlier, frequently linked to writing. Luther "Addes to Christs prayer" and creates a new religion. Coscus's "Assurances," drawn up "In parchments . . . large as his fields" (l. 87), prompt the satirist to note "that men (in our times forwardnesse) / Are Fathers of the Church for writing lesse" (ll. 87–90). This point receives yet another spin when Coscus's legal legerdemain is compared to commentaries on scripture or controversial writings:

> But when he sells or changes land, he'impaires
> His writings, and (unwatch'd) leaves out *ses heires,*
> As slily'as any Commenter goes by
> Hard words, or sense; or in Divinity
> As controverters, in vouch'd Texts, leave out
> Shrewd words, which might against them cleare the doubt. (ll. 97–102)

Finally, one of the changes resulting from Coscus's refashioning of the community is compared to one of the chief points controverted by reformers and Catholics: "But (Oh) we'allow / Good workes as good, but out of fashion now, / Like old rich wardrops" (ll. 109–111).

Since the satirist clearly aligns himself with the dispossessed, who are in turn repeatedly compared to Roman Catholics, it is tempting to place the satirist on the side of the old religion, to find a particularly Catholic component in his courtly self-presentation. Grierson sees in lines 71–73 an allusion to "the patient Catholics or suspected Catholics whom he [Coscus] wrings to the bar and forces to disgorge fines. Coscus, a poet in his youth, has become a Topcliffe in his maturer years."[42] If Grierson is right, line 75 on "Sodomy in Churchmens lives" would seem calculated to obfuscate any clear identification with Romanists. Donne's satires often represent the satirist as a kind of recusant, but we ought to be cautious about interpreting this as solidarity with Catholicism. Donne could, as Strier asserts, be "speaking for 'recusants' of all kinds."[43] I would only add that Donne's strongest "impressions," to use his word from the autobiographical preface to *Pseudo-martyr*, of recusancy would have come from his Catholic family experiences, and so his representations of recusant experience take a "Catholic" form.[44] The poems capitalize on the experience and discourse of Catholic recusancy as a particularly rich and often equivocal response to historical change and Elizabethan ideology.[45] In Satire 2 the recusant subject position is discernible here and there, in such instances as those noted above, where it frequently merges with Whigham's tropes of courtesy to produce, through its account of the career of Coscus, a satirical history of the Reformation. At the same time, the satirist claims to "hate / Perfectly all this towne" (ll. 1–2); yet within the space of nine lines we read that poets, like Papists, are "not worth hate" (l. 10). The subject of satire is, as we say, hard to read—which is exactly what Elizabethan authorities said about recusants.[46]

Satire 2, then, activates a number of rhetorical and literary complexes, including Whigham's courtly tropes of ambition, Marotti's coterie communication system, and conventions of classical and Renaissance satire, none of which should be used alone to position the satirist. The poem is mainly concerned with change (Coscus's change from poetasting to law practice, social change, religious change) and power (Coscus's power, the power of "th'huge statute lawes," "the Power and glory clause"), and disturbing linkages between aspects of both. While the satirist claims detachment from both change and power, I hope to have suggested his entanglement in them. This contradiction produces what might be called a recusant subject of satire, a subject whose equivocal position is epitomized in the riddling conclusion of the poem: "but my words none drawes / Within the vast reach of th'huge statute lawes."

The Subject of Satire

The interrelationship of power, change, and the subject is more fully and clearly manifested in Satire 3 as the problem of historicism. Donne's attempts to grapple with Renaissance historicism vis-à-vis religion leave him in something close to a "new historicist" predicament. His "strange way" is the place of a new subject of history.

37

Since Satire 3 has long occupied a central position in the Renaissance canon, it is perhaps inevitable that it has dropped out of sight in current de-centering representations of the Renaissance. Still, the poem ought to concern us, especially now, if only because it rehearses all the major themes of new historicist criticism of the Renaissance. Jonathan Dollimore's subtitle for *Radical Tragedy*—"Religion, Ideology, and Power"—suits Satire 3 nicely. And form follows content. The poem opens by worrying about authority ("thy father's spirit"), moves through a brilliant ideological analysis of religions toward what looks like some kind of affirmation of a possible truth beyond ideology, only to finally turn upon itself in a meditation on power as chiastically ambivalent and unstable as a new historicist could desire. In brief, Satire 3 is constructed along the lines of a good new historicist essay.

In another vein, the satire rehearses the vexed question of self-fashioning in Renaissance culture. Someone looking very much like an individual, an autonomous self even, seems to be hiking up the hill of truth. This self is glimpsed as an episode on the way to the soul's envisioned but not achieved rest before "age, death's twilight." As I hope to show, this apparitional individual appears in other Donne poems too, where a defiant rejection of certain cultural codes and structures is juxtaposed with an ingenious clearing of space for a "private" experience—on a hill, in a flea, in a bed—which, in turn, finally opens on to an attempted but never entirely successful resolution of the contradictions exposed by the interrogation. It's the oscillation between these positions that links the projects of Donne and recent historicist research and criticism.

In *John Donne, Undone,* which opens with a chapter on "Displacement and Eccentricity: The Struggle with History," Thomas Docherty offers a post-structuralist interpretation of this instability of the subject, valorizing it as the mark of historicity itself, and identifying it here and elsewhere in Donne with the figure of the woman. In Docherty's deconstructive account, "The Name of the Woman . . . which in Satire 3 is identified as the true religion or true church, is that which allows the poet to *escape* from individuated personality; for he here betrays a patriarchal filiation in some way and replaces the stability of an eternizing truth with the mutable and historical or secular discourse of Folly."[47] Docherty, I shall argue, is too quick to replace stability with mutability, but he correctly identifies Donne's historicist dilemma: "Oh where" is True religion to be found in history? What might be valid methods of arriving at a reliable historical account of true religion? What is historical Truth? Docherty answers that it is (for Donne) what men say about women—it is shifting, promiscuous, mutable; it is not what we generally think of as truth at all.

In sharp contrast to this reading is Strier's brief for a "genuine" and "Impossible [i.e., quite possible] Radicalism" that "constitutes the poem's deepest and poetically most distinguished strain."[48] Where Docherty's post-structuralist critical practice disperses the subject of the poem into a discourse of folly, Strier's close-reading strategy produces an autonomous self that resists totalizing political and religious systems in ways that comport with aspects of the thought of Erasmus, Sebastian Castellio, and Luther.[49] Strier's notion of autonomy in Satire 3 should not be confused with an idea of complacent bourgeois subjectivity that often serves as the straw man for poststructuralist or new historicist critiques of the subject. Donne's autonomy, in Strier's account, is in effect a defense of "suspension of commitment."[50]

This formulation of Donne's subject-position comes very close to my own sense of the poem, but I want to note two reservations that mark an important distinction between our readings. First, I find Strier's emphasis on Donne's "suspension" to be undercut by his own project of "rescuing Donne" as a radical hero of conscience. There is a revealing tension in "the subject of Donne" as it is constructed in Strier's essay. A disparity between Donne the writing subject and Strier the reading subject is opened by Strier's intervention in the academic subject of Donne, represented in Strier's essay as a struggle between radical Empsonians and conservative or cynical historicists. In his introductory chapter Strier claims that "When arguing for the presence of a theme in a work, I have not argued that the theme in question is the only one in the work or even the 'central' one"; in the Donne chapter, however, I have already noted that he explicitly privileges the radical strain in the poem by arguing "that it constitutes the poem's deepest and poetically most distinguished strain."[51] Again, Strier's frame of an academic contest between radicals and conservatives is, I believe, also an accurate account of the satirist's own struggle in the poem; but to commit the subject of satire to the radical position as Strier seems to do is, in my view, to resolve the struggle for Donne.[52]

My second reservation has to do with the role of desire in the poem. This is perhaps more a matter of emphasis, but I do find the sense of autonomy in the poem to be crossed by the satirist's desire—that is, his *lack* of wholeness. Docherty's linking of the satire with the love lyrics and the Anniversaries is important because it introduces into the satire this subject (again in the current, nuanced sense) of desire: the desire for true religion is a subject of the poem, but the speaking subject of the satire is also constituted by a lack, a desire of the Other—that is, the true religion. More specifically, the search for true religion is represented through a masculine discourse of desire—"Is not our Mistresse faire Religion?"—complete with oedipal inflection. "and shall thy fathers spirit" (Carey and Docherty invoke *Hamlet*) "heare / Thee, whom hee taught so easy wayes and neare / To follow, damn'd" (ll. 11–15).[53] This Law of the Father is, as Freud would have it too, both threatening ("heare / Thee . . . damn'd") and empowering ("hee taught so easy ways and neare"—seek "our *Mistresse* faire Religion," I take it, not *Mother* Church) and so produces a true psychoanalytic ambivalence in the subject; in Donne's words, "This feare great courage, and high valour is" (l. 16).

A similar ambivalence characterizes Donne's gendering of "faire Religion" in Satire 3. While she is "worthy'of all our Soules devotion," "faire Religion" can also be said to fall under a masculine regime of discovery and control—true religion is something to be achieved, above other achievements of the Renaissance man catalogued in lines 17–32, and then kept.[54] The search for true religion is represented as man's work of discovery and possession. However, this aspect of Donne's representation of the search is marked by contradiction at precisely the point at which it becomes most obvious—in the brilliant review of religions in lines 43–68. Each religious position is, of course, related to a type of woman, but also, and more significantly, each is compared to an inadequate male response to women, ranging from Mirreus's fetishism—which Donne dangerously links to obedience to the Prince (and, if standard dating of the poems is followed, this would be a female prince too), to the aptly-named Phrygius's "frigidity," to Graccus's promiscuity. To complete the figure, I would point out that these male responses are, psychoanalytically speaking, strategies of denying lack. In the terms of Donne's allegory, this failure to acknowledge one's lack (i.e., lack of the truth) results in a flawed religious choice.[55]

Donne's admission of desire into the poem by means of the witty figure of "our Mistresse faire Religion" can be interpreted as a destabilizing move with respect to subjectification; in working through the implications of the erotic analogy, he is able to suggest how the desire to locate and fix the truth can be a compensatory reflex for one's experience of lack of truth. The subject is divided by a desire for truth and the truth of desire. This is how the subject of desire is called to the "strange way" of "inquiring." At the same time, the imaging of true religion as a woman and the invocation of the father serve to pin down the seeker within interrelated structures of desire and power. One must not just "stand inquiring," but "stand inquiring right"; "unmoved thou / Of force must one, and forc'd but one allow; / And the right; aske thy father which is shee . . ."; "That thou mayest rightly obey power, her bounds know" (ll. 78, 69–71, 100). These lines make it clear that the subject of desire is also a subject of power, another division in the poem, roughly symmetrical to the "kind pitty" and "brave scorn" of its opening line. Donne's quest is both eroticized and politicized. That is, the subject of the satire is constituted (and divided at the same time) by the erotically construed search for what is lacking—true religion—and by a set of relationships to power.

The issue of power returns us to the problematic of new historicism. Like the new historicist, Donne opens his interrogation of the subject of power with a marginal discourse—"Can *railing* then cure these worne maladies?" This position of the railer is charged with ambivalent possibilities. As Robert C. Elliott demonstrated, in a work that anticipated some themes and procedures of new historicism, the railer occupied a special place in the Elizabethan and Jacobean imagination, perhaps due to a cultural residue from a period when railing was both respected and feared for its power to harm or heal its objects. Elliott explains: "railing has an apotropaic function; it drives away evil. He who rails, then (in the appropriate circumstances), will be cherished." But this beneficent aspect of railing is always accompanied by a dark potential for inflicting injury or causing disorder: "On the other hand, railing and ridicule and invective can be dangerous and he who uses them may have to be punished, perhaps ritually punished in such a way that he will bear on his shoulders the bad luck of the group."[56] The railer is at risk; his free speech might be read as sedition.

Thus Donne's railing at Mirreus produces a dangerous analogy that attempts to "cure" Mirreus of his malady: "He loves her [Rome's] ragges so, as wee here obey / The statecloth where the Prince sate yesterday" (ll. 47–48). This debunking of the papacy also looks irreverently towards the monarchy; if it denies the ultimacy of papal power, it also raises a question about the basis of royal power. Is obedience to this power a sort of idolatry? The attack on Anglican Graius makes a similar demystifying statement with respect to the union of church and state:

> Graius stayes still at home here, . . . because
> Some Preachers, vile ambitious bauds, and lawes
> Still new like fashions, bid him thinke that shee
> Which dwells with us, is onely perfect. (ll. 55–58)

After such interrogations of power, the railer urges in the pivotal section of the poem a process of private inquiry that will eventually result in what we might call an authentic form of religious commitment. What is truly daring here is the suggestion that there may be a religious position outside of those currently accepted: "To'adore, or scorne an image, or protest, / May all be bad . . ." (ll. 76–77). This possibility ("*May* all be bad") is difficult to reconcile with the earlier assertion of the necessity ("must," l. 70) of choosing "one" religion, "And the right." Strier usefully comments that this thought very nearly "returns to the viewpoint of Phrygius, who 'doth abhorre / All,'" and he explains this discrepancy by suggesting that perhaps Phrygius and Graccus (the religious "indifferent") are wrong not so much in their views as in their way of holding those views. More important, Strier characterizes this stage of the poem (ll. 74–77) as "the swing back to autonomy."[57] Again, Strier's "autonomy" is a much embattled position, which can include "hesitation," "uncertainty," lack of clarity, and—in the famous passage on the hill of truth— "no sense of progress."[58] In his reading of the closing section of the poem, however, these ambiguities tend to get resolved into a solidarity between Donne and "three of the most radical notions of the European sixteenth-century [*sic*]."[59]

I want to support Strier's sense of radical possibilities in the poem, but it seems significant that Donne's free speech often takes the shape of gnomic verse or riddle. Is Donne really saying established religions "May all be bad," or just that certain practices of those confessions are so? The line leading up to that assertion—"Hee's not of none, nor worst, that seekes the best" (l. 75)—is a nearly impenetrable tongue-twister; Donne seems to be defending the seeker, or what Weimann calls "the ideology of seeking, examining and trying which was so critical of authority," yet even Strier must admit that "it is not clear what it means to say that such a figure is 'not of none.' "[60] Indeed, Donne's hill of truth is encircled by paradoxes and problems, including the lines already quoted on force, the riddle of truth and falsehood (ll. 72–73), the regressive interrogations of fathers (ll. 71–72), and the puzzling lines on "hard knowledge" and "mysteries . . . dazling, yet plaine to' all eyes" (ll. 87–88).

Here again the experience and discourse of recusancy, "certaine impressions of the Romane religion" in which Donne was raised, seem pertinent to his improvisations on power. In *The Soul of Wit* Murray Roston suggests "an unmistakable parallel between the Jesuit concept of prevarication and the witty, quibbling, and shifting word-play of Donne's verse, which sought out beyond the deceptive plausibility of existence some ultimate authenticity."[61] Donne's riddling style can be read as an attempt to preserve what Robert Southwell, under interrogation on the matter of equivocation (in this instance the variety known as mental reservation), called "the secrecy of man."[62] As Margaret Ferguson has written, "A paradoxical mode of rhetoric which prevents the reader from knowing where the author's beliefs lie is clearly useful for an inquiry into ideologically sensitive matters."[63] At the same time, a case can be made that this rhetoric cuts across Roston's "ultimate authenticity" or Ferguson's "author's beliefs," that these equivocal moves represent a split in the subject of the discourse. Southwell's phrase, "the secrecy of man," is itself richly ambiguous. Along these lines, Steven Mullaney has pointed out that such rhetoric ("amphibology"), particularly as it occurs in the discourse of treason, not only "presents authority with a considerable dilemma," but also always threatens to overtake the subject who uses it.[64]

The evidence for the second of these alternatives in Satire 3 lies in the kinds of contradiction that Carey observes in the poem between the aspirations stated in the hill of truth section and the rest of the poem or that I would highlight in the poem's closing meditation on power.[65] The problem inscribed in the closing lines on power preoccupied a wide range of Elizabethan writers.[66] Donne's management of the problem of secular and spiritual power resembles a variety of Elizabethan arguments, ranging from those of Hooker to those of Catholic loyalists, that depend upon a deferral or obscuring of the relationship between the two orders. Southwell's *Humble Supplication to Her Maiestie* ("a document of the first importance for an understanding of the environment in which Donne grew up," according to R. C. Bald) is particularly instructive and historically timely.[67]

The publication data on this volume are themselves a kind of riddle. Composed in 1591 as an answer to the Proclamation of that year which identified recusancy with treason, it was first published in 1600 bearing a false imprint of 1595, the year of Southwell's execution. The argument is itself a kind of pathetic paradox, a plea for toleration from one who knows he is about to be crushed by the very power he addresses. In addition to addressing Elizabeth as "sacred" six times in the course of his complaint, Southwell explicitly ratifies the system which is about to destroy him in his own representation of the monarch's power:

> Every one trampleth vpon their ruines, whom a Princes disgrace hath once overthrowen, Soveraignes favours being the best foundations of subiects fortunes, and their dislikes the steepest downfalls to all vnhappines. Yet a Prince supplying the place, and resembling the person of Allmighty god, should be so indifferent an Arbiter in all Causes, that neither any greatnes should beare down Iustice, nor any meanenesse be excluded from mercy. (1)

The difficulty of Southwell's position is already apparent; his appeal to an ultimate spiritual authority here and elsewhere in the pamphlet is crossed by the resemblance, here represented in terms of positionality ("supplying the place"), between Prince and God. Southwell thus tries to critique the proclamation without attacking the royal author; attributing the order to "a racking of publique authority to private purposes" of counselors, he asserts that the "Soueraigne stile" has been "abused to th'authorizing of Fictions." By characterizing the discourse of power as fiction Southwell makes it available for ideological analysis, and he is highly successful in disclosing the contradictions of the government's position:

> If we live at home as Catholiques, professing our owne, and refusing to professe a Contrary Religion, we can neither keep our places in the Vniversity, nor follow our studies in the Innes of Court, but we are imprisoned for Recusancy, impoverished, troubled and defamed. And yet if we leave all, and seeke free use of our Conscience, and departe the Realme, taking such helpes as the Charity of other Cuntryes affordeth vs, we are straight reckoned for *unnaturall Subjects.* (3)

But Southwell's ideological criticism generates an historicized understanding of religion that is subversive not only of Elizabeth's proclamation but of his own appeal to ultimate authority (Roston's "ultimate authenticity") as well. Answering the charge of sedition against Archbishop Allen and Robert Parsons for providing "Sanctuaries for persecuted and succourles soules" in the English colleges at Douay and Rome, he argues,

> It was noe *Sedition* for many in Queene *Maryes* tyme to be harboured in *Geneva,* maintained then by those that now enveigh against vs. It is noe *Sedition* to admitt such multitudes of strangers as for their Faith swarme

into *England* out of all *Cuntries*. It is thought *Charity* to ayde the States of *Flanders* in the behalf of *Religion.* (4)

Southwell's historical perspectivism would seem to call for a separation of religious and political authority that runs counter to their union in a sacred monarch. As Bald observes in his edition of the *Humble Supplication,* "Southwell's own feelings, no less than his experience in the mission had taught him the vital necessity, if English Catholicism was to survive, of reconciling loyalty to Church and State" (xxii). Southwell writes, "All bonds and duties both of nature and grace, invite us to love *god and our Cuntrie* more than our lives" (3; my emphasis).[68]

Southwell is dealing as a Catholic with a general problem created by, in Weimann's words, the "forced, inconsistent, and often indifferent cohabitation of church and state under one supreme head."[69] In the closing passage of Satire 3 Donne returns to this issue of "religion 'politized,' " which had been earlier introduced in the satirical sketches of Mirreus, Crants, and Graius.[70] Donne works to distinguish between secular and spiritual power, or rather, as Strier insists, between obedience to the two kinds of power. Like Southwell and like many Protestant writers on this topic, Donne emphasizes the limitations of "mans lawes by which shee [the soul] shall not be tryed / At the last day" (ll. 94–95).[71] Not part of Donne's representation is what Stephen L. Collins characterizes as Hooker's sense of the "creative relationship between man, the law, and social order and the further relationship between order and the historical perspective of change."[72] Donne's response to historicism seems much less assured than Hooker's; change in the laws is suspect, "still new like fashions" (l. 57). Perhaps this explains his rather sudden move from a bounded notion of power ("That thou may'st rightly obey power, her bounds know") to the image of the continuous "stream" of power ("As streames are, Power is"). The simile suggests the one origin of all power, while the earlier notion of boundaries insists on knowing the limits of power.

In other words, the question of how to obey power is complicated by the image of the stream. Strier writes that "the poem, unlike the political tradition, is not interested in charting the ways in which power becomes abusive. Donne is interested in how the individual is to act once power has become so." This statement, it seems to me, dwells uneasily with Strier's preceding claim that "The difference between the churches was not on whether resistance 'for some causes' was allowable or necessary but rather on how such resistance was authorized."[73] How can one know when resistance, however authorized, is called for without knowing first "the ways in which power becomes abusive"? To say that Donne "is not interested" in this problem is to ignore the cunning shift from talk of knowing "bounds" to the image of the stream, which can carry over the notion of bounds but yokes it with an idea of continuity. One might say the political problem is "disappeared," not by recourse to some absolute authority of individual conscience, but by way of a poetic image—a solution, I would add, that requires our continued work on the problem.

Donne's unsettledness is suggested by what Strier calls the "wildly disjunctive" shift of focus from the stream of power to the "blest flowers that dwell" at the head.[74] The passage replaces a concept of "rightly obeying" with an imaginary relation to power in the image of the "blest flowers" at the head of the rough stream of power's "calme head." The issue shifts from knowing the limits of power to positioning oneself at the source. At least two distinct projects are undertaken here. The personification of the flowers that "dwell" or "leave their roots" encapsulates the ideological move of constructing a centered and coherent subject out of the disparate representations of power; a natural image represents a "natural" relation to power. The image is, of course, a misrepresentation, a pathetic fallacy, since flowers do not "dwell" or "leave" anywhere. At the same time, the image seems to work on behalf of theories of passive resistance to tyranny which are at least as old as Tyndale; "blest flowers" would here convey a Reformed understanding of the individual's conscience as, in Catherine Belsey's summary, "the faculty which identifies the will of God"[75] There is even the hint of a meaning of "election" here, the elect being those "blest" who "thrive and do well." In either case, the point to be emphasized is that the fixed relation of the flowers contradicts the agency and motility of the subject as truth seeker.[76] If individual conscience "dwells" in some fixed relation to absolute power, then how can individual conscience also be invoked as the justification for *seeking* the correct relationship to ultimate power—that is, true religion? Again, Satire 3 seems to valorize the radical form of seeking, condemned as the work of "false prophets," by the moderate Richard Bancroft: "it hath ever been noted as a right property of heretickes and schismatikes, alwaies to be beating this into their followers head: *Search, examine, trie, and seeke:* bringing them thereby into a great uncertainty."[77] But through the magic of the image, Donne exchanges Bancroft's "uncertainty" for blessedness. The radical seeking of the "new, subjective type of author-ity" is finally replaced by the flower, always already dwelling at the source of the "authority of power."[78] If, as Strier remarks, it is not clear how either the "blinde Philosophers" or Donne's father got to heaven (ll. 11–12), it is equally a puzzle how the seeker of truth becomes a blest flower.[79] The closing passage is, it seems to me, a mystification rather than an explanation. In so characterizing this image I do not presume to be disclosing a truth concealed by ideological illusions; rather, I mean to highlight some gaps in the discursive process whereby Donne negotiates his place vis-à-vis the stream of power.[80] It is clear that power becomes increasingly "tyrannous" as it flows away from the source and that souls who "more chuse mens unjust / Power from God claym'd" (ll. 109–10) "are lost" (l. 108). What is not clear is how one lives this critique of power and becomes, as Strier puts it, "the Lucretian sage, watching from his secure height."[81] Again, I want to say that Donne's position at the end of the poem is an imaginary one; Donne is not, as Strier maintains, "occupying (dwelling in) the position of Truth,"[82] but imagining what it would be like to do so. This imaginary subject-position is created through work on the "bounds" of discourse, on the faults between the "neare twins" truth and falsehood, "the mindes indeavours" and "mysteries," "the rough streams calme head" and "the streames tyrannous rage."

What also deserves notice here is the similarity of Donne's and some recent historicist representations of the subject of power in the Renaissance. In both models an attempt to delineate local, bounded, historically contingent circulations of power gives way to a unified theory that supports the possibility of a unified subject. In Donne, the relation to power of the "blest flower" functions as an ideological representation in the Althusserian sense of "the imaginary relationship of individuals to their real conditions of existence."[83] This ideal of a harmonious and fixed relation to power, expressed in the natural image of the flower, contrasts sharply with the dynamic mountain climber who takes his stand "in strange way," occupying a no-man's-land where conventional social relations seem suspended. In new historicist representations of the Renaissance, one often finds a similar contrast: local, highly particularized sets of social relations get inscribed into an oppressive, totalized representation of power that critics suspect of hiding (in a sort of postmodernist priest-hole) a recusant, liberal individualism.[84]

As a Renaissance historicist, truth seeker, and satirist, Donne belongs somewhere "betwixt and between." My invocation of Victor Turner, whose work on "structure and anti-structure" has greatly influenced new historicists, bespeaks my own investment in a new historicist approach and anticipates my next point: that new historicists who emphasize the processual aspect of the subject's relation to culture take up a similar liminal position. I want to suggest that we do so because we are also, in our own time and place, deeply invested in the historicist problematic that Donne and other Renaissance writers helped inaugurate. In making such a claim I do not believe I am reverting, as Jonathan Crewe has written of new historicist anthropologism, "to a realm of imagined cultural powers, conquests, and options scarcely compromised by history but rather dominating it," since I would locate anthropological discourse inside, not outside of this problematic.[85]

As is evident here (and as will be evident later in this book), I would like to push a bit further on this point, into Turner's notion of the "metaphorical liminality" of literature and its applicability to Donne's writing. Metaphorizing his account of the liminal activities of the ritual subject in rites of passage, Turner argues that this literary liminality allows the writer to "play with the factors of culture, to assemble them in random, grotesque, improbable, surprising combinations," and "to generate not only weird forms but also models highly critical of the status quo."[86] Thus here I have tried to emphasize how

Donne's threshold position as a railer enables a satirical production of ideology in passages like that on Mirreus and the rest.[87] But this type of production of culture is also, I would argue, very close to a new historicist production of the Renaissance. For example, Montrose's opening of "A *Midsummer Night's Dream* and the Shaping Fantasies of Elizabethan Culture" with Simon Forman's dream about the queen enables his production of Elizabethan culture as a kind of dream text of symbolic inversions such that the culture becomes in part, a creation of Shakespeare's play. New historicism's concentration on drama, playing, and its broader valorization of play testify to an interest in this notion of liminal experiences.[88]

It's the "in-betweenness" of Donne's position, then, that I would emphasize, as distinct from Docherty's "replacement" of "an eternizing truth" with a "mutable and historical . . . discourse." And this is the in-betweenness, the equivocal, chiastic rhetoric of the new historicist reproduction of the Renaissance. Liu argues that "the New Historicist interpreter is . . . a subject looking into the past for some other subject able to define what he himself, or she herself, is; but all the search shows in its uncanny historical mirror is the same subject he/she already knows: a simulacrum of the poststructuralist self insecure in its identity."[89] Without going as far as Docherty in making Donne out to be a poststructuralist writer, I suggest that the Donne of the Satires is engaged in such a search. Like new historicists, he is involved in, again quoting from Liu's characterization of new historicism, "*searching* for the subject, *any* subject able to tell us what *it* is (authority, author, identity, ideology, consciousness, humanity) that connects the plural to the dominant, historical context to literary text."[90] How, Donne asks, might my satiric texts be connected to history? Satire 3 raises this question in a particularly powerful way, as it attacks shallow historicizations of religion and then works equally hard to imagine a way of rescuing "true religion" from history. I do not find that Satire 3 produces a definitive statement on this problem, but this is not to say that the poem, one of the great poems of the age, accomplishes nothing. It creates not so much a hero of conscience as a practice of writing—a brilliantly nuanced, "suspended," and deeply valued literary subject that continues to shape our difficult relation to history.

The Authority of Satire

At the end of Satire 2, the subject of history took the form of the new historicist's equivocal confession of powerlessness—in the face of the legal texts written by Coscus, the butt of the satire, Donne writes: "but my words none drawes / Within the vast reach of th'huge statute lawes" (ll. 111–12). Is this, as Milgate suggests, a boast of the truthful, and therefore unindictable, quality of his text?[91] But this would fly in the face of the thesis of the satire, that the all-encompassing law is corrupt and so not sensitive to matters of truth or falsehood. By the end of Satire 4 the confession is itself made to confess its secret:

> though I yet
> With *Macchabees* modestie, the knowne merit
> Of my worke lessen: yet some wise man shall,
> I hope, esteeme my writs Canonicall. (241–44)

If this "wise man" is also a powerful man like Sir Thomas Egerton, who is directly addressed in Satire 5, then one might argue that Donne's Satires gesture beyond themselves *as texts* toward that "history" that is not a text, towards what Liu sees as new historicism's promise of "a rhetorical notion of literature as text-cum-action performed by historical subjects upon other subjects."[92]

The appeal to a wise reader at the end of Satire 4, however, is problematic in the extreme. Its representation of a hoped-for textual empowerment of the satirist in terms of canonical debates continues the foregrounding in the Satires of the problem of writing with power and as an historicist. As Hester and others have shown, Satire 4 draws powerfully on the Catholic recusant experience.[93] Throughout the poem references to Catholicism are accompanied by reminders of persecution, including in manuscript versions the naming of the most notorious "Pursevant," Topcliffe, the torturer of Southwell. If the "wise man" addressed at the end of the poem is Egerton, a man with recusant experiences of his own,[94] the reference to canonical disputes takes on added dangerous overtones by suggesting that a coterie of ex-Catholics might be needed to clean up the court—instead of the "preachers" sarcastically mentioned in line 237 (remember the pimping preachers of Satire 3). Again, I do not mean to suggest the satirist's commitment to the Catholic religion; as if to balance the controversial allusiveness of the poem, Donne notes of Macrine the courtier that he

> protests protests protests
> So much as at Rome would serve to have throwne
> Ten Cardinalls into th'Inquisition;
> And whisperd 'by Jesu,' so'often, that A
> Pursevant would have ravish'd him away
> For saying of our Ladies psalter. (ll. 212–17)

The point of all the allusions is that both courtship and religion are practiced at considerable risk to the subject of power. Recusancy works particularly effectively in the poem to aid in the representation of this power as a vague but insidious and enveloping system that forestalls any genuine communication or community.

The representation of power here is insidious and decentered, resembling Foucault's formulation in volume one of *The History of Sexuality* as "the multiplicity of force relations," something "produced from one moment to the next, at every point, or rather in every relation from one point to another."[95] This court, a dystopian version of Castiglione's Urbino, is a place in which to be afraid. The source of fear is always absent—felt, but not visible. The missing center of the court is matched by a satirist who, like the scholar of Satire 1, seems unable to account for his own behavior and therefore undermines any claim to moral authority and autonomy. The opening assertion of detachment, like the "perfect hate" of "all this towne" in Satire 2, does not hold up for long:

> My minde, neither with prides itch, nor yet hath been
> Poyson'd with love to see, or to bee seene,
> I had no suit there, nor new suite to shew,
> Yet went to Court. . . . (ll. 5–8)

The tortured syntax figures a satirist who does not know his own motives. He compares his visit to court to a joke that turns against the joker:

> But as Glaze which did goe
> To'a Masse in jest, catch'd, was faine to disburse
> The hundred markes, which is the Statutes curse,
> Before he scapt, So'it pleas'd my destinie
> (Guilty'of my sin of going,) to thinke me
> As prone to'all ill, and of good as forget-
> full, as proud, as lustfull, and as much in debt,
> As vaine, as witlesse, and as false as they
> Which dwell at Court, for once going that way. (ll. 8–16)

The comparison foregrounds the question of motive. Why would one attend mass as a jest? To prove something? To entertain oneself? To satisfy curiosity? The analogy points to a division in the subject—he was only joking but he was "guilty." The reader is also divided against the satirist and placed on the side of the Statutes: Glaze-satirist got what he deserved. Having approached the court as a self-confident outsider, the satirist found himself constructed as a courtier—"As vaine, as witlesse," and so forth.

It is helpful to position Donne's account of a visit to court among some of the "radical tragedies" of court life recently analyzed by Jonathan Dollimore. Like such works as Marston's Antonio plays or Chapman's *Bussy,* Satire 4 is radical not so much by virtue of its overt attacks on court corruption (although I do not mean to minimize the force of those attacks) as by its representation of the discontinuous, contingent, and constructed identity of the satirist. After problematizing his motivation and playing with recusancy as a possible subject-position in the opening sixteen lines, the satirist, even more vigorously than in Satires 1 and 2, begins the work of self-definition by a xenophobic representation of the satiric other as an alien being—"Stranger then strangers" (1. 23). Perhaps the strongest proof of the other's monstrosity is his language— either "one language," according to Milgate, made up of "all tongues" or "no language," according to Grierson, following some manuscripts. Yet, and this is the crucial point, "He names mee" (l. 49) and engages the satirist in a conversation about "the best linguist" (l. 53). The shift in power relations at being named by the courtier seems to be registered in the satirist's extremely cautious reply, which balances the Calvinst Beza against "Some Jesuites" (ll. 55–56), and in his equivocal and often ironic style of conversing with the courtier. He does score direct hits against the court by invoking Cicero and by linking the court to pornographic display: "Not alone / My lonenesse is. . . . Aretines pictures have made few chaste; / No more can Princes courts, though there be few / Better pictures of vice, teach me vertue" (ll. 67–68, 70–72). But each point scored against the Court must also go against the satirist, since these attacks serve only to remind us of his mysterious motives in going to Court. Aside from these self-wounding barbs, the satirist's remarks seem designed to fend off any real debate or communication with the courtier, even though he tells us that the courtier "tells many'a lie" (l. 96). But what is especially puzzling is the satirist's characterization of reports of the queen's frowns and smiles, murder, bribery, sodomy, and so forth, as lies and "triviall houshold trash." Isn't this the stuff satires should be made of? The satirist has compared "Princes courts" to "Aretines pictures" (ll. 70–71), but when presented with the evidence of vice at Court, he impugns the honesty of the messenger.

There seems to be a duplicity here that would condemn and save the Court in the same breath. It may be that by characterizing the courtier's satiric speeches as libels, the satirist invests the poem with what might be called "plausible deniability." Donne's coterie, then, would be expected to read through this politic device to get at the truth about bribes and entailed offices at the Court. At the same time, Donne may be addressing the coterie in another manner here. Insofar as Donne and his circle have styled themselves as aspiring courtiers, the figure of the libellous court fly serves as a convenient humanist explanation for what seems to be a systemic problem; if Hester's Christian humanists or "good courtiers" like Donne and friends ran things, this argument would go, then all would be well at Court. What is most striking about Satire 4, however, is the satirist's failure to achieve a stable humanist identity or moral center in the poem. In his conversations with the courtier he finds himself constructed as the other and envisions his fate as a subject of power:

> I more amas'd then Circes prisoners, when
> They felt themselves turne beasts, felt my selfe then
> Becomming Traytor, and mee thought I saw

50

One of our Giant Statutes ope his jaw
To sucke me in. (ll. 129–33)

So defeated at court, the satirist attempts a reconstruction of moral autonomy in "wholesome solitariness" (l. 155). Appropriating Dante's sureness and
control, the satirist dreams of the Court as inferno and himself as a fearless
and free observer:

Such men as he saw there,
I saw at court, and worse, and more; Low feare
Becomes the guiltie, not the'accuser; Then,
Shall I, nones slave, of high borne, or rais'd men
Feare frownes? And, my Mistresse Truth, betray thee
To th'huffing braggart, puft Nobility?
No, no. (ll. 159–65)

But the medieval dream vision gives way to a more distinctly Renaissance
conception: "Me seemes they doe as well / At stage, as court; All are players"
(ll. 184–85). Staging the Court allows for greater immediacy in the satiric
representations, but it also tends to deny the satirist a privileged position as
observer; all the usual extravagant courtiers "in flocks, are found / In the
Presence, and I, (God pardon mee)" (ll. 178–79). While Macrine is laughable
in "his skirts and hose" (l. 200), the already-cited comparisons between
his language and religious persecution shift attention from the satiric object
toward the satirist. Glorius, another Doppelgänger of an Elizabethan satyr who
"Jeasts like a licenc'd foole, commands like law" (l. 228), is also associated
with persecution, his face as "ill / As theirs which in old hangings whip
Christ" (ll. 225–26). The "tyr'd" satirist retreats, "As men which from gaoles
to'execution goe" (l. 230), his autonomy suffering its last indignity while
passing the gigantic Beefeaters: "I shooke like a spyed Spie" (l. 237).

All critics mark the movement of the satirist from a marginal position in
Satire 4 to a place inside the circuit of power in Satire 5. The poem begins
on a less ambivalent note than does Satire 3, to which the opening lines seem
to allude: "Thou shalt not laugh in this leaf, Muse, nor they / Whom any
pitty warmes" (ll. 1–2). What sort of writer, Donne asks rhetorically, could
represent "Officers rage, and Suiters misery" and then "jest" about them
(ll. 809)? "Pitty," however, hardly seems the appropriate word to describe
Donne's attitude towards courtiers by the time we reach line 19, where they
are compared to shit, or line 27, where (perhaps picking up on the comparison
of suiters to food in line 22 by punning on "wittail," meaning "victual") they
are compared to "wittals," that is, husbands who complacently accept and
even facilitate their wives' infidelities.

Marotti is right, I think, to stress "Donne's conflicts and ambivalences"
concerning his new position.[96] Indeed, the speaking subject of the poem is

hard to locate with any syntactical precision, even in a passage explicitly dedicated to doing so:

> Greatest and fairest Empresse, know you this?
> Alas, no more then Thames calme head doth know
> Whose meades her armes drowne, or whose corne o'rflow:
> You Sir, whose righteousnes she loves, whom I
> By having leave to serve, am most richly
> For service paid, authoriz'd now beginne
> To know and weed out this enormous sinne. (ll. 28–34)

The missing (or displaced to line 32?) preposition "by," needed in line 31 to complete the chain of command from Elizabeth to Egerton to Donne, is probably the result of exigencies of meter; even so, the missing link matches other gaps in the system, notably that already mentioned between Elizabeth and the abuses of power in her court; as in Satire 3, Donne wants to say "As streames are, Power is," and again the "calme head" is imagined as somehow detached from the river's flow. The move to exculpate the ruler through a mystification is one commonly found in Elizabethan Catholic writing against persecution and one we are familiar with from the 1980s in "beltway" investigations of Reagan and the Iran/Contra affair.[97] In Satire 5 this move is countered by demystifications of "Faire lawes white reverend name" and divine power itself. I have already referred to Renaissance ambivalence concerning the law and lawyers in my discussion of Satire 2; here in Satire 5 reverence and loathing combine in an image that idealizes and then trashes the law:

> Oh, ne'er may
> Faire lawes white reverend name be strumpeted,
> To warrant thefts: shee is established
> Recorder to Destiny, on earth, and shee
> Speakes Fates words, and but tells us who must bee
> Rich, who poore, who in chaires, who in jayles:
> Shee is all faire, but yet hath foule long nailes,
> With which she scracheth Suiters; In bodies
> Of men, so'in law, nailes are th'extremities,
> So Officers stretch to more then Law can doe,
> As our nailes reach what no else part comes to. (ll. 68–78)

The image has a particular force here if we recall the earlier identification of suiters and excrement (l. 19) and if we glance ahead to the next line with its quibble on "baring": "Why barest thou to yon Officer? Foole, Hath hee / Got those goods, for which erst men bar'd to thee?" (ll. 79–80). The "strumpeting" of "Faire lawes white reverend name" is here given a more specific, sodomitical representation.[98] But this attack on "deviant" behavior by officers and suitors at Court is contradicted by hints of a deeper, systemic dysfunction; drawing again on the image of the stream of power, but to a sharply different end, the satirist notes:

> powre of the Courts below
> Flow from the first maine head, and these can throw
> Thee, if they sucke thee in, to misery,
> To fetters, halters . . . (ll. 45–48)

In this instance Donne carries the interrogation of power to "the first maine head" itself in a striking improvisation on Psalm 82. The psalmist compares earthly and divine justice in order to attack corruption in the courts of kings:

> I say, "You are gods,
> sons of the Most High, all of you;
> nevertheless, you shall die like men,
> and fall like any prince." (Psalm 82: 6–7)

Donne also threatens earthly princes, but in his version the fall of princes is ascribed to the workings of a system of bribery in God's court. The psalmist's metaphor is first worked for a feeble pun:

> Judges are gods; he who made and said them so,
> Meant not that men should be'forc'd to them to goe,
> By meanes of Angels . . . (ll. 57–59)

This contrast between the two systems is then developed only to be reversed in a surprise ending which implies the two systems are completely analogous:

> When supplications
> We send to God, to Dominations,
> Powers, Cherubins, and all heavens Courts, if wee
> Should pay fees as here, daily bread would be
> Scarce to Kings; so 'tis. (ll. 59–63)

Donne's revisionist production of the psalmist's analogy of power here turns against the mystification of power inscribed in the image of "Thames calme head," yielding both a bitter protest against Renaissance monarchy and a radical interrogation consonant with other late Elizabethan challenges to providentialist belief.[99]

Through such contradictory productions of Elizabethan ideology Donne practices a relation between text and historical context; he constructs his subject of satire. This subject is neither the humanist recluse of Satire 1 nor the dispossessed poet of Satire 2 nor the radical individual conscience of Satire 3 nor the retired Christian humanist of Satire 4 nor the authorized servant of the "Empresse" of Satire 5. Although Donne repeatedly attempts to construct such essential subjects by way of creating his satiric "others," the distance between self and other just as repeatedly breaks down.

The Satires invite readers to identify with the authority derived from authorship and writing—to identify, that is, with either the author or the wise man who confers authority on the texts. This identification with "author-ity" is a key aspect of the literary ideology to which Donne contributes.[100] He ruled, wrote Carew in his famous elegy, "The universall Monarchy of wit." But an equally powerful effect of the poems is to render both sovereignty and the subject—Weimann's "bifold authority of power" and the "new, subjective type of author-ity"—as contestatory and discursively produced. In post-Reformation England, Weimann writes, "Authority constituted itself not so much at the beginning of discourse, where traditional sources might be cited as valid by consensus, but rather in the perception of meaning as *process*."[101] Within this context Donne creates satire whose truth, in Eagleton's phrase, "is not an essence but a practice—the practice of its relation to ideology, and in terms of that to history."[102] Approaching the Satires as a practice itself constitutes something like a paradoxical "resistant practice," an "impossible radicalism." It entails resistance to seeing the Satires as "done" and the "wise man" as oneself, even as one's own writing esteems those "writs Canonicall."

❖ T W O

Donne's "Disparitie": Inversion, Ideology, and the Subject of Love

The Power of Love

THE QUESTION I want to ask of Donne's love lyrics has to do with the large issue of the relationship between discourses of power and love in the Renaissance, a relationship at the center of a great deal of new historicist work as well as feminist critiques of it. How is love poetry related to ideological structures and practices of the late Elizabethan and early Jacobean periods? One way of focussing this inquiry is to recognize that it is also imbricated with the history of twentieth-century Donne criticism. Several ways of framing the question in such terms are reflected in what follows. New Criticism, as Dayton Haskin has reminded us in his new historicist account of the "Donne Revival," overturned the nineteenth-century habit of reading Donne biographically and constructed Donne's texts as just the well-wrought urns Donne boasts about in "The Canonization."[1] Both the strength and the weakness of this formalist approach can in part be explained by its complicity with claims made in many of Donne's poems and with the larger movement in Renaissance literary history towards some theory of literary autonomy.[2] The New Critical perspective on Donne also turns out to mesh smoothly with contextual studies by intellectual and literary historians who, following the paradigm of autonomy, tend to lift the poems out of biographical and social conditions of their production into a relatively pure and stable realm of ideas and literary forms. Finally, all of these critical projects are supportive of a humanist criticism of Donne's lyrics as what might be termed (honoring Donne) ecstatic texts, brilliantly paradoxical distillations of Renaissance culture in the high, Arnoldian sense. This Donne affords if not a critical purchase on the subject of power then an alternative, compensatory poetic discourse of power. This poetic discourse is,

55

in turn, related to a specific ideological project, namely the construction of a private world ("each hath one, and is one") that privileges a particular type of heterosexual relationship over other forms of social relation.

Against this critical history, Arthur Marotti has put forward the most extended argument both for a return to biographical criticism and for reading Donne's love lyrics within a network of politically-charged discourses. I view what follows as a continuation of this project. Interestingly, however, Marotti's style of reading often produces another, though much less ecstatic, version of Anglo-American formalism's paradoxical and ironic Donne. Where New Critics found a kind of transcendence or at least superiority in Donne's irony and paradox, Marotti finds precisely the opposite. Thus he argues that "courtship and courtiership shared the same social milieu" and that coterie readers of his most socially and politically defiant lyrics "knew that Donne passionately longed for the worldly advancement he pretends to scorn . . . just as Sidney's readers had known how to interpret his disingenuous denial of interest in the national and international events mentioned in the thirtieth sonnet of *Astrophil and Stella*."[3] Paradox and irony, that is, signify Donne's material and ideological dependency on a specific socio-semiotic system. In his book-length study of Donne's relationship with the patronage system, Marotti, rather like John Carey, adds a psychological dimension to the social scene of Donne's writing, arguing, for example, that "The Canonization" asserts "an intellectual and rhetorical mastery that, if only momentarily, could psychologically counteract the helplessness of his actual social condition."[4]

Marotti corrects naive modern readings of Donne's socially defiant lyrics, but I believe he invests too much authority in his coterie as a ground of meaning for Donne's texts. Whenever doubt arises as to Donne's intentions or attitudes, we are always returned for reassurance to the relevant coterie, which is presented as a stable interpretive community within or sometimes against which Donne fashions himself. As noted in my opening chapter, from the perspective both of current semiotic approaches and of recent critiques of new historicist work, this coterie system looks too finished. In the language of social semiotics Marotti aims at a study of the "discourse" of patronage in Donne's work; the focus would be on what Robert Hodge and Gunther Kress term the "semiosic plane"—that is, "the social process by which meaning is constructed and exchanged." In practice, however, he treats the poems as "text," defined by Hodge and Kress as "a structure of messages or message traces which has a socially ascribed unity. . . . Its primary orientation is to the mimetic plane, where it has meaning insofar as it projects a version of reality."[5] Donne's poetry, indeed his entire career, is treated as the *product* of a unified system of patronage. Missing, then, is a sense of both the subject and the coterie as contingent and continual processes of social construction. Thomas Docherty's fully engaged poststructuralist play with Donne's texts and biography also points to the need to see Donne's writing as symptomatic of Renaissance historicism, as a "scene not of stable meaning but rather of precisely the opposite: change of meaning."[6]

The other reason for revising Marotti's socially engaged reading of Donne in this chapter has to do with questions of gender and love. Simply put, I think Marotti underestimates the problematic character of heterosexual love in Donne's lyrics, particularly as it is related to the *process* of identification with and through a male coterie. The strength of his account is also its weakness; aggressively defamiliarizing the coterie's attitudes towards sexual love (although I hope to show that in the last analysis the attitudes are not that unfamiliar), Marotti also, it seems to me, assumes Donne's complete solidarity with a set of attitudes "out there." In addition, Donne's coterie communications need to be seen as crossed by other discourses of sexuality, love, and marriage that thicken his descriptions of love life. I argue that the poems are part of a process of constructing (and holding on to) an attitude towards heterosexual love, particularly as such attitudes take shape in a homosocial context.[7] To put it another way, I want to suggest that Donne's love poems explore the difficulty of heterosexual love in what Thomas Laqueur and others have described as a one-sex system of sexuality.[8]

I begin, then, with a conviction about the importance of Donne's love poetry to his culture and with a critical interest in different attempts to historicize that importance. If Marotti, for example, accounts for the production of the lyrics by placing them in their highly specialized social context, his socially informed reading ironically allows for the splitting off of poetic discourse from the language of politics, a move Marotti's book so forcefully opposes. Lyrics such as "The Canonization" are "*poetically* brilliant, but unsuccessful, attempts to justify his marriage and witty, basically sociable, *recreations* to relieve the pain of Donne's placeless, hopeless state."[9] Jonathan Goldberg, on the other hand, challenges such a distinction, arguing that "discursivity characterizes the real as fully as the imagined" and thereby isolating the "shared impulses of writer and ruler," "patterns of replication that extend the political domain until we arrive at the private bedchamber" of "The Sunne Rising." The *Songs and Sonnets* are often "rebellious and atheistical in their manipulation" of Royalist tropes, but, Goldberg insists, Donne remains a writer whose "self-constitution is absolutist."[10]

Annabel Patterson, Alan Sinfield, and, most recently, David Norbrook have questioned Goldberg's tendency to allow for subversive uses of the King's rhetoric only to close off any real possibility for subversion.[11] In what follows I mean to support Sinfield's characterization of "the literary text not necessarily as subversion, but as a site of contest," and, more particularly, his point that "the role of the writer as writer is likely to stimulate awareness of the importance of ideological production in the sustaining, negotiating, and contesting of power in the state."[12] The contest, however, is not between Donne and the king, but between men and women; or rather, the subject position of the writer in the social order is negotiated in these poems through a production of gender ideology. This process also engages the reader in ideological work on gender, that is, in "sustaining, negotiating, and contesting" the forms of power invested in the reader's position in the system of patriarchy.[13]

I begin with "The Indifferent" and "Confined Love" because their ironies seem to substantiate the "radicalism contained" thesis of some new historicist work. It might be objected that such obviously playful poems should not be made to bear an argument about ideology, but it is precisely this sort of playfulness that affords "a site of contest" in many Renaissance texts. Arnold Stein discussed these poems years ago as examples of "witty inversion," which he regarded as "the self-justifying play of mind, the immediate purpose of which was to provide intellectual pleasure."[14] I want to push the concept of inversion a bit harder, importing from anthropologically-oriented criticism the notion of "symbolic inversion" and from social semiotics the closely related idea of domains of inversion. Symbolic inversion is defined by Barbara Babcock as an "act of expressive behavior which inverts, contradicts, abrogates, or in some fashion presents an alternative to commonly held cultural codes."[15] As noted in my discussion of the Satires, Victor Turner has related this kind of inversion to the "metaphorical liminality" of literature, which allows the author to "play with the factors of culture, to assemble them in random, grotesque, improbable, surprising combinations," and "to generate not only weird forms but also models highly critical of the status quo."[16] The discourse of inversion is ideologically charged, a consideration perhaps obscured by Babcock's notion of "expressive behavior" or Turner's emphasis on play. This is where the social semiotic understanding of inversion becomes useful. As Hodge and Kress summarize, "Domains of inversion are specific sites in social space or time where antigroups produce antilanguage forms, under relatively controlled conditions." But, as the various attempts to explain inversions as safety valves or subversions attest,

> The social meaning of [the] domain of inversion is unstable and ambiguous, since it is established by an ongoing struggle between two groups. From the point of view of the dominant, a domain inverts or neutralizes the subversive meanings expressed in it, labelling them as permitted transgressions incorporated into an overall order. From the point of view of an antigroup, this label is always liable to be contested.[17]

The key phrase here is "ongoing struggle." In the discussion that follows, my aim is to register this sense of struggle in terms of gender.

When applied to Renaissance representations of sex differences, inversion also takes on a special meaning, as Laqueur has reminded us. According to Galenic tradition, which seems to have persisted until the end of the seventeenth century, "Women . . . are inverted, and hence less perfect, men."[18] In such a one-sex system, as Laqueur demonstrates in his readings of a wide range of discourses on sexuality, the connection between biological sex and gender is unstable: "So-called biological sex does not provide a solid foundation for the cultural category of gender, but constantly threatens to subvert it." As a result, Renaissance representations of the sex-gender system are marked by surprising slippages and combinations instead of fixed certainties of difference:

> in the world I am describing there is no "real" sex that in principle grounds and distinguishes in a reductionist fashion two genders. Gender is part of the order of things, and sex, if not entirely conventional, is not solidly corporeal either. Thus the modern way of thinking about these texts, of asking what is happening to sex as the play of genders becomes indistinct, will not work. What we call sex and gender are in the Renaissance bound up in a circle of meanings from which escape to a supposed biological substratum is impossible.[19]

Laqueur's work is relevant to my inquiry in two respects. First, Donne's inversions are staged on these disputed, permeable boundaries of Renaissance gender. Specific tropes of gender instability such as hermaphroditism and transsexualism play an important part in some of Donne's most celebrated poems. Second, and more important, the ambiguities explored by Laqueur and exploited by Donne also are powerful incentives to achieve the opposite, to stabilize gender; in their context of homosocial exchange, Donne's poems begin to look like tests run to confirm distinctions based on gender.

A final aspect of literary inversion is related to Louis Montrose's assertion, a type of inversion in itself, that "the categories of subject and structure are interdependent" (a view similar to Turner's conception of the "ritual process"); thus it is possible to see the literary text as "not only a cultural production but a representation of cultural production."[20] Donne's poems of inversion depend upon this slippage or inversion between cultural production and representation of cultural production. Erica Harth has suggested that literary texts "rework ideology for pleasure,"[21] and this is the effect of many of the Songs and Sonnets. By taking pleasure in this ludic representation of ideological production, however, the reader inevitably gets caught up in the work of ideological production as well.

Difference and Indifference

"The Indifferent" offers a convenient starting point because of its obvious concern with the cultural code of Petrarchism.[22] As many commentators have noted, Donne inverts Petrarchan conventions to create an antiworld of "indifferent" lovers; like one of his prose paradoxes, the speaker's argument for a new orthodoxy of inconstancy in love engages the informed reader by inviting the "heretical" (but, of course, entirely conventional) Petrarchan counterargument.[23] That is, the speaker's effort to break away from Petrarchan discourse paradoxically depends upon that Petrarchan subtext; a poetic norm of love—Petrarchism—must be evoked, placed hierarchically above the speaker's heresy, and then displaced in a reversing move by the speaker in order for the wit of the poem to have its effect.

The social stakes of these discourses have been much discussed in recent scholarship,[24] and Marotti is certainly correct in identifying the libertine speaker of "The Indifferent" with an Inns of Court coterie which challenged through this kind of writing the courtly, Petrarchan code of deference which we associate with Elizabethan courtship. The particular focus of the hazing of Petrarchan die-hards also points to at least two levels of sexual politics in the poem. By initially identifying the Petrarchan heresy with women, the speaker discloses fears concerning his masculinity and mastery when women start taking seriously the ideal constructed for them by Petrarchan poets. And given the Elizabethan Court's manipulation of Petrarchism, the poem must be registering a closely related political anxiety as well.[25]

Yet, as Marotti himself is quick to add, the frequently ironic treatment of the libertine pose must prevent a hasty homologizing of sexual and political codes here. I would also resist the ironic reading that, as Stanley Fish points out, is so often invoked to save Donne from the consequences of his rhetoric.[26] Donne attempts a representation of the ideological work that goes into creating an Ovidian stance by means of play with binary oppositions. Donne, that is, seems to be identifying Petrarchism and Ovidianism as ideological projects even as he is, so to speak, constructed by them. This awareness does not, however, lead to a breakthrough in the form of a new ideology of love; what it does produce is a feeling of discomfort that could be available for either revolutionary or reactionary projects.

The indifference of Donne's confidently rebellious argument is compromised in several ways. Most obviously, he is not, as he claims, "indifferent," since there is one type of woman he cannot love—a "true" woman ("I can love any, so she be not true").[27] As we learn through the urgent questioning of the second stanza, this true woman poses a threat to the swaggerer of the first stanza, who seems to be speaking at once to a particular woman who would be true and to womankind. It becomes clear that the indifference is not a function of a large sexual appetite but, rather, is produced by fear of a "fixed" relation to a woman, a relation expressed in terms of binding and subjection (ll. 16, 18). Donne manages this fear by projecting it onto the woman—"doth a feare, that men are true, torment you?" (1. 13); in the process he draws on the misogynistic commonplace of woman's "natural" inconstancy (ll. 10–12), here tamed by fear of a superior male constancy, only to deny any difference between the sexes (ll. 14–15). However, a natural sexual difference, which allows for the domination of one sex by the other, is restored in lines 17–18 when the misogynistic tradition about the Fall is used to make indifference appear in the best possible light as a desire for independence from sin, here conceived as sexual bondage: "Must I, who came to travaile thorow you, / Grow your fixt subject, because you are true?" The earlier radical proposal of free love—"Let mee and doe you, twenty know" (l. 15)—is contradicted by this appeal to a conservative myth of origins.

This use of tradition is complicated by the polyvalent address of the poem to Marotti's coterie, to a particular woman, to womankind (and, we are surprised to learn in the last stanza, to the Goddess of Love herself)—each of which will have a different interest in, as opposed to "indifference" to, the argument of the poem. The punning phrase "came to travaile" epitomizes the division of the indifferent's argument among his various audiences. For example, his general sexism, which might contribute to a solidarity with the male coterie, would appear, to his particular addressee, compromised by his sexual relation with her. The indifferent engages in a practice that conflicts with his theory. The sexist moral geneology covers other anxieties of origin— more precisely, of motherhood, of having come "thorow" a woman. Women, fair and brown, dry and "spungie," "her, and her, and you, and you" can be mothers; the particular addressee might become a mother, thanks to the indifferent's coming "to travail" through her. The language of binding ("binde me not," l. 16) and growing ("Grow your fixt subject," l. 18) registers fears about being infantilized and mothered, perhaps also about the possibility of having impregnated the particular "you" of the poem, an act that might "stablish . . . constancie" (l. 25) of another sort. The question—"Must I, who came to travaile thorow you . . . ?"—is not a rhetorical one, and it should be heard to resonate with the earlier question: "Will it not serve your turn to do, as did your mothers?" Together these nervous questions frame anxieties about male autonomy which border on a fantasy of being "not of woman born" (*your mothers,* not my mother).[28]

Unlike Fish, then, I think there is something behind the rhetorical display here—namely, fear of women, and perhaps fear of turning into a woman. Petrarchism is identified with effeminacy, and insofar as the Elizabethan Court is structured along Petrarchan lines, the poem can be seen to express the sorts of anxieties expressed in Castiglione's *Book of the Courtier* about men sliding into femininity in the act of fashioning themselves as courtiers. Perhaps more relevant to this poem is the closely related fear that what Laqueur calls "heterosexual sociability" in general poses a threat to sexual identity.[29] I see no ground for claiming that Donne is dramatizing this attitude, though, in order to critique it. He is in its grip. Marotti believes, to the contrary, that Donne "assumed that his reader was able to perceive 'The Indifferent' as a love poem, a piece that converts a fashionable libertine stance into one of affectionate responsiveness." Although I find his sensitive reading very attractive, it is, again, dependent upon the notion of a coterie audience *out there,* a privileged audience "that was fond of antisentimental Ovidianism" but "could also appreciate its ironic undoing." This coterie—priviledged, educated, and enlightened—looks very much like a professor of literature. In Marotti's study, as in much Donne criticism, there is an attempt to identify the best Donne poems and then to connect this literary excellence with "the kind of mutuality in loving celebrated in those Shakespearean romantic comedies for which Inns men [enlightened beings that they were!] were such an appropriate audience."[30]

This view of the romantic comedies has, of course, been much contested both by new historicists and by feminists using a variety of methods.[31] A central theme in this work has to do with the conflict in the plays between heterosexual and same-sex relationships which is part of a structure of gender distinctions and the anxieties produced by it.[32] Viewed within this problematic, the first two stanzas of "The Indifferent" seem to be reinforcing solidarity with the male coterie by means of several strategies of containment of women. As objects of heterosexual love, they are represented as interchangable—except for the all-important "true" woman. As already mentioned, male autonomy even in heterosexual love is nervously asserted in the identification of women with their mothers while tacitly denying a male relationship with mother; this autonomy is then reasserted and at the same time undone in the final two lines of the second stanza. The interrogative mood of stanza two, however, suggests growing uncertainty and conflict.

Donne attempts an escape in the third stanza, which surprises the reader by placing the argument into a narrative and introducing a third character, a dea ex machina in his love story: "*Venus* heard me sigh this song" (1. 19). As Marotti suggests, the stanza operates as a metapoetic frame. This aestheticizing of the first two stanzas serves to advance the ideological project of constructing autonomy through male solidarity: Donne strengthens his solidarity with the male coterie by jokingly misrepresenting libertine speech as sighing and singing and simultaneously demonstrates self-sufficiency by a metapoetical move—"See, I know this is just a poem; that wasn't me speaking; I'm in control; nothing to worry about." Donne inverts another "factor of culture" consonant with the shift to narrative: the goddess inverts a romantic theme by undertaking for Donne's inverted Squire of Dames a quest for virtuous women. Venus's finding, that "alas, Some two or three / Poore heretiques in love there bee" (ll. 23–24), encloses what can now be called the speaker in yet another irony: his heretical stance, we discover, is in fact the norm; the true heretics are those "Which thinke to stablish dangerous constancie" (1. 25). The indifferent swaggering lover of stanza one is exposed as the orthodox devotee of Venus, while those who would have truth, those committed to a Petrarchan discourse of love, are discovered to be dangerous heretics. In either case, women seem to come out on top.

As Clay Hunt noted years ago, "by the time Donne began his literary career, the tendency to poke fun at the artificiality of the Petrarchan conventions had already become simply another of the Petrarchan conventions."[33] What makes "The Indifferent" more than a debunking exercise is its thematizing of this fact, its gradual exposure of the speaker himself as a subject constituted by ideologically invested conventions. The conflict in the poem is not between a subtext of Petrarchism and the "naturalism" of the speaker, but rather, between equally conventional treatments of love and women. Neither the speaker nor Petrarchists can claim more than a conventional authority for their arguments about love and women; even Venus, the goddess of love and court of final appeal in the poem, renders a judgment reached by many a questing knight in Medieval romance.

The result of this play with cultural commonplaces is not simply a New Critical tension or entrapment of the speaker by irony. Donne uses ironic entrapment as an ideological device for containing the sorts of contradictions he falls into in stanza two. For example, the libertine argument in stanza two indirectly treats a problem in his society's attitude towards women: the coexistence of the belief in the "naturally" passionate nature of women with the strictest standards imaginable for their sexual conduct before and after marriage.[34] The indifferent proposes to resolve this contradiction by means of his doctrine of free love. In the process of advancing his new order of sexual equality, however, he discovers the old standard of fidelity firmly in place. His rhetorical solution to this problem is to turn gender ideology in on itself by representing the woman's *resistance* to his libertinism (i.e., her constancy) as just another manifestation of her willful nature, restlessly trying out new behaviors (ll. 10–12) or jealously fearing an imagined male constancy (l. 13), not as the result of legal, moral, and religious constraints (including the Petrarchan ideal of our subtext) imposed from without. In the third stanza this new order of sexual relations is ironically "validated" by appropriating an old romance motif. This literary solution by irony does not, however, resolve the problems released by the conflict between Petrarchism and Ovidianism. Donne's play of wit is not subversive in the sense of directly challenging any ideology, but neither is it orthodox in the sense of reflecting an ideology. The poem discloses some of the secrets of sexual relations only to conceal them again in irony and paradox. This process, I suggest, is ideology at work containing fundamental contradictions in sexual attitudes and practice.[35] In Victor Turner's formulation, Donne's inversion "develops a language for talking about normative structures,"[36] and that language is irony, a literary language that makes it easier to live with contradictions.

Or does it? "The Indifferent" does not put me completely at ease. Wilbur Sanders has written well of the "feeling of distaste" one can experience after reading some of Donne's poems, even some of the most celebrated ones such as "The Canonization," and he relates this dissatisfaction to problems with Donne's irony: "It seems connected somehow with a feeling that the complexities of response in which Donne is dealing are self-indulgent, wanton, factitious. . . . The irony becomes *dis*integrative."[37] The twists and turns of Donne's irony in "The Indifferent" do not quite succeed in concealing vulnerabilities and inconsistencies in the subject of love. The poem opens with its jaunty ironic claim that indifference and loving are not opposites, that indifference, on the contrary, is for the speaker a condition for loving. Freud wrote that "The most striking distinction between the erotic life of antiquity and our own no doubt lies in the fact that the ancients laid the stress on the instinct itself, whereas we emphasize its object."[38] Donne would seem to be advocating a return to the primacy of the instinct, until, at the end of the first stanza, we learn that one kind of love object, the "true" one, has a (negative) determinative influence on desire. This "turn" in the argument (Donne's argument takes more turns than he accuses women of in line 11, a fact that aligns him with the women he so obviously fears) is the result of having broken with Petrarchan notions of truth; uncannily, an obsession with the love object returns, another "true" woman, though she douses the instinct instead of firing it. In the second stanza, as we have seen, this object is then analyzed according to some cultural commonplaces about women in order to put distance between the no-longer-indifferent subject of love and this object. But in advocating promiscuity (i.e., indifference) for the stubbornly "true" love object, a promiscuity that would presumably make her desirable to him, the indifferent subject in effect tells *her* to be more like *him:* "Oh we are not, be not you so, / Let mee and doe you, twenty know." The promiscuity that had been ascribed to "your mothers" earlier (l. 11) has been transformed into a practice of men which the indifferent now wishes to share with women. This shift is perhaps an index of the level of anxiety turning the ironies of stanza two: better to let copulation thrive on both sides than to "grow your fixt subject."

Having "crossed the threshold" of Petrarchan resistance, as William Kerrigan and Gordon Braden phrase it, Donne seems to be struggling with a problem of residual Petrarchanism. At the end of their survey of "Petrarch Refracted" Kerrigan and Braden write, "There is something Petrarchan in our souls."[39] I prefer to argue that poems like "The Indifferent" disclose our culture's tendency to construct love or sexuality around oppositions like promiscuity and fidelity, sex and love, male and female. The disclosure can open these constructions to review and critique, but perhaps its chief effect is one of discomfiture. Again Freud's meditations seem pertinent, both as comment upon and as exemplification of this process of construction by opposition. Martin S. Bergmann has recently discussed the contradiction in Freud's attempt to explain the difference between love and the sexual instinct, on the one hand, and his insistence on a link between them, on the other. As a result, Bergmann summarizes, Freud found it difficult to integrate the sexual instinct with an enduring relationship: "The human being in this view must either sacrifice stability and permanence in his most basic relationship, or sacrifice the full capacity for sexual pleasure."[40] Lacan follows suit on this point, insisting on the mutual exclusion of love and desire, and adds an ironic twist of his own: since love is basically narcissistic in this scheme, love of a woman would seem to be a step in the direction of identification with her.[41] Again, the defensive ironies of Donne's indifferent seem to some degree provoked by the fear that in constantly loving a woman he may become a woman.

"The Indifferent," then, constructs the subject of love along the lines of Freud's antithesis: One must be either an Ovidian or a Petrarchan, it would appear. The unsettling, interrogative force of the poem, what exceeds the considerable intellectual pleasure it offers, is never stated but is bound up with *how the speaking/reading subject feels about this arrangement of love life*.[42] In this last respect it seems to me that "The Indifferent," like many of Donne's most brilliant exercises of wit, is a perplexed and unhappy poem. The jocular mythologizing of the last stanza needs to be qualified by the consideration that the libertine seems to be disturbed by one of the "two or three" Petrarchan heretics, his sexual indifference having collapsed in the face of its opposite (again, a genuine indifferent would not be bothered by a "true" love object). His plenitude as the indifferent is crossed by a lack—he cannot love one who is true. A certain disparity in sexual relations is made to seem inevitable, embarrassing, or even sad, though it would be the sadness one feels for the consummate cynic: "You shall be true to them, who'are false to you" (l. 27). The "minds of the fair sex" are not perplexed by Donne's writing. Rather, Dryden's famous criticism of Donne—"he affects the metaphysics . . . and perplexes the minds of the fair sex with nice speculations of philosophy, when he should engage their hearts, and entertain them with the softnesses of love"—captures a deep division *within* Donne's indifferent subject of love.[43]

"Confined Love," an inverted "Indifferent" for women, talks even more overtly about the asymmetry of normative structures, and it returns us to the gendered subject of love. If "The Indifferent" is powered by a fear of women and of turning into a woman, "Confined Love" projects fear of the reverse, that women might become men. The poem has recently been understood as a paradox in the Donnean sense of an "alarum to truth"—an argument designed to provoke the reader "to find better reasons against" it.[44] But we ought not to rest easy with that undoubtedly correct approach to the poem, for the very process of finding better reasons against the female speaker is also on trial in this poem. This feature of the poem is historically (in the best sense) interesting given the cultural placement of the speaking woman in the Renaissance. Ann Rosalind Jones has sketched out "the link between loose language and loose living" that "arises from a basic association of women's bodies with their speech." If "verbal challenges from women were perceived as sexual challenges as well," Donne's impersonation of a powerful speaking woman (Donne as *donna*) might be seen as an opening analogous to what

Jones calls "the scandalous openness" of the female body that proscribed women's speech.[45]

In the spirit of the Renaissance *querelle des femmes,* the speaker of "Confined Love" invents a radical myth of origins to critique orthodox views on sexual relations. Denying any basis in nature for the standards of sexual conduct imposed on women, the speaker advances a Machiavellian explanation for the origins of such prescriptions. The law confining female love, she reasons, was a means of compensating for male "unworthiness"; unable, through moral ("being false") or physical ("or weake") means, to possess a woman, the male created a law designed to reduce the "pain" and "shame" accruing from female infidelity, the "natural" response to male inadequacy. Here Donne's wit cuts at least two ways. More obviously, the speaker demystifies monogamy by representing it as a device for reducing male anxiety caused by inherent male weakness; unable to control the effects of love on himself, he tries to regulate the cause of those effects. More ingeniously, Donne undercuts the speaker's naturalistic argument before it even begins; even in its original condition, human sexuality is marked by behavior and feelings ("false," "pain," "shame") not shared by the elements of the natural world treated in stanza two. And, of course, the argument of stanzas two and three is itself fallacious and clinched with a quibble on "good."[46]

However, our detection of a flaw in the speaker's argument does not allow us to mock her from a comfortably fixed position. A key component of the fun of this poem is the fact that the woman's speech is composed for her by a man. This inversion, a poetic analogue to the durable British satiric tradition of female impersonation, allows Donne to play with sexual codes in their relation to male desire. Like much transvestite sexual satire, Donne's poem in drag is ambivalent: on the one hand, it critiques gender stereotypes by the technique of exaggeration; on the other, it releases the sorts of fantasies that help to produce the stereotypes. Thus I agree with Marotti's insistence on the importance of the male coterie to this and other poems featuring female speakers. I would add to Marotti's account the point that, as in transvestite performances, so in "Confined Love," and as we shall see especially in "Sapho to Philaenis," the relationship between the sexual fantasy and the satire is highly unstable. "Confined Love" offers little in the way of prurient interest, but its fantasy of a sexually free and active woman is an enduring topos in pornographic discourse. When the fantasy is presented through female impersonation, we can see a particularly exaggerated version of the process whereby women are constructed by men: the woman is a man, literally the embodiment of a male fantasy. The result of such impersonation can be sexually exciting and satirically devastating all at once.

As a combination of sexual fantasy and satire the poem seems both to produce subversive views on sexual roles and relations and to contain them.[47] Again, the woman constructed in the poem is both desirable and threatening.

This matches the poem's formal indebtedness to paradox. As a paradox, "Confined Love" allows for the simultaneous recording and containment of radical points of view. Containment is achieved in "Confined Love" by logical fallacy and equivocation. Of course, as Rosalie Colie and others have noted, there is "nothing" to a Renaissance paradox but language. And that is just the point. "Confined Love," like many of Donne's *Paradoxes and Problems,* thematizes the interplay of orthodoxy and heterodoxy by representing it as a contest of language; the "defense" of orthodoxy proceeds by linguistic entrapment, that is, by reversing the equivocal movement of heterodoxy. Thus, paradoxes seem hospitable to both radical and conservative readings. Donne's self-consuming artifact is, on the one hand, productive. Writing on *The Praise of Folly,* Joel Altman has illuminated this feature of paradox; the inconsistencies and equivocations of Dame Folly, the greatest female speaker of paradoxes, have the purpose not only of mocking her arguments but of making us "respond emotionally to them, test the validity and provenance of our responses as the viewpoints grind with murderous innocency one against the other, and . . . weigh the value and limitations of each."[48] Pretending to be the sexually riotous woman of physiological theory[49] and folk tradition, Donne's speaker challenges the reader to test that belief and the male response to it. However, while encouraging us to entertain multiple perspectives on a problem, the poem also provides the means for reducing the problem to a single perspective. This reduction, however, is never entirely satisfactory, for the play of ideas has disclosed problems—for example, the split between desire and love in "The Indifferent" or the problem of sexual freedom and sexual possession in "Confined Love"—which resist the easy solution of mocking the speaker and thereby fixing the subject-position of the reader.

Inversion and male fantasy also encircle one another in the elegy "To his Mistres Going to Bed." As Thomas M. Greene observes in a brilliant reading, the second line of the poem raises questions about the speaker's "powers": "Come, Madame, come, all rest my powers defie, / Until I labour, I in labour lye."[50] Donne the plowman changes places with the woman laboring to deliver the fruit of his tillage; Donne would seem to be saying, "I'm just like you, except that I have this huge erection (I'm not like you)." At the end of the poem he is further metamorphosed into a midwife in a comparison that, taken together with the conceit of labor pains, seems decidedly ineffective rhetorically, if the poem is read as a persuasion to intercourse:

> Then since I might knowe,
> As liberally as to a midwife showe
> Thy selfe. . . . (ll. 43–45)

Does a woman want to think about getting pregnant at a time like this? I do not know. Once again the topic of motherhood disturbs an Ovidian performance (Donne brings it up again in the elegy "Loves Warre"). Donne's male coterie might have enjoyed the thought, and it would seem to agree with the obtrusive erection jokes that have made this poem a preeminent example of phallocentricism in Donne's poetry.[51]

But the fantasy goes further and allows Donne to imagine himself in the position of male and female at once. This double identification is perhaps most titillating when Donne's stiff penis fuses with the woman's corset: "Off with that happt buske, whom I envye / That still can be, and still can stand so nigh" (ll. 11–12). I shall have more to say about this interchange between the penis and the woman in my discussion of "Aire and Angels"; here I only want to remark that what appears to be an intensely phallic moment in the poem is marked by a fantasized passage of the phallus over to the woman. In the terms of psychoanalytic debate over the relationship between phallus and penis, one might say that the sexual power Donne associates with his penis here is detached from the penis and moved to the woman through the mediation of the "busk."[52] Donne seems exceedingly anxious to affirm the penis as the signifier of sexual difference in this poem, but in the fantasy equation corset = penis it seems to efface difference.[53] This equivocal movement of phallic signification is consistent with another striking feature of the poem; as Carey and Greene both observe, there is no woman to be seen in Elegy 19; in Greene's words, "The poem is a tissue of *coverings,* analogical garments which apparel the 'full nakedness' the text seems to celebrate but actually withholds."[54] Donne's descriptive tour de force is a classic account of the fetish as a substitute for the (missing) maternal phallus, that is, as a defense against the fear of castration. I will not insist upon a rigidly psychoanalytic articulation of the references to clothing, women's underwear, and giving birth, but the psychoanalytic theme is consistent with the functioning of Donne's phallic exhibitionism in this poem. It is autoerotic. The final inversion of the poem—"To teach thee, I am naked first"—underscores the point that the fantasized striptease has actually discovered the male speaker. And when Donne finally approaches the joys of the woman's "full nakedness," he imagines her covered again, with a man.

If "To his Mistres Going to Bed" is a hymn to the phallus, "Loves Progress," like "Going to Bed" one of the poems not licensed for publication in the 1633 edition, is ostensibly Donne's elegy to the vulva.[55] Inversion operates quite literally in this poem, as it advises male readers to start at the bottom, instead of the top, in their approach to the beloved's "Centrique part." Figuratively, too, Donne inverts the Petrarchan convention of praise of the beloved in her "parts," what Nancy Vickers calls "scattered woman and scattered rhyme."[56] Indeed, the poem works as both writing guide and sex manual; the most efficacious arrangement of a blazon of the beloved will correspond to the most efficient form of foreplay. The poem makes for an interesting comparison and contrast with "To his Mistres Going to Bed"; here body parts abound—hair, brow, nose, lips, teeth, tongue, and so forth, to the vulva—and it is the body parts that are fetishized and thereby block access to the "one thing" that is the "right true end of love." In this poem the erection jokes are replaced by jocular and mainly low-register names for the woman's sex organ: in order they are, "thing," "pits and holes," "the Centrique part," "her India" (the exception, although, as Gardner points out in her edition, it connotes wealth not beauty and thus supports an economic theme in the poem; see ll. 15–16), "that part," "purse," and "mouth." The search for the true end of love coincides with a search for the essence of woman:

> But if wee
> Make love to woman, Vertue is not shee,
> As Beauty's not, nor Wealth, Hee that strayes thus,
> From her to hers, is more adulterous
> Than if hee tooke her mayde. (ll. 23–27)

Particular stress is placed on the attribute of beauty; the point is not to identify woman with beauty because "when we are come" to the beauteous parts "Wee anchor there, and think our selves at home, / For they seem all" (ll. 53–55; this is said of the lips). Thus Donne would seem to be critiquing Petrarchan fetishizing of the female body. Donne finds nothing beautiful to write about the vulva, choosing to treat it instead as a site of economic activity.[57] Indeed, it resists visualization in the poem, another aspect of the poem's anti-Petrarchism.[58] This point is reinforced by the metaphysical conceit which finds "some symetrie" between the foot and the vulva ("lovely enough to stop, but not stay at" [l. 76]; Donne is not a foot fetishist and makes the modern reader suddenly aware of the absence of legs in the erotic inventory of Renaissance poets, since he sees nothing but "this empty and etheriall way" between the foot and the vulva), perhaps by way of Katherine's "le foot" in *Henry V:*

> Least subject to disguise and change it is,
> Men say, the devill never can change his.
> It is the embleme that hath figured
> Firmness; 'tis the first part that comes to bed. (ll. 77–80)

Donne's joke on Petrarchan conventions of praise is many-faceted. He counters the decentered, "scattered" woman of the blazon with a woman centered by some "thing" not seen and therefore "least subject to disguise and change." Donne's insistence on, and even detachment of, the vulva is consistent with "pin-up" pornography. In what Annette Kuhn calls the "split-beaver" shot, the woman is "reduced to one part of her anatomy, . . . the single, irreducible signifier of sexual difference."[59] Like the foot "that hath figured / Firmness," the vulva stabilizes the woman's identity but, more important I think, confirms male identity by "figuring" the "firm" penis; the vulva can only be seen as the penis. Thus the site of sexual differentiation is, through the foot/vulva comparison, also marked by a paradoxical identification of male and female.[60]

Like the scattered Petrarchan woman, Donne's gynocentric woman is also silent; he is particularly averse to "beginning at the face" and the upper of the two mouths produces "Syrens songs." The two mouths of the two purses are also "aversely laid" (perpendicular to each other but also averse to each other). Privileging the lower mouth would seem to deny the upper. He converts Petrarchan idealization and worship of woman into materialist "tribute" paid to her "purse." Love, then, is represented as a business transaction (see also "Loves Exchange" and "Loves Usury") rather than as a feudal courtship; the entire poem, of course, is aimed at showing up Petrarchism as a waste of time ("what this chace / Mispent, by thy beginning at the face").[61]

Donne's essentializing of woman by her "purse" is suggestive of the way socioeconomic relations and sexual relations are wrapped around each other. There are signs that Donne is not entirely happy with the commercial sex object he has constructed. Cupid is "an infernall God, and under ground / With Pluto dwells, where gold and fyre abound" (ll. 29–30). The misogynistic joke (woman = vulva) covers anxieties perhaps assuaged, as noted earlier, by adding the penis to the equation. Furthermore, the concluding couplet—"Hee which doth not [follow my advice], his error is as greate / As who by Clyster gave the stomach meate"—seems at once unconscious and too curiously considered. The tenor of the comparison insists on the primacy of genital sexuality, but the vehicle complicates the eroticism of the poem by enlisting oral and anal drives in the promotion of genitalism. The joke constructs a scene of forcible penetration that contrasts sharply with the commercial language of purses and exchequers used to represent the genital sex act. It may be appropriate that a poem praising 1) intercourse as a commercial transaction and 2) an orifice close to the anus should end with an enema, and an inverted one at that. But Donne's praise of genital heterosexuality also seems to slide in these lines from crude jocularity to violent defensiveness.

To complete this reading of the pornographic Donne, I turn now to what appears to be the most "Freudian" of Donne's inversions, his heroical epistle "Sapho to Philaenis."[62] On the basis of internal evidence of subject matter and style, Gardner places this poem among the Dubia even though it appears in 1633 and in the Group II manuscripts. I follow Grierson and Shawcross in accepting it as Donne's work. Both Grierson and Gardner seem to find the homosexual content distasteful, but Gardner finds the style lacking too: "repetitive," "lacks Donne's habitual progressiveness," "metrical dullness . . . matched by the poverty of its vocabulary," "monotonous." Grierson is divided by content and style as evidenced by this cautious sentence: "whatever one may think of the poem on moral grounds," he writes, "it is impossible to deny that Donne has caught the tone of the kind, and written a poem passionate and eloquent in its own not altogether admirable way."[63] Recent studies differ sharply on the poem's construction of lesbianism. James Holstun and Elizabeth Harvey both find the case to be one of lesbianism contained: Holstun argues that while " 'Sapho to Philaenis' does consider lesbian eroticism with considerable sympathy, it finally masters this eroticism by subordinating it to a patriarchal scheme of nature, history, and language"; Harvey finds Donne's "ventriloquistic appropriation of the feminine voice" to be "a censorship of its difference," while his masquerade of the lesbian "marginalizes her within a utopian world that . . . is narcissistically sterile."[64] Janel Mueller writes more affirmatively of the poem as a text that interrogates Renaissance heterosexuality, friendship, and marital customs through its construction of a lesbian erotic utopia. Finally, Paula Blank has recently questioned, rightly I think, whether lesbianism is really at stake in the poem, finding the elegy instead to be one instance of a recurrent failure of " 'homopoetics'—the cultural making of likenesses"—in Donne: "a strict opposition between heterosexual love and homosexual love breaks down over the course of the poem, and difference emerges as the only inviolable, invariable feature of erotic experience with an other."[65]

Marotti's thesis of the coterie inclines me to approach this poem as a heterosexual male fantasy and to read its employment of "lesbianism" in that light. I have suggested the relevance of pornographic conventions to "Love's Progresse," and while Donne's poem cannot be simply equated to a layout in *Penthouse* or a porn loop, I do believe that the use of "lesbian" lovemaking in such publications/films is a helpful orientation to Donne's poem. Lovemaking between women is installed in a variety of ways in heterosexual pornography—as a prelude to heterosexual sex, as a substitute for it, as report on or verification of feminine desire, and so forth, but always *in relation to* heterosexual activity. I would suggest that "Sapho to Philaenis" also needs to be read in the context of Donne's other, heterosexual love poetry. In this context, the poem works somewhat like a lesbian episode in conventional pornography; as Judith Roof writes, "lesbian episodes are represented as excursions into the mysterious realm of female sexuality," which promise "to present what is presumably a privileged view of the forbidden secrets of female sexuality especially for the spectator's eye (and pleasure)."[66] The poem is for men; or, to borrow Gary Day's phrase, it is an instance of men "looking at women." Like straight pornography, the poem seems to use the "lesbian" to present a truth "not only about the female body but also about female sexual behaviour," and like pornography, it fails to do so.[67] But where pornography fails because the women are portrayed to please the male viewer and/or their sexual behavior mimics heterosexual lovemaking, Donne calls attention to the failure and attributes it to a failure in the system of representation: "Where is that holy fire, which Verse is said / To have?" (l. 1). The poet's failure is owing to the beloved's incomparability, her independence of the representational system:

> Thou art not soft, and cleare, and strait, and faire,
>   As *Down,* as *Stars, Cedars,* and *Lillies* are,
> But thy right hand, and cheek, and eye, only
>   Are like thy other hand, and cheek, and eye. (ll. 21–24)

Like her body, their lovemaking cannot be represented but only contrasted with the foreplay of "some soft boy" and the "tillage of a harsh rough man": "of our dallyance no more signes there are, / Then fishes leave in streames, or Birds in aire."[68]

Donne's nonrepresentation of the female body and lesbian lovemaking complicates the already complicated possibilities for identification one finds in the straight pornographic use of lesbianism. As Day notes, in the latter, "not only is the male identifying with male behavior as expressed through a female body, but, in wanting to be desired, he is also, by extension, identifying with each woman's desire to be desired. . . . What is happening here is that the sexual difference on which pornography insists is losing its clarity."[69] "Sapho to Philaenis" seems to offer its male readers little in this line. It may be that the "soft boy" and the "harsh rough man" enter the scene of fantasy in the ways described in Day's account, though Sappho explicitly denies them participation. But the male reader is teased, I believe, until near the end of the poem, where two distinct points of identification are offered. The first is Sappho's masturbatory fantasy (another porn commonplace which equates female sexuality, autoeroticism, and lesbianism[70]):

> Likenesse begets such strange selfe flatterie,
>   That touching my selfe, all seemes done to thee.
> My selfe I'embrace, and mine owne hands I kisse,
>   And amorously thanke my selfe for this. (ll. 51–54)

Donne explicitly relates her autoeroticism to narcissism—"Me, in my glasse, I call thee" (55), a move which Harvey and Holstun read as a critical containment while Mueller finds it, with its accompanying autoeroticism, one of the "self empowering pleasures . . . by which an acculturated female invests her body and her psyche with a sense of worth and gains the confidence to be a subject, not merely an object, of desire."[71] At the same time, however, the trope of the masturbating female in pornography can suggest a more complex alternative that implicates the male reader/voyeur. As Day notes, the autoeroticism of the model "suggests her sexual self-sufficiency: not only is she not available but she also has no need of men." However, Day continues, the narcissism cuts two ways: "her auto-erotic pleasure . . . mirrors the man's auto-erotic pleasure as he looks at her. Her image thus becomes a reflection of his own activity and indicates that gazing at a pin-up [in Donne's case, imagining an autoerotic Sappho] is analogous to Narcissus captivated by his own image in the pool."[72] Again, the distinction between the lesbian and the heterosexual breaks down. Following the myth to a fault, Donne dissolves this pleasure in water: "But alas, / When I would kisse, teares dimme mine *eyes,* and *glasse*" (l. 56). Finally, in a dazzling sequence, a wish for lesbian *jouissance*—"restore / Me to mee; thee, my *halfe,* my *all,* my *more*" (ll. 58–59)—also returns the beloved, perhaps through a pun on his wife's name, to representation. Using the terms of conventional Petrarchan blazonry, Donne recuperates the "lesbian" beloved as an object of heterosexual love:

> So may thy cheekes red outweare scarlet dye,
>   And their white, whitenesse of the *Galaxy,*
> So may thy mighty,'amazing beauty move
>   *Envy'*in all *women,* and in all *men, love*" (ll. 59–62)

Thus Donne's "apparitional lesbian" is returned to a male gaze and conventional gender roles: women may "envy," men "love" the beloved.[73]

While Donne, as Mueller argues, veers away from the homophobic tradition of commentary on Sappho, his Sapphic impersonation does not, it seems to me, necessarily construct an alternative to heterosexuality. Roof's comments on the pornographic convention again seem relevant here:

> Parts of unhappy love affairs, the lesbian affairs are never quite successful. . . . Staging, thus, an uncompleted or perpetuated desire that they arouse but do not assuage, they constitute a kind of crisis, a roving unfixity. . . . As an element in a larger narrative, lesbian sexuality is quickly made a part of a heterosexual system where its seemingly liberalized variety ultimately assures a heterosexual trajectory for female sexual development.[74]

But to say "Sapho to Philaenis" simply reinforces sexual "norms" is to assume too much and miss the truly interrogative power of the poem. What is the "sexual norm?" Donne seems to be asking. In the great central passage of the poem, for example, Donne makes lack of the penis, or what Valerie Traub might call the "(in)significance of lesbian desire,"[75] a means to greater freedom and plenitude in sexual relations:

> Thy body is a naturall Paradise,
>   In whose selfe, unmanur'd, all pleasure lies,
> Nor needs perfection; why shouldst thou than
>   Admit the tillage of a harsh rough man?
> Men leave behinde them that which their sin showes,
>   And are as theeves trac'd, which rob when it snows.
> But of our dallyance no more signes there are,
>   Then fishes leave in streames, or Birds in aire.

> And betweene us all sweetnesse may be had;
> All, all that Nature yields, or Art can adde. (ll. 35–44)

Precisely how this fantasy might position male speaking or reading subjects, how it might affect a male coterie, is not entirely clear. From a psychoanalytic perspective, for example, it could be read as an instance of castration denial; the love described is phallic in the Lacanian sense in its plenitude, wholeness, self-sufficiency; "Sapho" and "Philaenis" need no man because they have the phallus.[76] But for just this reason the "lesbian" body remains connected to phallologocentrism. As I think Blank is also suggesting, the poem challenges definitions of heterosexuality based upon "a strict opposition between heterosexual love and homosexual love."[77] Jeffrey Weeks suggests that desire is not "a relationship to a real object but is a relationship to phantasy"; by means of the "lesbian" fantasy, "Sapho to Philaenis" registers the potentially disorienting motility of masculine desire.[78]

I want to stress, then, that by putting ideological invention in motion, these poems of inversion allow for the possibility of a reproduction of ideology that is, at least provisionally, open to a variety of interventions. Tony Bennett's provisional synthesis of formalism and Marxism summarizes my practice in arguing for a double movement in Donne's paradoxes: "The concern, within such an approach, is with the *different* sets of formal devices through which *different* forms of writing work upon ideology so as to produce it in *different* ways—sometimes distancing it, sometimes underwriting its effects by sealing its enclosures."[79] In particular, as paradoxes the poems reproduce processes whereby norms are generated, imposed, and violated. Thus my argument has come round to the familiar topic of paradox as a marker of Donne's writerly texts. But not so common in discussions of Donne's paradoxes is the ideological significance of this sort of rhetoric. Like many writers of the period, Donne clearly saw the usefulness of paradox to the scrutiny of ideology, since it hinders readers from knowing with certainty the views of writers.[80] But this formulation implies a certain superiority of the writer to ideology. Ideological work is, as Sinfield argues, writers' work, and writing always takes place within ideology. Donne's paradoxes of gender seem more focussed on the activities of identifying and managing contradictions within ideology.[81] I want to press this view with particular force here because these poems deal with gender, which I take to be, as Teresa de Lauretis argues, "a primary instance of ideology, and obviously not only for women."[82] I claim not that Donne covers his views through a kind of "plausible deniability," but rather, that his own position is very much under construction. Indeed, to say, as I have said, that these poems represent ideological work is somewhat redundant. Rather, the poems exemplify de Lauretis's proposition that "The construction of gender is the product and process of both representation and self-representation."[83]

"Some lovely glorious nothing"

"Aire and Angels" is something like Donne's Exhibit A in the construction of gender. The critical heritage of this poem provides illustrious evidence of the value of Bennett's notion of the "reading formation" as a set of discursive relations that construct the text and position the reader in specific ways.[84] As Peter De Sa Wiggins notes, the poem has been treated by all the "major figures" of Donne criticism "as if it were a touchstone for criticism of Donne's secular lyrics." And, Wiggins continues, so disparate are interpretations of the poem that they "look as if they could not have arisen from scrutiny of the same object."[85] In light of my earlier discussion of the lyrics as imitations of ideological production, and the construction of gender in particular, Wiggins's exasperated statement is precisely the point needing to be understood. The stated interests in these many readings of the poem are diverse and very high— the character of Donne, his thinking on the body/soul question, his doctrine of love, poetic unity—but what emerges from a reading of most of the criticism is an earnest concern with the failure or success of the speaker's discourse. As Wiggins writes, "In reading criticism of 'Aire and Angels' from C. S. Lewis to the present, one loses the poem amid a fracas of conjecture about the nature of Donne's poetry" (87). Of particular interest are the ways in which these conjectures are gendered, in the sense that arguments and conclusions about the poem, or "the nature of Donne's poetry" said to be raised by the poem, generally turn upon a decision concerning Donne's views on the nature of women, about "just such disparitie."

In his compelling formalist reading Wiggins faces squarely the critical problem with the poem: "Virtually every reading we have of the poem, from Lewis to the present, gets caught in an exasperating contradiction that would force the lover to defeat the purpose of his persuasion" (92). Helen Gardner, for example, is forced to conclude that it is "not a wholly successful poem" because Donne's intention remains unclear.[86] Although Wiggins writes of a "lover" rather than Donne, this speaker is never distinguished from the author, and his reading proceeds from an assumption about unity of intention shared with Gardner: "If one is to be as sophistical and as reverent as the paradoxical lover in 'Aire and Angels,' one must at least be passionately consistent about it, and the extraordinary symmetry in the double-sonnet structure of this poem would appear to suggest that consistency is important. If the lover declares his beloved to be an angel at the opening of the poem, she must remain an angel to the closing lines" (92). To resolve the apparent contradiction in the poem, Wiggins substitutes for the apparent shift of angelic identity from she to he a shift in the signification of "love" across the two stanzas, from "a passion in search of an object" to "the object of a passion" in line twenty-five ("So thy love may be my loves spheare"), a shift mirrored in the corresponding eleventh line of the first stanza ("And therefore what thou wert, and who"), in which the word "thou" ceases to mean the imperfect glimpses of the lady in other women and settles on the lady addressed by the speaker (94). This slippage enables a brilliant inversion: in line twenty-five "the speaker's love *is* the woman and the woman's love *is* the speaker, so that a plain paraphrase of the lines should read, 'So may *I* be *your* sphere' " (94). "Just such disparitie" is highly unexpected and complimentary.

Wiggins is forthright in stating that he seeks resolution in his reading; the alternative is to dwell "on contradictions that render it a poetic riddle whose key lies in its cultural context" (98). Against such a position, Docherty works at "undoing Donne," a project that "expands the concerns of these texts, obscures and mystifies them and makes them available for re-reading." Although like Docherty I emphasize contradiction, I prefer to think of the text as a site of cultural production rather than his scene of "failed confessions."[87] My reading of text and context emphasizes contradiction in the interest of the historical side of my argument—that "Aire and Angels" both represents and participates in a process of defining heterosexual relations in terms of a construction of gender.

By positioning the poem within a system of courtly compliment of great ladies, Marotti correctly, I believe, makes the problem of "Aire and Angels" the problem of the subject. What I want to restore to Marotti's account of "Aire and Angels" is the gendered subject of love, which seems to drop out of his sociopolitical reading. Joan Kelly-Gadol offers a way of thinking across political and sexual courtship (and, for my purposes, a bridge from "Confined Love" to "Aire and Angels") in her well-known essay, "Did Women Have a Renaissance?" Demystifying Bembo's discourse in *The Courtier,* Kelly-Gadol notes that while the lady appears to be served by her courtier, "this love theory really made her serve—and stand as a symbol of how the relation of domination may be reversed, so that the prince could be made to serve the interests of the courtier." But the courtier achieves this by adopting " 'women's ways' in his relations to the prince":

> To be attractive, accomplished, and seem not to care; to charm and do so coolly—how concerned with impression, how masked the true self. And how manipulative: petitioning his lord, the courtier knows to be "discreet in choosing the occasion, and will ask things that are proper and reasonable; and he will so frame his request, omitting those parts that he knows can cause displeasure, and will skillfully make easy the difficult points so that his lord will always grant it. . . ." In short, how like a woman—or a dependent, for that is the root of the simile.[88]

We have observed Donne's "dressing up" in "Confined Love," but it may be that female impersonation of another sort was a problem endemic to the Renaissance courtier's career and one figured in the work of fashioning a masculine subject of love in "Aire and Angels."

As several commentators have noted, it seems to be a somewhat chastened *indifferent* ("Twice or thrice had I lov'd thee") who speaks here and recalls "The Good Morrow," perhaps the most universally praised celebration of "mutual" love in Songs and Sonnets. My reading imports some of the unsettledness noted in both "The Indifferent" and "Confined Love" into "Aire and Angels," a poem which struggles with the same sort of contradictory definitions of women in its attempt to argue for the possibility of a fulfilling sexual relation between man and woman. These contradictions are staged as competitions between ways of speaking about love (Wiggins suggests the *dolce stil novo* and Latin elegiac tradition, and I hope to display others) that the speaker strives to bring under his control. Again, I wish to emphasize the process and well as the product of this project of representation. In the terms of my argument with Gardner and Wiggins, I propose not only to reconstruct the intention of speaker or poet but to position intentionality as an element in the ideological projects we undertake in analyzing this poem. Although my argument is not rigorously feminist or psychoanalytic in method or aim, the writings of post-Lacanian feminists like Jane Gallop offer a powerful formulation of the sort of interplay of sexuality and reading evoked by this poem: in Lacanian terms the speaker's or reader's success might be seen as a victory for phallologocentrism and hence as a defeat of the possibility of a real sexual *relation;* on the other hand, what escapes or resists control might be felt as an exciting alternative for reading and sexual relations, but one which, like the paradox it is, is always contingent on the closure it resists.[89] Judith Butler's recent reflections on gender and "performativity" capture the movement of Donne's constructions: "The 'performative' dimension of construction is precisely the forced reiteration of norms. In this sense, then, it is not only that there are constraints to performativity; rather, constraint calls to be rethought as the very condition of performativity. . . . constraint is . . . that which impels and sustains performativity."[90]

Undoubtedly, as Wiggins argues, "consistency is important" to the poem; indeed, an ideological analysis would make consistency the central issue of the poem. The poem opens by invoking and immediately problematizing the Petrarchan convention of praise of the beloved as an ideal, spiritual being.[91] The speaker represents this ideal, the source of his desire, as a power originating outside himself: "So in a voice, so in a shapelesse flame, / Angells affect us oft, and worhip'd bee" (ll. 3–4). Robert H. West notes that "In the common interpretation, at least, they [angels] stood to man's dazzled eyes for God himself whenever, as in the burning bush or the plains of Mamre, he showed his will to man more directly than usual."[92] The angel analogy represents the woman as a kind of stand-in for God, but this representation is immediately challenged and then exposed as a mystification. Donne first cleverly exploits the dispute between Catholic and Protestant theologians on the worship of angels (Catholics allowed for a kind of adoration, since angels were higher beings, while Protestants vigorously opposed any worship of them) to prod the reader into deciding for or against Petrarchism (i.e., the worship of angels). In the next two lines the speaker rewrites his praise as a paradoxical encomium, a praise of nothing (or no thing): "Still when, to where thou wert, I came, / Some lovely glorious nothing I did see" (ll. 5–6).

This line is one to linger over. Gardner directs us to Neoplatonic love theory, noting Ficino's insistence that "The passion of a lover is not quenched by the mere touch or sight of a body."[93] This is persuasive, although we also need to consider what has happened to the theory in these lines. Again, a Lacanian account of the definition of woman helps me describe the movement of the opening lines of this poem: "As negative to the man, woman becomes a total object of fantasy (or an object of total fantasy), elevated into the place of the Other and made to stand for its truth. Since the place of the Other is also the place of God, this is the ultimate form of mystification."[94] The speaker seeks authority for his desire outside himself, in an Other, but his attempts to name this Other in terms of angelology and the discourse of praise disclose it as a mystification, a form of idolatry and a paradoxical praise of nothing.

But the improvisation on Neoplatonic themes also seems related to the poem's drive to construct love in terms of gender difference and thus also encourages an earthier reading that encapsulates this equally paradoxical project. Donne is also praising "the Centrique part" of love mentioned in "Love's Progress," although the phrasing foregrounds the impossibility of doing this in Donne's phallologocentric terms: it means seeing no thing. Luce Irigaray's comment on the relation between castration and the gaze in Freud is suggestive with respect to this level of meaning: "Woman's castration is defined as her having nothing you can see, as her *having* nothing. In her having nothing penile, in seeing that she has No Thing. Nothing *like* man."[95] Joel Fineman's account of Shakespeare's move from a discourse of vision to one of the "perjured eye" is also pertinent here, although not in precisely the terms of Shakespeare's Dark Lady: still, in Donne, as in Shakespeare, to look at the woman is to see difference; she is "an image that calls forth what it is not."[96] "Some lovely glorious nothing." But the paradox of seeing difference in terms of no "thing" is quickly abandoned as the speaker strives to represent the love object as something visible, as a body and as something not from without but from within the speaker. The gender stakes of this move are concisely stated by Irigaray: "The idea that a 'nothing to be seen,' a something not subject to the rule of visibility or of specula(riza)tion, might yet have some reality, would indeed be intolerable to man."[97] Here we might begin to understand why Neoplatonism generally makes Donne nervous. The Neoplatonic construction of the object of love as the soul, "a shapeless flame," is a sort of redemption or mystification of the woman's otherness. In "Aire and Angels" this Neoplatonic "specula(riza)tion," to invoke Irigaray's term, is crossed by a punning prospect of radical difference constructed around a "no thing to be seen."

And so Donne's alternative genealogy of love, which is not quite the logical move suggested by his transitional "But since" (l. 7), functions in two ways: as a critique of Neoplatonism and as a response to the "intolerable" difference of no thing. These lines employ an inverted Neoplatonism, using its commonplaces against its own premises, to generate a specific, material beloved out of the unspecified spiritual love originating in the lover. As the speaker's soul informs his body, so does his love (child of his soul) inform the body of his beloved (7–14).[98] It may be that Donne wishes this broad parody of incarnation (Gardner and Wiggins note the theological overtones of "assume" in line 13) to be read in light of the "annunciation" scene of the first four lines, although the speaker's claims to have controlled this process disturb the parallel:

> And therefore what thou wert, and who,
>   I bid Love aske, and now
> That it assume thy body, I allow,
> And fixe it selfe in thy lip, eye, and brow. (ll. 11–14)

Precisely how the speaker "allows" this process is uncertain (OED offers about a dozen meanings available to Donne, ranging from "accept," to "surrender," to "permit"), but the grammar seems to favor the reading that the speaker permits the incarnation. If this reading is allowed, then the speaker seems to be claiming to have created his love object. This "fixing" of love in the beloved's "lip, eye, and brow" corresponds to the naming of a woman ("what thou wert, and who"). The shapeless flame or voice of the opening lines has been given a local habitation and a name: the word has been made flesh; the "lovely glorious nothing" has been made visible and therefore subject to the rule of the male lover's gaze.

By now I think it is clear that the project of defining love is inseparable from the project of representing its object, and that the demystification of love is also a program for gaining control of its object and effects. The first stanza juxtaposes two accounts of love, as a response to something originating outside the lover—a relation of dependency, and as a spiritual desire originating within the lover and incorporated in a what and who, a body and a name—a relation of supremacy. These accounts of love's progress correspond to standard, if contradictory, representations of woman—here, the mysterious angel and the synecdochic lip, eye, and brow of the material girl. The speaker's meditation on love seems bound up with the problem of subject position and a corresponding concern with the conventions of praise of a woman. This reflexivity—the entangling of problems of the subject of love and the poetics of praise—is, as Fineman reminds us, a convention of

Petrarchism.[99] If we follow Wiggins and read "Aire and Angels" as a double Petrarchan sonnet "turned upside down" (88), this inversion can be seen as a means of at once honoring and interrogating this conventional reflexivity. As noted earlier, in the opening "sestet" the speaker's attempt to speak of love by praising an ethereal beloved gives way to a paradoxical praise of nothing. In the "octave" he comes to rest momentarily in another convention, praise of physical beauty, that will be overturned (or, more exactly, sunk) in the second stanza. In both instances, the speaker's efforts to account for his love are linked to his efforts to represent woman, the "what and who" he loves. The definition of his love depends upon a construction of gender—again, in de Lauretis's phrase, "the product and process of both representation and self-representation." Thus, Wiggins's shift from "a passion in search of an object" to "the object of a passion" is a slide that permeates the speaker's discourse and constitutes the poem's divided "subject"—its doubled topic, the discontinuous subject position of woman across the various discourses of the poem, and the divided subjectivity of the speaker produced on this "site of contest."[100]

By the end of the first stanza the speaker has replaced an emanation theory of the origins of desire and its paradoxical discourse of praise with a psychologically more compelling model of desire issuing in the blazon of lip, eye, and brow; love is a kind of identification, a reunion with a lost part of oneself, the child of the soul that has assumed the body of the beloved. In the second stanza this identification of desire and its object, with its corresponding language of praise, is ruptured. Donne's return to a narrative past tense in line 15, as opposed to the "now" of line 12, is another metapoetic move like that in "The Indifferent," reminding us that the poem is an account, a story, of love; that is, as suggested already, the poem is about both love and talking about love (praising the beloved). The "wares which would sinke admiration" are, of course, the physical attributes of the beloved, but they are also the tropes of praise. The double project of fixing love and praising the beloved is threatened. As Theodore Redpath notes, lines 15–19 make a fine ironic distinction: where Donne had aimed to avoid capsizing his love boat he has ended up in danger of sinking it.[101] His predicament resembles that recounted by Adam in Book VIII of *Paradise Lost* as he describes for Raphael the disturbing effect Eve has on his subject-position in the famous Miltonic ratio of the genders.

This challenge to the speaker's fixed position is inseparable from the problematizing of love's language. Most obvious is the sinking of admiration through excessive praise ("wares which would sinke admiration"), a problem addressed in Shakespeare's Sonnet 130. More controversial is the play of the signifier in Donne's treatment of the conventional ship metaphor. D. C. Allen stresses libertine, Ovidian associations while Peter Dane sketches Platonic and Petrarchan contexts.[102] My reading must emphasize the competition between sources—the slang meaning of "pinnace" (whore) favoring Ovid, the speaker's fear of capsizing or sinking evoking Petrarchan commonplaces. This dissonant playing on literary conventions returns us to the problem of passion and object of passion noted earlier, for the image seems to equivocate between references to the lover and the beloved.

Here, at the turning point of Donne's definition of love, the ambiguities of political and sexual courtship are underscored by the instabilities produced by the one-sex system. Whether or not the addressee of "Aire and Angels" was a patroness such as Lady Bedford, the speaker's courtship has led him into an indeterminate subject-position. The most striking instance of this decentering is the pun—we would call it a Freudian slip—in line 18: "I saw, I had loves pinnace overfraught."[103] This pun, a sexy inversion of the lover's sight of no thing in stanza one, *is,* in the senses outlined above, the subject of the poem, encapsulating the problematic interrelationships between male passion, female object of passion, and signification. The signifier of sexual difference has been unveiled, or, in the parlance of Galenic tradition, inverted; we have temporarily lost our sexual bearings.[104]

The challenge of punning to the fixing of passion in praise of lip, eye, and brow is also spelled out as a disparity between signifier and signified, passion and object of passion:

> Ev'ry thy haire for love to work upon
> Is much too much, some fitter must be sought;
> For, nor in nothing, nor in things
> Extreme, and scatt'ring bright, can love inhere. (ll. 19–22)

The work of praise again undoes itself. Having interrogated discourses of praise of woman as body and as ethereal Other, the speaker reverts to his original analogy, in inverted form—*he* is now like the angel. This move at once attempts to regain the coherent subject-position challenged in lines 15–22 and, paradoxically, reminds us again of slippage between passion and object of passion, signifier and signified in the poem. Characteristically, Donne's return to the analogy draws attention to another, more vexing, controversy about angels. As West notes, there was much less unanimity within denominations on the question of angelic substance than on the question of worship of angels alluded to earlier in the poem.[105] Donne's confident resolution of his love problem with the assertion that angels assume bodies of air oversimplifies a notoriously subtle, unresolved, and "indifferent" theological debate: How many angels can stand on the head of a pin? In one respect, the analogy is not particularly compelling for the theologically informed reader, since a much contested and indifferent matter is being used to demonstrate a truth about the complementary relation of the sexes. On the other hand, the very contestedness of Donne's vehicle here opens the claims about complementarity to inquiry.

And, of course, the indifferent status of the question of angelic bodies, if carried over to the issue of relations between the sexes, radically undermines the subject-sustaining difference of gender ideology which the speaker seems to invoke at the close of the poem.

A gap also appears in the juxtaposition in rhyme of two types of soul-and-body, male-and-female relations posited by the notions of "inhering" (l. 22) and "wearing" (l. 24).

> For, nor in nothing, nor in things
> Extreme, and scatt'ring bright, can love inhere;
> Then as an Angell, face and wings
> Of aire, not pure as it, yet pure doth weare,
> So thy love may be my loves spheare. (ll. 21–25)

As Gardner suggests, "inhere" carries theological overtones of a permanent relationship.[106] The relationship implied by "wearing," on the other hand, is explained as follows by a prominent seventeenth-century angelologist: angels have appeared in human shape, "but bodies were not united to the Angells, as to their forme, as the bodie is to the soule, which is its forme, nor was the human nature body and soule, united to the person of any Angell, but they tooke bodies to them as garments which they tooke up, and laid down upon occasion."[107] This relation, which is essentially the one advocated by the speaker of "The Indifferent," does not quite square with the idea of inhering or with the relation of "intelligence" to the sphere proclaimed (recommended?) in line 25. The "disparity" between "wearing" and "inhering" challenges Gardner's confident assertion that "love is regarded as a soul seeking a body, that is, form seeking matter to inform."[108] Donne seems to be emphasizing the near equality in terms of purity of substances ("not pure as it, yet pure"), but the *relationship* between these substances (i.e., angels and their airy bodies, men's and women's love[109]), which is really the point at issue in the poem, varies across the rhymes "inhere," "weare," and "spheare." Each of these words suggests a significantly different way of representing the love relationship, including, but not limited to, lasting mutuality or communion ("inhere"), temporary cohabitation ("weare"), domination (the ruling intelligence of "my loves spheare"), and just plain intercourse ("thy love may be my loves spheare"). The poem concludes by fixing attention on the slightness of the "disparity" of substance. As Gardner so aptly writes of these lines, Donne's version of sexual hierarchy here "is the orthodox view of women, put kindly."[110] This "putting it kindly" is part of the ideological work performed by "Aire and Angels." But Donne's gallantry does not really resolve the other disparities in the poem which are generated by his struggle for a sexual identity and for a language to represent a sexual relation between a man and a woman.

Love in Text and Context

My own ideological work has been on the side of maintaining "disparitie" in "Aire and Angels."[111] Gardner and Wiggins, on the other hand, work at demonstrating poetic coherence, a demonstration that is related to an argument about gender relations. More tentative than Wiggins, Gardner suggests resolving the closing lines of the poem by means of orthodox views of woman's inferiority, views which she claims Donne uses to validate his angel analogy. Her stated reason for preferring this reading is to save the poem from being "artistically trivial."[112] Gardner's historical scholarship, then, supports a kind of defense of poetry; the identification of an orthodox tradition in the history of ideas is brought to the support of a hypothesis about the unity of the work or of the poet's intention upon which rests the value of the work as literature.[113] On the other hand, Gardner is careful to particularize Donne's relation to the tradition: "In the light of the universal assumption of the superiority of masculine love Donne's close seems aimed to diminish the distinction between man's love . . . and woman's."[114] Part of the literary value of the work would seem to be related to this intention.

Where Gardner finds Donne softening the tradition, I find him struggling to maintain and understand it and, in the process, creating divisions in the subject of love not entirely resolved by the polite conclusion. But the "tradition" is itself less monological than phrases like "universal assumption" might suggest. A case in point is a text cited by Gardner as evidence of "the universal assumption of the superiority of masculine love" in her commentary on "Aire and Angels":

> Nonne (ut Plato inquit) cum alter sit dimidium alterius, uterque appetit dimidium sui? . . . Sed cur foemina magis appetit virum quam e converso? Quod innuere videtur Arist. dum ait. Materia appetit formam, sicut foemina virum. An, quia vir perfectior est: et imperfectum magis appetit perfectum, quam e converso? Propterea materia appetit formam, et non forma materiam. An (ut alii opinantur) foemina appetit virum, id est esse virum, ut sortiatur meliorem sexum et statum? Est itaque mutuus amor inter eos: quamvis ardentior sit in minus perfecto.[115]

> Is it not (as Plato asks) that, since the one is half of the other, each seeks half of itself? . . . But why does a woman seek a man more than vice versa? Which Aristotle seems to nod to [agree with?] when he says matter seeks form just as a woman seeks a man. Or because a man is more perfect: and the imperfect seeks the perfect more than vice versa? Therefore, matter seeks form and not form matter. Or (as others opine) does a woman seek a man, that is, to be a man, in order to obtain a better sex and status? And so there is a mutual love between them: albeit it is more passionate in the less perfect.

This sixteenth-century explanation of sexual difference is in a "probative" rather than a "magistral" style, to use Bacon's terminology, moving restlessly from metaphysical principles ("But why does a woman seek a man more than vice versa? . . . matter seeks form just as a woman seeks a man. . . . a man is more perfect") to psychological and social demystifications ("Or [as others opine] does a woman seek a man, that is, to be a man, in order to obtain a better sex and status?"). Neither answer to the question overturns the principle of male superiority, but the second suggests that some (presumably male) commentators think that some women think that (male) superiority is there for the taking. Georgius's style represents "tradition" in a way that could allow the discovery of an alterity in his text.

Such a reading, it could be argued, is more "historical" than Gardner's contextualization. As recent studies have reminded us, there was a Renaissance "debate" about women, conducted at several levels of discourse, from the high register of *Il Cortegiano* to the pamphlet controversies of Tudor and Stuart England (which included pamphlets written by women). One English controversy developed around the social practice of women adopting male attire ("does a woman seek a man, that is, to be a man, in order to obtain a better sex or a better status?"). In opening her survey of the debate in England, Linda Woodbridge alerts the reader to the many paradoxes generated by the controversial literature, noting, for example, that "the purpose of attacks and defenses was (from at least one perspective) the same," and "that Renaissance attacks on women are more congenial to modern feminism than are Renaissance defenses of women."[116] In their collection of pamphlets from the English controversy, Katherine Usher Henderson and Barbara F. McManus also acknowledge the problematic nature of this writing, but they do allow us to hear other voices in, for example, the sinuous wit of Jane Anger's play with and within "universal assumptions": "The Gods, knowing that the minds of mankind would be aspiring and having thoroughly viewed the wonderful vertues wherewith women are enriched, lest they should provoke us to pride and so confound us with Lucifer, they bestowed the supremacy over us to man, that of that Cockscomb he might only boast. And therefore, for God's sake let them keep it!"[117] Gardner is ultimately right, I think, about the masculinist tenor of Donne's polite analogy, but those nice manners do not entirely succeed in silencing what is both a threat of otherness in the poem and the paradoxical decentering caused by the slightness of the "disparitie" defined and defended in the poem. The inversion performed at the end, whereby she (the angel of stanza one) is replaced by him, constructs a gender relationship of power; but this strategy of inversion at the level of gender relations is matched by the destabilizing sex inversion that precedes it.

The debate about women did not take place in a vacuum. Work on Renaissance women, and their representation in drama particularly, has suggested that an emerging model of the affective family became a site of contradiction in the social definition of woman. In Catherine Belsey's formulation, "Murderous or demonic, whores and saints, women were placed at the margins of the social body, while at the same time, in the new model of marriage they were uneasily, silently at the heart of the private realm which was its microcosm and its centre."[118] Georgius's puzzling over the relationship between the sexes assumes a particular urgency in Protestant marriage literature of the seventeenth century. In his manual *Of Domesticall Duties* (1622), for example, William Gouge follows a chapter on "an husbands superioritie over a wife" with one entitled "Of a fond conceit, that husband and wife are equall": "Contrary to the forenamed subjection is the opinion of many wives, who thinke themselves every way as good as their husbands, and no way infereior to them." Gouge's explanation hinges on the fine "disparitie" of status: "The reason whereof seemeth to be that small inequalitie which is betwixt the husband and the wife: for of all degrees wherein there is any difference betwixt person and person, there is the least disparitie betwixt man and wife."[119]

These developments have not usually found their way into Donne criticism and will be treated in greater detail in the following chapter. In the readings above, I have tried to follow through a few poems some disparities concerning women in the literary discourse of love. "Aire and Angels" attempts a beautiful resolution that might also be seen to participate in this early modern project of remodelling the family into a unit controlled by affective (Gardner's "the orthodox view of women, put kindly"), as opposed to political, relations of power.[120] In Belsey's committed language, "by this means liberalism opens a gap for the accommodation of an uncontested, because unidentified, patriarchy."[121] In the case of "Aire and Angels," however, the patriarchy also seems to me to be under pressure; writer and reader must labor manfully to keep the overloaded "pinnace" up. What at once binds the poem to its ideological matrix and makes us feel its difference from it is the tentative, or as Frederic Jameson might put it, the "imaginary" nature of this resolution executed in the supersubtle language of angelology.[122]

And so we ought to approach Wiggins's celebration of mutuality with some caution; mutuality creates as many problems as it resolves for Donne, as we have seen, and for Wiggins. Wiggins appears to interrogate the orthodoxy brought to bear on the poem by Gardner since his argument requires a revision of the usual metaphysical argument from matter and form in line 25. But, rather like the Renaissance "defenses" of woman's position, Wiggins's more palatable modern reading of the poem is, in a crucial respect, not far at all from Gardner's adherence to orthodoxy. Where Gardner wishes for manuscript or biographical evidence to resolve the problem of the writer's intention, Wiggins rescues Donne by means of a formal analysis that I have tried to link to the ideological work of containing contradictions, of "putting it kindly." This aspect of Wiggins's project is most tellingly revealed in the stirring summation of his argument where the male speaker of the poem is elided with humankind: "This lover engages our sympathy, because his cause is as much our own as if he were defending, not just himself, but all humanity against a charge of being tainted" (99).

So much depends on writing and reading love poetry. As Julia Kristeva has it, "*Love is something spoken, and it is only that;* poets have always known it."[123] Predictably, it was Shakespeare who most paradoxically put in question this subject of love, in a poem addressed to a man: "If this be error and upon me proved, / I never writ, nor no man ever loved." This connection between love and the poet's writ also famously interested Donne, and it is to this topic that I will turn in the next chapter.

❖   T H R E E

Mutual Love and
Literary Ideology

IN *The Reinvention of Love,* Anthony Low has recently argued that Donne's love poetry transcended and eventually transformed the conditions under which it was produced: "Donne was a chief actor and influence in what may be called the 'reinvention of love,' from something essentially social and feudal to something essentially private and modern." Low's general argument, and his thesis on Donne's pivotal role in the process of reinventing love, are underwritten by his "faith," eloquently stated in his Preface, "that poets are far more sensitive than most of us to the broad cultural and political transformations in society that impact on our individual lives."[1] This chapter attempts to sketch the connection between that literary faith and Donne's construction of love in two of his best known poems. My argument tends to invert the structure of Low's assumptions by suggesting that the faith in poets that grounds Low's project is in part owing to Donne's ideological work on love. To put it another way, I mean to emphasize not so much the reinvention of love by the poet Donne as the creation of poetic authority through Donne's reinvention of love; the product of Donne's love poetry is the literary faith that informs the thesis of Donne as a "pivotal figure" in the history of love.

The chapter is divided into two parts. In part one I begin by supplementing Arthur Marotti's reading of the coterie system with other stories of love and power in the period. Behind this strategy is an assumption—namely, that Donne and his coterie engaged in their metacommunications under pressures from a variety of sources, including not only careerist ambitions and demands for "political correctness," but also alternative discourses on love and power that challenged this hermeneutic circle of writers and readers. Drawing on these discursive contexts, I discuss how Donne's defenses of love turn into defenses of poetry; his lovers are constructed as the authors of a love story, the text of which is bequeathed to a faithful community of knowing readers. The literary subject of this textual practice is, as numerous critics have noted, a masculine one. The second part briefly comments on complications in this masculine subject position in light of Donne's play with androgyny and his wonder at the possibility of an autonomous woman with a sexual history of her own.

Safe Sex—Love and the Ideology of the Aesthetic

I propose "The Canonization" as a bridge from the poems of masculinist anxiety discussed in the preceding chapter to the poems of mutual love. It is Donne's *Antony and Cleopatra,* a hyperbolic performance that, like Shakespeare's, seems to comment on its own hyperbole while at the same time asserting a transcendence through erotic self-destruction. Marotti's corrective reading helpfully suggests "that love and ambition are connected" here, but in the end I find his argument troubling. His claim that "Irony, not moral or aesthetic idealization, was Donne's purpose" seems paradoxically dependent, like moral or aesthetic idealizations, upon maintaining a sharp division between private and public, erotic and political desire. The construction of such a division is, it seems to me, the aim of the poem and thus should not be taken for granted but examined. In this respect, Marotti's reading is in step with recent work on the politics of love, which tends to correct earlier transcendentalist interpretations by resolving conflicts between love and politics in favor of politics. In Marotti's case this results from his privileging of the male coterie relationship, a move that has the added effect of recuperating for Donne a sort of transcendence through a shared perspective with the all-knowing, ironically-cued coterie; if Donne is the victim of circumstances beyond his control, he is still a master of discourse and knowledge: "Though this poem is a rhetorical tour de force that contains an attractive fantasy of love's triumph over social disadvantages, Donne knew and was aware his coterie readers knew that neither poetry nor wit could solve the serious difficulties he faced in his painful social exile."[2] Through the author-function, Donne's authority is saved even in his admission of powerlessness.

As noted in the preceding chapter, Marotti's coterie system is one historical structuration of what Eve Kosofsky Sedgwick has termed "male homosocial desire." Sedgwick uses the category of homosociality as a means to focus on the interplay of discourses of sexuality and politics; in particular, she stresses that "[t]he exact, contingent space of indeterminacy—the place of shifting over time—of the mutual boundaries between the political and the sexual is, in fact, the most fertile space of ideological formation." In this space "[t]he two sides, the political and the erotic, necessarily obscure and misrepresent each other—but in ways that offer important and shifting affordances to all parties in historical gender and class struggle."[3] Donne's love poetry was composed in such a space. While it undoubtedly reinforced the homosocial community by means of irony, that irony was also productive of an emergent ideology of literature.

In "The Canonization" the subject of love takes shape between misrepresentations of political and sexual pursuits that are aligned with scenes of public achievement and private retreat. While acknowledging the importance of Donne's coterie audience to his handling of this conflict, I would like to consider both Donne and the coterie on this matter in the light of contemporaneous perceptions of the problematic relationship between public and private life. The debates most pertinent to "The Canonization" occurred in the areas of marriage theory and religious controversy.[4]

Dayton Haskin has recently pointed out that the prominence of "The Canonization" "is almost entirely a result of the attention accorded the poem since 1940" and also that biographical readings relating the poem to Donne's marriage "are the product of twentieth-century criticism."[5] Haskin convincingly attributes these facts of literary history to the powerful influence of Izaak Walton's treatment of the poetry and the life in his *Life and Death of Dr. John Donne.* At the end of his article Haskin offers a brilliant close reading of Walton's own "conflicting feelings about the Donne-More relationship, courtship, and marriage" that suggests a possible linkage between Walton's opinions about Donne's marriage, on the one hand, and his poetry, on the other.[6] In what follows I do not take a position for or against the biographical reading. On the basis of its language I do, however, locate "The Canonization" in a context of contemporary discourse on marriage, and I do argue for a decisive connection between the poem's treatment of marriage discourse and its aestheticizing and privatizing motives which have been celebrated and deconstructed since 1940.

In her excellent study of marriage in English Renaissance drama Mary Beth Rose argues that "Evidence from the drama and from Renaissance sexual discourse indicates clearly both an emerging awareness of an increased sense of conflict between the demands of public and private domains and a profoundly anxious cultural perception of that disjunction as problematic."[7] On the way to describing in Jacobean tragedy an emerging valorization of private life and a "heroics of marriage," she analyses three wedding sermons by Donne as powerful examples of a conservative, patristic attitude towards marriage that was revised in Protestant discourse on sexuality and explored in all of its contradictions in a Jacobean tragedy such as *The Duchess of Malfi.* Rose finds the connection between Donne's rather gloomy preaching on marriage and his marriage for love "not surprising," given his Augustinian views on desire and sexuality.[8] Although I agree with Rose that Donne was not persuaded by Protestant teaching on marriage and sexuality, I think his poems of mutual love do negotiate problems similar to those exemplified in the Protestant heroics of marriage. Donne's particular creation, however, was an aesthetics, not an heroics, of marriage.

In "The Canonization" Donne misrepresents both the public domain he claims to have renounced and the erotic life he claims to embrace by denying any possible connection between them. Each domain is represented in a "pure" state that launders it of any patriarchal linkage to the other. Among the links I have in mind here is the homosocial relationship between the speaker and the interlocutor; Donne proclaims an end to bonding with his male coterie, but his extended and ingenious defense of the heterosexual love that replaces his same-sex bonds suggests that his connection to the coterie still matters to him. This double motive makes the poem available to conservative and subversive readers. Donne wants to have it both ways—a successful defense of heterosexual love will paradoxically strengthen his homosocial relation to the coterie. This cultural fantasy, which has been much commented upon in Shakespeare studies,[9] is behind the careful development of Donne's particular version of androgyny—"The Phoenix ridle"—in the third stanza. Donne's love can finally be both male and female, which again means that it can be construed both as an alternative to gender codes and as a reinforcement of them.

Working most powerfully for male hegemony is the frame of the poem as an address to a male observer. In this context, "The Canonization" is a tale of survival, a proof-text of masculinity. At the center of Donne's poem is a claim to have had great sex and to have remained "the same," nonetheless. Sedgwick's comment on Shakespeare's sonnets is appropriate here: "to be fully a man requires having attained the instrumental use of a woman, having *risked* transformation by her."[10] "She and I do love," I have lived to tell of it, the world goes on. From the perspective of a male coterie reader, then, the mystery celebrated here is that the male lover is *not* changed by the experience: "We die and rise the same" would mean *I* die and rise the same.

But this is only half the story. The lover seeks permission (the repetition of "let me love") to love and, it is implied, will be able to love only in the silence ("hold your tongue") of the observer, who here functions in several distinct and sometimes opposed ways. On the one hand, this silent other is represented as everything rejected by the defiant speaker—the pursuit and rewards of patronage, deference to a hierarchical system. At the same time, the addressee assumes several features of the Lacanian Other. That is, the addressee is the site of the symbolic order, language, here the language that speaks the "rebellious" lover, since his discourse in stanza one is a pastiche of speeches on behalf of or from the place of the Other. The silent hearer occupies the site of intersubjectivity, in Lacan's words "the locus in which is constituted the I who speaks with him who hears." The lover seems able to represent himself to us only as he is presented to himself by the Other. This Other functions as something like Lacan's Name-of-the-Father, which denies Donne his love but with which Donne must also identify. Finally, this Other can be associated with the unconscious, the "other scene" in which the subject of desire, as distinct from the boisterous, defiant ego of "For Godsake hold your tongue," is spoken.[11]

The point of invoking Lacan's Other here is to suggest how the lover's discourse on love is bound up with his relation to another male as well as to the woman. The open challenge to the symbolic order of the Other (here, the silent observer) is, as Marotti explains in terms of the patronage system, constructed in the field of the Other. Donne struggles with the problem of representing a fulfilling heterosexual relation in a homosocial system of signifying sexual relations. The strain produced by this paradox becomes especially evident in the third stanza:

> Call us what you will, wee'are made such by love;
>   Call her one, mee another flye,
> We'are Tapers too, and at our owne cost die,
> And wee in us finde the Eagle and the Dove;
>   The Phoenix ridle hath more wit
>   By us, we two being one, are it,
> So, to one neutrall thing both sexes fit.
>   Wee dye and rise the same, and prove
>   Mysterious by this love. (ll. 19–27)

Here the lover at once subjects himself to the Other ("Call us what you will") and lays claim to another form of interpellation independent of the Other, or, more precisely, a construction by another Other ("wee'are made such by love") that controls both the lovers and the observer's calling them lovers.

In the famous third stanza of "The Canonization" Donne wants to draw a distinction between the construction of heterosexual love in a language of patriarchy ("Call us," "Call her . . . [call] mee") and an experience that is claimed to exceed that structure ("Mysterious"). To accomplish this, he improvises upon the rich and polyvalent notion of androgyny. Donne's "phoenix ridle" draws upon a time-honored symbol of marriage, what Gayle Whittier terms the "sublime androgyne," to figure the rebirth from destruction brought about by his sexual union in marriage.[12] On the other hand, the stanza's imagery of depletion, combined with Donne's phrasing in the elaboration of the phoenix image in line 25, allows the masculinist anxieties of the Ovidian source-text of transformation to be heard:

> sic ubi conplexu coierunt membra tenaci,
> nec duo sunt et forma duplex, nec femina dici
> nec puer ut possit, neutrumque et utrumque videntur.
> (*Metamorphoses* IV.377–79)

Ovid warns, "quisquis in hos fontes vir venerit, exeat inde / semivir" (IV.385–86); Hermaphroditus loses his sexual identity.[13] "Wee dye and rise the same" looks at once like a rebuttal of Ovid's warning about loss of sexual identity—no metamorphosis occurs after love—and like a confirmation of it—the lovers are now "the same." Donne's point of view is very difficult to focus here. The phoenix is chosen as the emblem of the lovers both because of its hermaphroditism and because of its power over death. Lines 23–27 seem equally interested in the victory over death ("over coming," as Christopher Ricks might have it) and in the creation of the androgynous "thing."[14] The two concerns can be forcibly united by reading "the same" as a double reference, to their unchanged condition after intercourse and to their sameness as the one "neutrall thing." As distinct sexual beings our sex acts are linked with death, but as "the same" being—the "one neutrall thing"—we are intact, nothing is lost (neither "just so much honour" nor semen?) in orgasm.

As many commentators have noted, Donne transforms the phoenix from Petrarch's image of the uniqueness of his love for Laura into a representation of *both* the lovers. The "one neutral thing" produced by the union of "both sexes" is a genuine "ridle"—at once a reinforcement of and a departure from the sex-gender system. Donne's figure draws upon a rich and complex tradition of commentary on the hermaphrodite/androgyne, brilliantly combining physical and metaphysical meanings.[15] At the level of physical sex, Donne imagines the "fitting" together of male and female genitals as a sort of recapturing of an original bisexuality. In terms of gender, the lovers fuse to form a being that joins the "masculine" eagle and the "feminine" dove.[16] At the most rarified level, A. R. Cirillo has traced Donne's hermaphroditic phoenix to the love theory of such writers as Ficino and Leone Ebreo, where it functions as an emblem of the perfect and transcendent soul-union that follows an ecstatic death in love.[17]

As James Grantham Turner has pointed out, Leone Ebreo's treatment of hermaphroditism is part of a tradition of commentary on Genesis that includes an hermaphroditic Adam and that reflects a deeply divided attitude towards sexuality. Leone, for example, "praises the benevolence of a God whose 'primary intent' is to divide the protohumans 'for their own good,' and thus initiate sexual reproduction. But in the same breath he equates division with sin itself."[18] This tradition, which exemplifies a paradoxical attitude towards sexuality—fear and loathing on the one hand, intense desire for an original whole-earth sexuality on the other, is highly relevant to Donne. The "one neutrall thing" is one of the most striking of Donne's assertions of oneness as a mysterious aspect of mutual love, and I think it harmonizes with several other poems of mutuality in its aim to dissolve difference. On the one hand, this move would seem to imply an overcoming of "disparity" as well as difference; it connects with the theme of "sublime androgyny"—as Kathleen Williams put it, "the hermaphrodite . . . as a symbol of marriage, but marriage as itself a symbol of the necessary concord of opposites on which the world depends and individual human welfare also."[19] On the other hand, hermaphroditism might also function to resolve the anxieties aroused by difference. This is another way of saying what many critics have noted about Donne's poetry of mutual love—that it pays little attention to praising women. The erasure of gender difference in representing a fulfilling heterosexual relation as unclassifiable ("neutrall") is the flip side of the offensive cynical portrayals of the Elegies, "Loves Alchymie," or "Farewell to Love," poems that do attend to women.[20] As we saw in the discussion of "Aire and Angels," Donne experiences great difficulties in describing the difference of women. In "The Canonization" the "she" is either absorbed into "we" or dissolved altogether into "one neutrall thing." As a result, the poem is focussed not on the relation between man and woman, but on that between the lovers and their critics or their devotees.

Donne also uses the word "mysterious" to describe his lovers. The term comes from Ephesians 5, where Paul outlines the "mutual" love of husband and wife, grounding his recommendations in *the* origin of the mystery in Genesis and in an allegorical interpretation of the Song of Songs: " 'For this reason a man shall leave his father and mother and be joined to his wife, and the two shall become one.' This is a great mystery, and I take it to mean Christ and the church" (Eph. 5. 31–32.).[21] I take it this is and is not what Donne means. His two becoming one flesh is a mystery expressed in the "one neutrall thing," but Donne then cuts blasphemously to the Bridegroom's resurrection for another analogue of the mystery.[22] The Pauline "mystery" of sexual union, hermaphroditic Adam, and risen Christ add up to something like a "Paradisal Marriage" regained.

Donne's echo of Paul's "great mystery" reminds us that this poem takes shape not only within a literary tradition but also within a context of ideological debate on marriage. Is it permissible to imagine a strong Protestant reading? If Marotti is right, the poem was certainly not written for such a reader. But is not that unintended reader something like another Other in the poem? What Donne fears and therefore excludes from his poem is a sexual relation lived as a "respectable" relation to a larger social existence. Donne prefers to think of his sexual relation as a high-risk heresy, love become a funeral pyre. The fact that such a representation has a long history should not obscure its historically specific force here. Donne's apparent capitulation to the friend—"Wee can dye by it, if not live by love," particularly as it is linked to the achievement of Catholic sainthood, is a position opposed to the emerging Protestant ideology of the companionate marriage.

Donne's vehement denial of any relationship between sexual love and society is in striking contrast to the new ideology of marriage which, as Rose explains, depends upon the "careful, fervent elaboration of the ancient analogy connecting the family, society, and the spiritual realm."[23] In his chapter on "due benevolence," the Pauline locution for conjugal love, William Whately comments specifically on the interdependence of sexual and social relations:

> Doth not euery mans priuate wel-fare, and the publike also for the most part, depend in a manner altogether vpon the successe of this societie? The hope of posteritie, the stay of old age, the comforte of weaknesse, the support of euery mans house and name, together with the flourishing and populous estate of euery Church and Common-weale, doth euen hang vpon the fruit of matrimony.[24]

Whately's emphasis here on "the fruit of matrimony," children, is in striking contrast to Donne's use of a literary and philosophical language that scrupulously excludes this aspect of sexual relations from consideration in the interest of establishing a privileged private space for intimate relations.

This moment in "The Canonization" also exemplifies what Empson and, more recently, David Norbrook and Anthony Low have identified as a utopian motive in Donne's lyrics.[25] But, like the original *Utopia* and other inversions, this aspect of Donne's work seems equally open to Marotti's ironic reading or Goldberg's new historicist importation of state secrets into an absolutist Jacobean politics of the bedroom.[26] Flooding stanza three with conflicting significations of sexual love, Donne seems to deny himself and the close reader a stable position of identification with a signifier.[27]

The problem of interpreting "The Canonization" is introduced into the poem itself when Donne turns to Roman Catholic doctrine and practice for a figure of his paradisal love regained:

> And by these hymnes, all shall approve
> Us *Canoniz'd* for Love.
> And thus invoke us . . . (ll. 35–37)

John Carey, the critic who has argued most forcefully for the influence of Donne's Catholic formation, treats Donne's turn to the Catholic doctrine of intercession of the saints as one of those habits of thought that return "when he feels himself threatened": in Carey's psychologically-inflected reading Donne is comforted by the fantasy of returning to the Church and thereby redeeming both his ruined career and his apostasy. In a more sociological vein, Low has characterized Donne's utopian inversions as an (imaginary) return to pre-Reformation rituals of carnival.[28] Considered as a socially symbolic act, however, this move in the poem can be read in a variety of ways, depending on the position of the reader. Marotti's coterie reader might have found the canonization amusing or daring, considering Donne's personal religious history. If, as Dennis Flynn has recently argued, Donne's early life as a courtier was formed by his relationship to "the ancient Catholic nobility," Donne's "return" to Catholicism here might be an instance of a political position shaping the discourse of love.[29] In this context Donne's opposition between peaceful love and love "that now is rage" resembles the opposition in recusant writing between the peace of a Catholic universalism and the present condition of heresies and schisms in England.[30] More precisely, the argument of "The Canonization" parallels the recusant narrative of the history of Catholicism in reformed England as the story of its transformation into a minority religion of "interior commitment."[31] I do not, however, wish to claim that Donne is sending a coded message to fellow Catholic readers; Donne's precise religious position at this time is notoriously difficult to ascertain, and references to Catholicism in poems certainly does not prove anything about religious affiliation. What I do want to suggest is that Donne's Catholic, and specifically his recusant formation, is reproduced in his construction of the lover as a divided and marginalized subject.

In a recent article on Donne's Elegies, Achsah Guibbory has supplemented Marotti's deservedly influential argument on the politics of love poetry by emphasizing the "*inter*relations between love and politics."[32] Following Guibbory, I would suggest that although "The Canonization" does betray its investment in the political world it pretends to reject, it is just as deeply interested in love itself as a political relationship and position. The specific politics of love in this poem is a "recusant" politics of a subject divided by conflicting relationships, here to the friend and to the beloved. Such a division is a constant theme in the political writing of Elizabethan Catholics. As Peter Holmes points out, "Elizabethan Catholic writers wavered between loyalty to the Queen and opposition to her,"[33] but both resistance and compromise were justified on the basis of a distinction between the subject's obligations to secular and religious authorities.[34] The problem of determining the correct relationship between these competing obligations produced, in Holmes's words, "a real tension in . . . casuist booklets, and elsewhere in the literature of the English Catholic community, between the desire for total alienation from the Protestant society, and the need for some contact and compromise with the enemy."[35] This recusant ambivalence describes Donne's relationship to the worldly friend in "The Canonization." The lover's alienation is expressed by his refusal to participate in courtship or commerce and by his experiment in sublime androgyny. On the other hand, solidarity with the friend is everywhere, including between the lines of the "rage" (not "peace") of the first two stanzas,[36] in the submission to the friend's views on love in the first lines of stanzas three and four, and in the phallocentric mystification of love as dying and rising.[37] The source of this instability is the construction of love as a minority position, one that affords Donne a critical perspective on the friend while it also fuels utopian visions of a future when "*all* shall approve" (my italics). It's not just the exaltation of the lovers but the eventual confirmation of that status by everyone that appeals to the spokesman of the love minority.

Donne's imaginative leap into the future in the last stanza of the poem suggests a further discursive relationship between poem and religious polemic. A recurring theme of recusant political writing is historical irony. In *A Humble*

Supplication to Her Maiestie, Robert Southwell, like many other Catholic writers, uses the Protestant Marian exiles to introduce a historical perspectivism that paradoxically supports an argument for the transcendent truth-value of the Catholic Church.[38] Donne's last two stanzas are constructed around a similar contradiction between time and timelessness; every line registers the pressure of time, and, in the last stanza, a change in the religion of love is envisioned, one that corresponds to the Reformation seen from a recusant Catholic perspective as a fall from "peace" into "rage." Despite this acknowledgment of change, Donne insists "all shall approve / Us *Canoniz'd.*"[39]

Of course, as Donne himself noted in his controversial work *Pseudo-Martyr,* his connection to recusancy was personal as well as political.[40] It seems significant that Donne's original and ongoing relationship with Catholicism was primarily through his mother, a descendant of Thomas More and lifelong recusant who left the country for a time because of her religion and who lived with her son (and survived him) after the death of her second Catholic husband. In light of this strong maternal influence, I find Julia Kristeva's theory of poetic language a rich and helpful analogy for describing the function of Catholicism in "The Canonization." I will use Kristeva to sketch the process by which Donne moves to his double "canonization" in the close of the poem.

Kristeva theorizes poetic language as the irruption of the "semiotic," a preverbal ordering of drives which she associates with the mother's body, into the patriarchal symbolic order. Kristeva relates this semiotic modality to the rhythm of poetic language, which, following Mallarmé, she posits as "the mysterious functioning of literature," that aspect of poetry which "pluralizes signification or denotation." By this means, Kristeva argues, poetic language questions "the very principle of the ideological," because it breaks up the "unicity" upon which it depends.[41] This *"transgression* of position" is not a transcendence of the symbolic order, however; Kristeva describes it as a death and rebirth. The parallels with Donne's moves in "The Canonization" may be best observed in the following remarks by Kristeva. Art, she writes,

> assumes murder in so far as artistic practice considers death the inner boundary of the signifying process. Crossing that boundary is precisely what constitutes "art." In other words, it is as if death becomes interiorized by the subject of such a practice; in order to function he must make himself the bearer of death. . . . But he is not just a scapegoat; in fact, what makes him an artist radically distinguishes him from all other sacrificial murderers and victims.

> In returning, through the event of death, towards that which produces its break; in exporting semiotic motility across the border on which the symbolic is established, the artist sketches out a kind of second birth. Subject to death but also to rebirth, his function becomes harnassed, immobilized, represented

and idealized by religious systems (most explicitly by Christianity), which shelter him in their temples, pagodas, mosques and churches.[42]

Other details of Kristeva's theory offer tantalizing perspectives on Donne. I have not, for example, commented on poetic rhythm, which Kristeva associates with the semiotic rupture, but the often-noted irregularities of Donne's "strong lines" are suggestive in this regard. (Needless to say, Kristeva's theorizing of rhythm and the maternal semiotic would clash dramatically with the critical tradition, initiated in Carew's famous elegy, of the "line / Of masculine expression" in Donne's verse.[43]) But I do not mean to import Kristeva's theory in all its details into Donne's poem. I do, however, want to claim that her theory of the signifying process of poetic language helps to explain, in broad outline, the movement of the poem. Donne's "breeching" or "pulverizing," to borrow Kristeva's terms, of the symbolic order is represented as a death, and his rebirth is imagined by means of a return to his mother's religion, or rather, by a reinvention of that religion as a textual practice.

How to "dye and rise the same?" Donne tells us: "by these hymnes." This creation of a literary subject is the most important "reinvention" in "The Canonization." The focus of stanza four is a textual practice, the construction of a love story in legend, sonnet, hymn. Thus the canonization envisioned here is mainly literary: Donne's recuperation of a sacred rite to authorize his secular writ constructs a fine and private place for his poems and a readership for those poems. Donne's construction of the subject of love in "The Canonization" is marginal, heterodox, and powerless—in brief, recusant—yet paradoxically so, since it also reflects ("such mirrors") and illuminates ("such spies") the world. This particular claim to literariness occurs within a specific set of biographical, historical, and ideological conditions, but many of its chief characteristics were beginning to appear in a variety of Renaissance literary works. David Quint has traced the development of the idea of literary autonomy in the Renaissance, and his assessment of the somewhat paradoxical result of this development is pertinent to Donne's achievement in "The Canonization":

> By obtaining a cultural autonomy from systems of authorized truth, literature gave up its right to be authoritative. It thereby found itself in a marginal position with respect to what would pass as the more central, more authentic disciplines of human thought. . . . Under the influence of idealist philosophy, intellectual historians have assigned the literary text a more or less passive role: literature reflects but does not embody, still less create, ideas. But the evidence suggests that the effort of the Renaissance literary text to reexamine the source of its authority, to define itself *as text,* is an event in intellectual history that intellectual history has not adequately understood or explained.[44]

Donne's use of canonization exemplifies the process Quint describes here and elsewhere in his book. In the context of the religious controversies of his day, Donne's appropriation of a religious language to name his secular love is not simply the continuation of a convention stretching back to the troubadours. It places his love in a position relative to other positions—a minority position. We are at once being told that this love is extraordinary and being reminded, despite the boast that "all" will do so, that this assessment is one we are free to "approve" or not.[45] The figure of canonization, then, both authorizes and undermines the poet's claims.

Canonization also locates the interpretative act in the readers. The Donne devotees of the future conceive of the lovers and, by extension, their love poems in both a passive and an active relationship to the world—as mirrors and spies. They reflect the social world beyond the love relationship, but "epitomizing" the world suggests a particular type of reflection that combines miniaturizing and idealizing or essentializing. My point here is that Donne matches the love celebrated in the poem with a mimetic theory of a literary work's relationship to history. That theory resembles in many respects Aristotelian mimesis as refracted by Renaissance literary thought. As Alan Liu reminds us, Aristotelian mimesis "first dictated to literary history not only the relation between unified structure and plural episode but the canonical relation of history to literature."[46] In Donne's version love and poetry are bound up with each other in the sense that the lovers construct an ideal imitation of life. However, by also characterizing the relation between lovers and world as a form of spying, Donne registers the sense of an unstable, even dangerous connection between this ideal imitation and the original. A spy would seek to intervene in the world for purposes of disrupting it rather than reflecting or idealizing it.[47]

But it is not clear to me what sort of action this intervention might have been. Although the "spies" suggest a subversive agency, the lover has argued in the first two stanzas that his love has no effect on the order of things. The only indisputable achievement of the lovers appears to have been the building of a private space for love, a space that turned out to be their tomb, although even this achievement, it must be recalled, is in the optative mood. This kind of self-irony prompts Tilottama Rajan to treat "The Canonization" and other Songs and Sonnets "non-mimetically as poems about the status of their own discourse as well as poems about concepts of love."[48] In the case of "The Canonization" I have tried to defer Rajan's thesis that the poem swallows its own tail long enough to consider the ideological work it does in conjoining the problem of love's place in the social order with the problem of literature's relation to life. "The Canonization" plots a movement of desire from erotic rupture and death toward recuperation and rebirth in a textual practice. It moves from a rhetorical "Apology for Love" to an aesthetic "Apology for Poetry."[49] In doing so the poem makes a special contribution to the larger cultural project of establishing distinct public and private domains, particularly as these were organized around the erotic life.[50]

Donne's aestheticizing move is a formalist "solution" to a personal and cultural predicament. His satirical, nonconformist lover, we quickly realize, is not really engaged in a defense of love in the sense of arguing for its value in a network of human relations. Again, that seems to have been the project of Protestant writers on marriage whose teachings are problematized in Milton and, as Rose has demonstrated, in Jacobean tragedy. Donne wants to claim the irrelevance of love to the social order. Accordingly, his commmunity is a church of alienated readers in search of some transcendent Idea or "pattern" of love. On the other hand, Donne imagines his future devotees as critics of a Sidneian disposition; they will use the poems ("hymnes") to create a golden world of love as ideal imitation of the social world. By staging the act of reader response, of course, Donne also seems to acknowledge that the ultimate value of poetry depends on the reader—on those who will (or will not) invoke him in the next age.[51]

By linking the problem of mutual love to the problem of Renaissance poetics—how is poetry related to the world?—I want to suggest two things. First, that Donne's poetry of mutual love is a complex attempt to manage conflicts between public and private domains: on the one hand it constructs the love relation as central, sometimes even literally so when Donne makes the sun revolve around the lovers, but its alliance with literary marginality seems to work against that. This contradiction seems to reproduce the instability of relations between public and private life in the period. On the other hand, Donne's "solution" is also a particular construction of an aestheticized private life with specific implications for literary and social history.

This "culture-poem," this "Canonization," works along the lines of many another Donne poem to stage subversion "safely." In this respect Donne's poems might be said to operate along the lines of Liu's characterization of various formalisms, including the "cultural poetics" of new historicism: "They shelter a place where Subject and Action may be mobilized (ambiguously or differentially) by claiming that such a place is all there is."[52] Donne's "Nothing else is" from "The Sunne Rising" echoes here.

Stephen Greenblatt has noted another paradox associated with this notion of autonomy in regard to the Renaissance theater: "the practical usefulness of the theater depends largely on the illusion of its distance from ordinary social practice. . . . Shakespeare's theater is powerful and effective precisely to the extent that the audience believes it to be nonuseful and hence nonpractical."[53] Although coterie poetics are not, like the theater, topographically zoned and walled off from other activities, they do depend upon "a separation of artistic practices from other social practices, a separation produced by a sustained ideological labor, a consensual classification."[54] Greenblatt cites Pierre Bourdieu on this process of establishing the "disinterested interest" of art:

> The constitution of relatively autonomous areas of practice is accompanied by a process through which symbolic interests (often described as "spiritual" or "cultural") come to be set up in opposition to strictly economic interests

as defined in the field of economic transactions by the fundamental tautology "business is business"; strictly "cultural" or "aesthetic" interest, disinterested interest, is the paradoxical product of the ideological labour in which writers and artists, those most directly interested, have played an important part and in the course of which symbolic interests become autonomous by being opposed to material interests, i.e., by being symbolically nullified as interests.[55]

Linking Donne to such a project would revise the portrait of the "amateur" writer in Richard Helgerson's compelling description of the Elizabethan/Jacobean "literary system," a portrait that matches in many respects Marotti's notion of the coterie writer. Helgerson argues that amateurs saw poetry as a means to a greater end, "a way of indicating their fitness for precisely the sort of service against which they were rebelling."[56] Marotti's biographically-shaped study tends to verify this thesis with respect to Donne. But, as Marotti's own more recent work on the invention of a literary canon in the seventeenth century points out, the boundaries between the amateur and the professional were being challenged by the publication of the Sidney folios of 1598, 1599, and 1604, even as the "amateur" Donne was writing poetry.[57] A letter of 1611 to Sir Henry Goodyer printed in the 1633 edition of Donne's poems suggests that Donne considered revising and publishing a selection of his poetry and prose.[58] Would such a volume have functioned *only* as an advertisement of Donne's "fitness for service"? To assume so is to miss the creative or productive aspect of Donne's work on ideology in "The Canonization." We need to recognize the importance of claims of inconsequentiality and disinterest to the development of an ideology of literature as a "disinterested" area of practice.[59]

In "The Canonization" Donne insists, falsely, that his love has no effect on the world of politics and business. Of course at least one of his loves did have an effect—on *his* place in the world, on Sir George More's plans for his daughter; by adding children to the world it might even add "to the plaguie Bill." But the claim of disinterestedness is not completely reversed by irony. Donne's poem does not simply reflect a pre-existing set of values oriented towards social and political involvement; "The Canonization" is also involved in a process of constructing a "relatively autonomous area of practice," an incipient ideology of literature, by joining an idea of love to an idea of art. Marotti is certainly correct, following Foucault, in noting that authorship is "a cultural product" rather than "a Platonic idea,"[60] but Donne's love lyrics do contribute to the production of an idea of the literary as a separate "world," to use a Donnean locution. The thematics of privacy and elitism in his love lyrics underwrites a privatized and elitist system of literary production that does construct an "author-function" for the poet as a marginal, recusant, politically skeptical agent.[61] The fact that, as Marotti convincingly demonstrates, this separation will not hold up should not obscure its potential to promote creative work on ideology.

" 'Twas but a dreame of thee"

Perhaps one of the greater mysteries of love celebrated in "The Canoniza-tion" is that the woman involved seems to be offered the position of co-author of the poem: "*We'll* build in sonnets pretty roomes" (1.32, my emphasis). Or perhaps I should say that the writing of the lovers' story is to be the task of the "one neutrall thing." In either case, Donne registers an awareness of the need to break free of the circuit of masculinist discourse within which the poem originates. That collaboration is not realized in "The Canonization" itself. Donne speaks for both lovers in the poem and he speaks largely to his own concerns: the satirical defense of love in the first two stanzas can only be effective insofar as it draws upon *his* situation as a failed courtier; the world well lost for love is a world lost to the male speaker, not his beloved. If, as Low suggests, "Donne's poems mark . . . the invention of an inner space, a magic circle of subjective immunity from outward political threat and from culturally induced anxiety,"[62] that threat and anxiety are, inevitably, perceived from the masculine point of view. Donne's invention of privacy as "subjective immunity" is androcentric. The beloved woman in this and other poems would not share in the motive of flight from a hostile public sphere of activity; for her, privacy would not be associated with the notion of refuge from the public world, since she is always already excluded from the career paths mocked by Donne in the first two stanzas.

Donne celebrates the creative power of the two become one. A compar-ison with *Astrophil and Stella* 21, which is also a response to the criticism of a courtly friend, is instructive. What Sidney puts forth against the "right healthful caustics" of the friend is simply the beauty of his beloved Stella. Donne's beloved barely exists as a separate being. His shift in stanza three from a defense of himself to positive claims about "we two" silently enlists the beloved in his fantasy, a male fantasy, of creating an alternative to the public world of achievement represented in the first two stanzas. Ideologically this might be processed in at least two ways. The speaker moves away from the masculinist positions caricatured in the opening speech in order to take up the position of the sublime androgyne; from this position the new s/he works the miracle of death and resurrection. At the same time, the mysterious love celebrated in stanza three does not seem to entail a comparable shift in position for the woman. Her lack of access to the world rejected by the speaker is reinscribed in Donne's "invention of an inner space."

As Janel Mueller has noted, such "asymmetry of outlook and sexual role" is an undeniable feature of Donne's construction of the private world of mutual love. But if "the lyrics of reciprocated love," represent "the male as the persuader and possessor, the female as the persuaded and possessed,"[63] some of them also register, even in their "masculine perswasive force," an otherness that fascinates and disturbs. On the margins of mutuality, "Love's

Deity" champions the idea that "it cannot be / Love, till I love her that loves me" (ll. 13–14) against the dominant, Petrarchan discourse of love, but finally collapses under the weight of its contradictions. The Petrarchan predicament of unrequited love is contrasted with an earlier time when, first, nature ruled and then a newly installed god of love worked "indulgently to fit / Actives to passives" (ll. 11–12). If the third stanza demystifies the "modern god" and imagines a rebellion, the last discloses a lover fully interpellated by Petrarchan codes of devotion (he is obsessed with a woman and fears "love might make me leave loving") and fidelity ("Falsehood is worse than hate").

But perhaps what is driving the poet into these paradoxes originates in his idea of "correspondencie," which involves fitting "actives to passives." This understanding of the perfect love match jars with a new notion of mutuality as a correspondence of active with active: "I love her, that loves mee." Again a comparison with Sidney's Astrophil is helpful. Stella refuses him because of "tyrant honor" ("Eighth Song"), the Elizabethan cult of chastity that rules them both.[64] Donne, on the other hand, finds himself in love with a woman who already loves someone else, that is, with a woman who has apparently broken with the tyranny of Love codified in Petrarchan convention. Donne withholds this information until the end of the poem, thereby increasing our sense of the novelty of the situation. All along we are made to think that Donne is complaining about a typically resistant cruel fair. Then, in a wonderful subordinate clause, Donne lets slip the truth: "she loves before." In the face of this independence, it is the rebel and atheist Donne who, ironically, reprocesses this active, loving woman according to Petrarchan norms in an attempt to preserve his dignity: "Falsehood is worse then hate; and that must bee, / If shee whom I love, should love mee" (ll. 27–28).

Is there a difference in the poems of assured, mutual love? J. B. Broadbent long ago argued that Donne is one of the earliest poets to write about love as a relation rather than "as something happening inside themselves," and he read "The Good-morrow" as a prime example of this quality: "This is Christian in Martin Buber's sense—'I and thou.'"[65] Broadbent's brilliant commentary comes from the side of the masculine "I" not the "thou." Like Carey, he insists on identifying Donne's beloved in "The Good-morrow" as a "girl." Perhaps this is related to an indeterminacy in the poem. Donne opens in a way that suggests both he and his partner are sexually experienced. The chief stroke of wit of this poem, however, is Donne's brilliant inversion in representing previous sexual experience: the evocation of Paul's weaning metaphor, noted by most commentators, receives an entirely fresh treatment when he describes something like an oral stage of sexual development. The coarseness of the verbs here—"suck'd" and "snorted"—strikes me as ambivalent. It is a set-up for the contrastive turn to souls in stanza two, of course, but I am less certain as to its immediate effect on the reader's evaluation of the relationship. Is Donne talking dirty to impress a girl, or is he talking frankly with a woman who can be expected to share his knowledge and perspective? One wonders, because Donne seems to forget his interest in the beloved's previous experiences when he returns to the I and thou at the end of the stanza. He cannot continue with the notion that they have both had sex with other partners but instead, as one sympathetic woman reader puts it, "he cannot stop boasting about himself and his conquests"[66]: "If ever any beauty I did see, / Which I desir'd, and got, 'twas but a dream of thee" (ll. 6–7). This dubious compliment provokes another question: What about *her* previous sexual experiences? Was she the shadow "beauty" to another one of the seven sleepers? Donne's emphasis on his power as sexual conqueror—he saw, he desired, he got—disturbs the striking mutuality of carnal knowledge assumed in the opening lines. The reader is forced to think about the difference between her sexual career and his and to wonder whether this line might not be used again to heighten another country pleasure.

Almost all readers find that these anxieties are resolved in the second stanza. This effect is achieved by a reworking of sexual hegemony such that each is offered power over the other. Ilona Bell is right to point out that Donne senses he has erred in referring to his earlier conquests,[67] but she fails to follow through on the observation and face up to the contradiction between what Donne says and what has just occurred:

> And now good-morrow to our waking souls,
> Which watch not one another out of fear;
> For love, all love of other sights controls . . . (ll. 8–10)

The shift from the sexually successful "I" at the end of stanza one to "*our* waking soules" (my emphasis) seems crucial here. Donne perhaps senses that, in light of his boasting, the woman *is* watching him out of fear—of being just another of his dream lovers. Alternatively, returning to the opening "wonder" concerning their previous sexual experiences, Donne could be settling his own fears—that she is not just "any beauty" or that he is not just another in her string of lovers. The assertion of the next line is intended to allay either or both of those fears: our eyes cannot rove anymore because as far as we are concerned this room is "an everywhere." The hyperbole is splendid, but, like the renunciation of worldly ambition in "The Canonization," it might carry slightly different charges for men and women readers:

> Let sea discoverers to new worlds have gone,
> Let maps to others, worlds on worlds have shown,
> Let us possess our world; each hath one, and is one. (ll. 12–14)

For men the microcosm of love can appear as just that—a miniaturization of the worlds of power and knowledge exemplified by the voyagers and the

103

cosmologists. The reduction of the sphere of action makes possession of this world possible. I don't believe it looks quite the same to the seventeenth-century woman reader. Instead of a contraction of the great world, a world to which she had little access, she is offered an imaginary expansion of her allotted space—the little room—into "an everywhere." The chance to "possess" this world is not, for the woman, a reduction or redirection of ambition but a rededication of herself to the little room, over which she now rules in partnership with a man. Taking possession of "our world," then, might mean something different to the I and to the thou of the poem. Donne's self-denial might be read as a mystification of the little room that serves to bind his beloved affectively to that "world."

The third stanza returns to the issue which opened the poem—the problem of creating a lasting heterosexual relation. How, exactly, does one possess this new miniature world, "if each hath one, and is one"? In place of the male gaze of stanza one ("if ever any beauty I did see") Donne imagines reciprocal gazes: "My face in thine eye, thine in mine appears" (l. 15). Not only is he looking at her but she looks at him; he too can be an object of the gaze. But it is a dazzling stroke that he discovers himself as the object of the gaze by seeing his own reflection in the eye of the other.[68] The image captures the difficulty of the new relation Donne is constructing in the poem. On the one hand, it means that he can see himself in her (or he is she) and she can see herself in him (or she is he); on the other hand, it captures the paradox of the claim that "true plain hearts do in the faces rest," since Donne seems to be divided between seeing the heart of his beloved resting in her face and seeing his own face reflected in the eye of the other. What he sees in the face of the other is his own desire, which is, as Lacan argued, always the desire of the other—that is, our desire *for* the other, but more, what we think the other desires.[69] "The Good-morrow" is what Donne thinks the other desires.

The product of this mirroring is again an androgynous subject, this time in the form of an evocation of the myth recounted by Aristophanes in the *Symposium:* "Where can we finde two better hemispheares?" In the context of references to the Renaissance voyages of discovery, this allusion enlarges the theme of the search which Aristophanes draws out of the myth. In place of the new worlds of stanza two, the lovers have spent their lives searching for each other and now "finde" their "better hemispheares." The discovery is redolent of paradise, "Without sharpe North, without declining West," the place of the original androgynous Adam.

The last three lines test the myth against Scholastic physics.

> What ever dyes, was not mixt equally;
>   If our two loves be one, or, thou and I
> Love so alike, that none do slacken, none can die.

The careful measurement of "disparitie" in "Aire and Angels" is here replaced by an equally meticulous concern for assuring the essential unity or likeness of the "two loves." The lines are difficult in themselves and in their relation to the rest of the poem. Gardner and Redpath both refer to Grierson's citation of Aquinas, who argues that corruption occurs where there is contrariety.[70] Donne seems to hesitate between imagining the lovers as a unity, perhaps recalling the Aristophanes myth, and emphasizing likeness (vs. contrariety) of men's and women's loving. There is manuscript evidence for believing that Donne himself tinkered with the ending.[71] Responses to the close of the poem vary, with the recent trend being a sense that the poem fails to live up to its early promise.[72] Redpath is, as usual, illuminating; after a careful sifting of the variants, he concludes, "I cannot help feeling that something may have gone wrong, and prevented this otherwise magnificent poem from achieving a truly satisfying ending."[73] "Satisfying" is precisely the right word. Redpath discloses the connection between our reading pleasure and the pleasure Donne is writing about. Both make satisfaction hinge upon the achievement of a perfect unity or symmetry. The acts of reading the poem and making "mutual" love both aim at achieving wholeness.[74] But Donne's somewhat technical fussiness about how this might come about in the case of loving works against the desired fulfillment.

I think the difficulty of the lines is also related to sex and gender. Bell argues ingeniously that Donne invites the beloved to "test the equality of their love . . . by the quality of their physical relationship. . . . If his sensitivity to her, and hers to him, has increased, then neither will slacken until they are both ready to die, to reach a climax together."[75] Her reading cleverly picks up on the technical aspect of the passage, and it would be like Donne to use Aquinas as an authority on sexual technique. I suggest that the confusing, hypothetical conclusion of the poem is also an attempt to connect an argument for mutuality as a sexual technique to an argument against traditional moral teachings on sexual relations and traditional gender politics. Line 19—"What ever dyes, was not mixt equally"—is a statement of the orthodox view that sexual relations are tainted with mortality (i.e., with sin); Donne boldly imagines, as in "The Canonization," a sex free of mortality, though here the freedom is achieved by means of power sharing and proper technique. In "The Canonization" the daring of such a thought is expressed by a blasphemy—to have sex without death and sin would be like being Christ. In "The Goodmorrow" the fantasy of sex without death is linked to gender equality—"Let us possesse our world, each hath one, and is one"—and equality of sexual performance. For Donne, however, both kinds of equality mean, finally, either being one or being the same: "If our two loves be one, or, thou and I / Love so alike." And the choice of the verb "slacken" just hints at a phallocentricity that is also suggested in the "great Prince" imprisoned in the androgynous "abler soul" of "The Exstasie" until "we'are to bodies gone," and that is more obvious in the "die, and rise" of "The Canonization" or that famous "fixt foot" which "grows erect" as Donne "comes home" in the "Valediction: Forbidding Mourning."

Donne seems to be aiming at the creation of a sexual identity or wholeness through the creation of likeness—what Paula Blank calls "a characteristic Donnean homoerotics, in which a subject attempts to possess its object by blurring the distinction between them."[76] Again, erotics is intertwined with poetics—in this instance the making of comparisons. Donne makes the achievement of a satisfying sexual relation seem to depend on the achievement of likeness. The poem compels attention because of its focus on the effort needed to construct this subject position. The new worlds of the Renaissance must be contracted; the self must be rediscovered through a complex process of mirroring in order to produce a new androgynous subject of love; love must be maintained through scientifically tested techniques practiced equally by sex partners. The lengths to which Donne could go in these efforts earned him his reputation as ruler of the "Monarchy of wit" and master of "masculine expression"; his work at making likenesses was gendered masculine.

I want to add that the elegies and songs and sonnets display not what Donne himself called his "masculine perswasive force" but masculinity *by* persuasive force. Force is needed because of opposition. If Mueller is right about a masculine asymmetry in Donne's writing on love, that writing does not quite succeed in negating difference. The other cannot be entirely assimilated; "comparisons are odious."[77] "The Good-morrow" opens and closes in uncertainty about the past and the future. The closing lines are a challenge and a question, and they circle back to the questions of the opening lines. In both places Donne addresses the beloved, but he also addresses himself. Opening in wonder and closing in the conditional mood, the poem registers the silence of another subject of love whose good-morrow, we are beginning to learn, was being sung elsewhere by other voices.[78]

❖ FOUR

The Obscure Object of Desire:
Elizabeth Drury and the
Cultural Production of
"the Idea of a Woman"

Reading into the Anniversaries

IN HIS RECENT book on Donne's Anniversaries, Edward Tayler complains that "[l]ike *Lycidas* and *Hamlet,* The Anniversaries have come to function as hermeneutical barometers in the sense that the commentary on them seems to betray rather more about the critics and their cultural climate than about the poems themselves."[1] This was so from the first readings of the poems. Ben Jonson damned them as blasphemies and Donne defended them as the expression of an "Idea of a Woman." Academic critics have always been drawn to the poems as representative of major intellectual and religious currents of the Renaissance and seventeenth century. Marjorie Hope Nicolson regarded the First Anniversary as "an 'epitome' of the intellectual universe in which Donne lived during the years that saw . . . the transformation of our world from medieval to modern. . . . [A] modern reader will understand better than from any other one poem what the Elizabethans had made of the world and the universe."[2] Two of the most important theories of seventeenth-century English literature to emerge between the New Criticism and new historicism were generated by work on the Anniversaries. Louis Martz's "poetry of meditation" offered not only an explanation for the structure of the poems but also an historical analogue to New Critical claims about poetry as the fusion of thought and feeling that could be used to analyze a wide range of religious poetry of the period. Barbara Lewalski's historical investigation of the particular "symbolic mode" of the poems was a prolegomenon to her theory of a "protestant poetics" which was presented as an alternative to Martz's scheme for understanding seventeenth-century religious poetry.[3] More recently, in something like a poststructuralist "Breaking of the Circle,"

Thomas Docherty argues that the poems play a pivotal role in a "symptomatic reading of a cultural crux between a competing theology and ideology, and of Donne's position within that crux or crisis."[4]

Aiming "to set the record straight," Tayler nonetheless presents another reading of the barometer by enlisting his study of the poems in a polemic against Lewalski's "symbolic" approach as well as an array of literary theories and approaches, including new historicism, deconstruction, Geertzian "thick description," and Victor Turner's concept of liminality, perhaps to inoculate readers against new historicist and other ideological interpretations that have yet to be written. "Theory," Tayler writes in his preface, "(now more or less synonymous with 'ideology'), . . . by its very nature actually authorizes the 'translation' of other people's words into alien terms."[5] What Tayler means to "get right" are the terms Donne thinks with so that we might understand how he creates his "Idea of a Woman." We must not, Tayler repeatedly insists, mistake this process for the creation of an anachronistic "symbolic mode." The payoff of right understanding, however, seems to me to dissolve the historical distance that Tayler wants to maintain from his subject. Those of us who get it right, who are "in the know" about the process of ideation in the Anniversaries, will "confirm our sense of ourselves as selves": "This is to complete the poetic circuit, in which the poet corresponds to poem corresponds to reader—if all are good, and if the reader knows it."[6]

A great deal seems to be at stake in Tayler's book. At least I find it difficult to believe that he regards his book as a paradox, that his passion and erudition have been deployed merely to show us what we (and he), as post-Cartesian selves, cannot be. The Anniversaries, again, have a way of drawing academic critics into discussion of large and even urgent questions—the intellectual world before Descartes, "the older poets . . . ourselves . . . our ancestors."[7] Additionally, Tayler reminds us, even as he deplores the situation, of the imbrication of big works like the Anniversaries in a tradition of scholarship. Tayler's thesis about the relationship between poet, poem, and reader would seem consistent with Antony Easthope's claim that "Literary value is a function of the reader/text relation." Tayler, however, seems unwilling to accept the consequence that, again following Easthope, literary value "cannot be defined outside the history in which texts—some [like the Anniversaries surely] more than others—demonstrably have functioned intertextually to give a plurality of different readings transhistorically; the greater the text, the more we are compelled to read it through a palimpsest of other interpretations."[8] Tayler needs the readings (and the terms) he rejects, if only to motivate his own reading. He has to rescue Donne from someone.

Most readings of the Anniversaries, as Tayler laments, have been devoted to determining *what* is being represented in the poems. More recently, aspects of the how and why of representation—social and material conditions of production—have been emphasized.[9] My reading attends to the urgency of the desire to identify the famous "shee" of the poem; it balances the recent new historicist critique of representation against a psychoanalytic notion of identification in order to argue for the importance of desire in the process of producing and interpreting the Anniversaries. I approach the two Anniversaries entitled "An Anatomy of the World" and "The Progres of the Soule," the poem entitled "A Funerall Elegie," the prefatory poems by Joseph Hall, and the critical tradition—the Anniversaries palimpsest—as a project dedicated to the production of a subject of Donne. As noted in the Introduction of this book, under "a subject of Donne" I include the following interrelated positions: the speaking subject who produces (and is produced by) Elizabeth Drury as the Idea of a Woman for Sir Robert Drury in the two Anniversaries; the academic subject "John Donne" produced by readings of the Anniversaries; and the reading subject who produces (and is produced by) that "John Donne" and who thereby also instantiates a relationship between the Renaissance and the present.[10] In all three processes of subjectification I mean to emphasize the psychological investment in the work of producing Elizabeth Drury as the centering "shee" of the poem; to explore the role of desire, particularly in the form of identification, in this production of the enigmatic "shee."[11]

Representing Elizabeth Drury

"Shee" has been variously represented by scholars as the idea of the decay of the world and its counterpoint, Queen Elizabeth, Astraea, the regenerate soul, image of Wisdom of God, Donne himself. Nearly everything written in this vein makes some sense. Or, if we heed Tayler, *none* of it makes sense, and thus, the proliferation of symbolic equivalents for Donne's "shee" must be brought to an end. The alternative, well, what is the alternative? It is worth pondering for a moment what is at issue here. For Tayler it is the historical study of literature, which is "Probably the most efficacious way to 'feel' outside the conceptual archetypes of our own culture." And one "feels" outside one's own culture by talking to the dead: "If we learn the lingo, Donne will speak to us, not without what used to be ambiguity and now is indeterminacy—but well enough to be heard and understood."[12] He will tell us his Idea of a Woman.

This desire, as Stephen Greenblatt suggests, is one shared by most of us in academic literary studies, but like Greenblatt, I want "to resist the integration of all images and expressions into a single master discourse"—in the case of Tayler's reading of the Anniversaries, epistemology.[13] My reasons for resisting differ from those of Greenblatt, who writes about the most social of literary sites—the theater, but they are just as obvious. Tayler, capitalizing on Donne's reported comment on the "Idea" behind the poem, compellingly demonstrates the importance of this discourse to Donne's poems, but I think it is a mistake to fix meaning in the structure generated by that discourse. We need to remember that the authorial voice always reaches us through a process of mediation: Donne's explanations of his purpose, as we shall see, responded to problems created by the poems in his circle of patrons; and his comment about the "Idea of a Woman" comes to us thirdhand—Drummond reporting Jonson's report of Donne's response to Jonson's criticism. What is more, the Anniversaries comprise one of the most spectacular Renaissance instances of a poet apparently failing to make his intended meaning stick. The readers who "misunderstood," Jonson and some of the great ladies courted by Donne in verse epistles, were hardly common readers.[14] Finally, Donne himself claims to have been divided in his own intentions; in a letter to his close friend Sir Henry Goodyer, he wrote, "I do not pardon myself, but confess that I did it against my conscience, that is against my own opinion, that I should not have done so."[15] Donne's Idea was in trouble from the start, engaging powerfully with contradictions in systems of patronage, courtship, and patriarchy.

And yet, perhaps more than any other Donne poems these challenge readers to make sense out of them. They do so for a variety of reasons: to save Donne from charges of insincerity, to demonstrate the poems' claim to greatness—that is, to celebrate the Anniversaries, to repeat the act of the poem. Why? As with Donne, I think, to reassure ourselves that we have a "rich soule," which is another way of saying to maintain a sense of wholeness, self-possession.[16] We do this by representation—by constructing the world and thereby constructing a self. This is what I mean by ideological work.

The Anniversaries construct the reader, the reader constructs the Anniversaries, in relation to "the *Idea* of a Woman." In the First Anniversary the Idea is mostly felt as loss. We feel the Idea only through the representations that fill in for her, an imagery of weakness and disintegration, "wherein," as the subtitle tells us, "the frailty and decay of this whole world is represented." The Second Anniversary gradually pulls away from the imagery of the world's decline, recuperating speaker and reader through a positive identification with Elizabeth as a religious master signifier of power.[17] This recuperation, we shall see, is also implicated in an aesthetic ideology; in Hall's prefatory poems the processes of idealizing Elizabeth and of anatomizing the dead world are presented as the work performed by art. That is, the Anniversaries perform an act of what Greenblatt terms "aesthetic empowerment" by which ideological work is transformed into the work of art.[18]

But Drummond reported that Donne claimed to have described the idea of a *woman*. In the many readings of the poems little is made of Donne's gendering of his idea, except in a broadly typological or symbolic register.[19] I think it is significant that the poems are occasioned by the death of a daughter of a would-be patron. In terms of the patronage relationship within which the poems originated, but which by no means contains them (witness the "misreadings" of Jonson, a poet of patronage, and some of Donne's female patrons), the *Idea* of a *Woman* is produced by a transaction between a lost daughter, a father, and her male celebrant ("let thy makers praise / Honor thy Laura," writes Joseph Hall in "The Harbinger to the Progres"). Lynda Boose's arresting thesis is pertinent here: "Inscribed within patriarchal narrative is something more specific than just a general erasure of woman. What is specifically absent is the *daughter*."[20] One might say that the daughter "is specifically absent" both in Donne's poems—that is what they are about, the absent daughter of Sir Robert Drury—and in commentary on the poems. This is another way of saying that the signifying economy of loss and recuperation that produces the reading subject of the Anniversaries is a male economy. This comes as no great surprise. My point is not to rediscover patriarchy in Donne's England. What interests me, again, are the ways in which Donne's particular mobilization of this system has been read into Renaissance culture and the possibilities for reading the system against itself that are released by both Donne's work upon ideology and the reader's work on Donne that the text seems to invite.[21]

Arthur Marotti has urged that the reading of Donne's poetry begin with study of the culture of patronage within and against which it was produced. In the case of the Anniversaries, he suggests that problems of interpretation might have originated due to the circumstances of their production. Donne's decision to publish, he argues, was not followed up by "making the necessary adjustments demanded by the more public circumstances of print."[22] What was appropriate for private, coterie reading was not necessarily suitable for public reading. Thus the problem of reading the Anniversaries was, from the beginning, a part of the critical tradition. As noted earlier, Donne seems to have offended some of the female coterie readers to whom he had addressed extravagant verse epistles to which the Anniversaries have often been compared. Hearing secondhand of the criticisms of these readers, Donne wrote in a letter, a genre suited to the "coterie" writer, his well-known defense: "that when I had received so very good testimony of her worthinesse, and was gone down to print verses, it became me to say, not what I was sure was just truth, but the best that I could conceive; for that had been a new weaknesse in me, to have praised any body in printed verses, that had not been capable of the best praise that I could give."[23] At least three points in this self-serving explanation deserve comment. Most obviously, the publication of the work calls forth a private explanation for it, an explanation that would probably not have been required had the piece been privately circulated. Donne is one of the earliest English writers to offer an interpretation of his own work, an interpretation embedded in a private genre and identified with his intention.[24] Second, coterie writing, it is implied, is distinguished from published writing on the basis of its truth-value: printed verses require ("it became me to say") more than the exact truth. At the same time, Donne blurs the distinction between his public and private writing in what has to be an aside to his female coterie reading over the shoulder of the addressee of the letter: I only praise the best. And finally, Donne's defense implies that the extravagance of the verse epistles addressed to the complaining ladies was not extravagance at all but "just truth"; Donne tries to use his published work here to support his status as a coterie writer.[25]

All three dimensions of the defense respond to a particular instance of what Jonathan Crewe terms "the scandal of authorship." In particular, the Anniversaries risk the scandal of a coterie or "amateur" writer going public. More broadly, they are scandalous in the sense suggested by Jonson's famous quip on the incongruence of their language and the object of their praise: they say too much. In their excesses, the Anniversaries exemplify Crewe's notion of "unredeemed rhetoric," a sort of scandalous literary exhibitionism. Modern historical critics have generally worked to dismiss this charge as just the *appearance of excess* by restoring (but actually constructing) their lost historical contexts. Scholarship and criticism of the poems, like the poems themselves, stage the project of redeeming rhetoric. Crewe's characterization of this work of recuperation is an apt description of the movement of both the poems themselves and critical writing about the poems: "there is . . . no major writer of the period who does not participate in the dream of healing and restoration, or seek the ultimate triumph in language of the erected wit over the infected will."[26] The literary enterprise of the Anniversaries—which includes the First and Second Anniversaries and "A Funeral Elegie" by Donne, two prefatory poems by Joseph Hall, and a long critical history that begins with Donne himself—is a wonderfully detailed exhibit in two programs for reading that Crewe finds anticipated in the "protestantization" of culture from the Tudor to the Stuart periods: reading as an act of aesthetic appreciation (see, for example, Hall's prefatory poems) and reading as reduction of offensive rhetorical excess (by means of, say, a generic convention, a Protestant poetics, or a history of an idea like Wisdom).

This work of healing and restoration, which Crewe finds inscribed in Renaissance ambivalence about literature, is ideological work. In the Anniversaries and commentary on them it is tightly focussed on the work of representation. The reader is informed in the subtitle of the First Anniversary that "by occasion of the vntimely death of Mistris Elizabeth Drvry the frailty and the Decay of this whole world is represented." Since the critical controversy about the Anniversaries has always been, from Donne's own time, a debate about the method, form, and content of representation in the poems, and since the First Anniversary advertises a theme of representing one thing by another, I think we are justified in treating them as poems about (among other things, of course) representation.

Cultural historians of various schools have discussed representation as a central activity in the production and reproduction of culture. Roger Chartier describes the work of representation in terms that suggest its relevance to Donne's Anniversaries: as an aspect of the general problem of signification, representation entails "the establishment of a relation between a present image and an absent object in which the one is a valid equivalent of the other because it is in conformity with it."[27] Historical critics like Frank Manley and Barbara Lewalski have argued that Donne's aim in the Anniversaries is to establish such a relation between the absent Elizabeth Drury ("Shee is gone") and an image of her as Wisdom or the regenerate "rich soule."[28] The aims of these historical critics are representational in other respects that are similar to Donne's. In this kind of historical criticism there is an attempt to establish a relation between the absent intention of John Donne and an image such as the regenerate soul or Wisdom; the idea is to make Donne present through a disclosure of his intentions in the poems. This desire to recover the lost Donne is related, as I noted at the beginning of this chapter, to a larger historical project. Like many other major literary texts, these poems have become representative of an entire historical period: the familiar lines on "the new philosophy" were long routinely employed to represent the Copernican revolution; in retrospect, Lewalski's Anniversaries book appears a harbinger of an Englishing and Protestantizing of English Renaissance literature which replaced the more Catholic, Anglican, Continental literary history of Eliot and Martz. One of the stakes of the Anniversaries debate for us, but not for Donne or Jonson, is the representation of the Renaissance in literary history.

The task of representation, however, is highly problematic, as the critical history of the poems which began with Donne himself suggests: the aims of representation do not always correspond to its effects on readers; or the relation between image and "absent object" can be contested. Moreover, the aims of representation themselves can be heterogeneous or conflicted. Marotti suggests, for example, that the representation of Elizabeth is bound up with, and even displaced by, the representation of Donne the poet of patronage, an idea given an interesting deconstructive spin by Docherty.

Unlike Jonson, most informed readers have solved the problem of representation posed by the Anniversaries by reading them symbolically. Tayler passionately disputes such readings, arguing that they turn on a crucial mistaking of Donne's "Idea" for "symbol"; rather, Tayler argues, we need to focus on "how Donne managed to convince himself that he could see an 'Idea' " and on "the cognitive processes by which he accomplished the task in the poems."[29] I share Tayler's interest in process, but where he writes of Donne's cognitive processes, I find the processes of representation and identification. I choose these terms to try to capture both conscious and unconscious elements in the ideological struggle I see underlying the controversy over the poems. The ideological foundation of the debate was first and most obviously revealed in Jonson's famous remark on the Virgin Mary, and it has persisted into Tayler's use of the poems to defend a particular historical approach to the study of literature. I believe it is more important to try to understand this controversy than to try to end it.

I think the text of the Anniversaries accommodates, and even provokes, an ideological reading. The First Anniversary famously employs the correspondence system of representation to comment just as memorably on the breakdown of correspondence theory. Donne saws away at the rotten branch he is seated on. This often-noted paradoxicality of the poems, highlighted in Joseph Hall's prefatory verses, tends to push the reader into an impossible position, but the result, I want to insist, is not simply another "self-consuming artifact." Or rather, the production of a self-consuming artifact is itself a recuperation of a stable subject-position. Donne's disparities demand resolution; they engage us as readers in the work of constructing ourselves and Donne as coherent subjects through representation, in particular through the construction of "an Idea of a Woman." In the last part of this chapter, I suggest this work is a gendered production of an aesthetic ideology. Here I merely want to stress that the Anniversaries strike me as profoundly orthodox in their ideological conclusions but that the work of constructing these positions around the master signifier "shee" is difficult and unsettling.[30] Reading the Anniversaries challenges assumptions about the heterodox and the orthodox, the subversive and the normal, in Renaissance culture. Orthodoxy is not always an easy, default position; it too, like resistance or subversion, can entail a struggle.[31]

The best introduction to the Anniversaries remains Joseph Hall's "To the Praise of the Dead, and the Anatomy." In this poem, a substantial piece of evidence in favor of Marotti's thesis on patronage as a determinant of Donne's poetry, the death of Elizabeth Drury is treated as a part of a literary project:

> Well dy'de the world, that we might liue to see
> This world of wit, in his Anatomee:
> No euill wants his good: so wilder heyres
> Bedew their fathers Toombs with forced teares,
> Whose state requites their los . . .[32]

As commentators have pointed out, Hall was remembered for a tour de force rhetorical performance on the decay of the world during his years at Cambridge, a discourse wherein, according to Thomas Fuller, "his position confuteth his position, the wit and quickness whereof did argue an increase, rather than a decay of parts in the latter age."[33] Hall makes much the same point in his praise of the "Anatomy": "how can I consent the world is dead / While this Muse lives?" (ll. 7–8). Still, it is remarkable that Hall chooses to treat the occasion of Elizabeth Drury's death so explicitly as a literary exercise, framing it in the terms of Donne's poem, for, as Hall's rhetorical question reminds us, the world has not died but Elizabeth Drury has. Even if Philippe Aries were right about a relative dearth of familial affection in the period, and this is by no means a settled question, Hall's poem, like Donne's, cannot entirely be explained by such a cultural difference.[34] His outrageous analogy of dissolute heirs crying crocodile tears over a father's grave is a grotesque inversion of the occasion being memorialized. So impudent and tasteless to a twentieth-century sensibility is Hall's puffery in these lines that one is tempted to see in it a perhaps unwitting revenge for past injustices (or, more likely, a feeling that divine intervention has redressed such injustices) that Hall felt he suffered while in the patronage of Drury.[35] Hall was certainly capable of consciously regarding his negotiations with the patronage system in ultimate terms, as evidenced by his account of an episode that occurred during his service under Drury; in his autobiography, *Observations of some specialties of divine providence*, Hall makes it clear that his enemy's death was punishment for attempts to come between Hall and Drury.[36] In any case, Hall rather neatly replaces Elizabeth Drury with John Donne:

> thou the subiect of this wel-borne thought,
> Thrise noble maid, couldst not haue found nor sought
> A fitter time to yeeld to thy sad Fate,
> Then whiles this spirit liues. (ll. 11–14)

We are from the outset made aware of the material conditions of literary production, the bid for patronage represented in and by the Anniversaries.

Hall's title, like the subtitle of the "Anatomy," involves the reader at the very outset in the problem of representation, here with respect to Hall's praise. Hall equates praise of Donne's poem with praise of the girl. He seems more comfortable, however, praising Donne than praising Elizabeth; one suspects that Hall, like Donne, was unacquainted with the girl and that he is uncomfortable with the claims made by the "Anatomy." He uses a conceit of praise to avoid the work of praising the girl—"A task, which thy fair goodnes made too much / For the bold pride of vulgar pens to tuch" (ll. 19–20). When he approaches praise of the girl Hall redirects it: "So these high songs that to thee suited bine, / Serue but to sound thy makers praise, in thine" (ll. 35–36); or again,

> For as by infant-yeares men judge of age,
> Thy early loue, thy vertue, did presage
> What an hie part thou bear'st in those best songs
> Whereto no burden, nor no end belongs. (ll. 41–44)

Hall's closing promise or wish—"Neuer may thy name be in our songs forgot"—sounds almost like a joke in view of the declaration earlier: "Enough is us to praise them that praise thee" (l. 21). On the other hand, Hall is making a serious point about his role in the circulation of praise: his function is to praise the poet who praises the girl who praises God. This also seems to entail dispraise of the marginalized, "love-sicke Parents" who "have bewayl'd in vaine" (l. 46). Such an attitude is perfectly conventional from both a literary and doctrinal point of view, and I do not wish to exaggerate its significance; but, taken together with the opening remarks on the *timeliness* of Elizabeth's death and the absence of any expression of sorrow in the poem, it works toward detaching the literary performance that is to follow from the real human beings who commissioned it.[37] Hall oddly alerts us at once to cultural contexts in the two senses suggested above, what in old Marxist terminology might be called the base and the superstructure of the poem—its mode of production and its religious ideology, but the relationship between these seems anything but clear. The problem of reading the Anniversaries begins before the beginning.

From the first Donne makes the reader and the act of reading a major concern of the "Anatomy." The opening lines posit a connection between the "rich soule" of the deceased girl and the reading subject's soul: "When that rich soule which to her Heaven is gone, / Whom all they celebrate, who know they have one" (ll. 1–2). This identification of self and soul, of the reader's soul with Elizabeth and of the reader's self with his soul, seems oddly placed here at the outset. It raises a question about motive: If all fit readers already celebrate Elizabeth, then why write the poem? Is there a joke here? No one celebrates her (i.e., no one has a soul), because, as the poem later asserts, the soul of the world (Elizabeth the representative regenerate soul) has departed. But this would conflict with the claim later that

> A faint weake love of vertue and of good
> Reflects from her, on them which understood
> Her worth (ll. 71–73)

—a claim that, characteristically for this poem, Donne then inflates to a point that requires him to produce another rationale for writing (and reading) the poem:

> (For all assum'd unto this Dignitee,
> So many weedlesse Paradises bee,
> Which of themselves produce no venemous sinne,
> Except some forraine Serpent bring it in)
> Yet, because outward stormes the strongest breake,
> And strength it selfe by confidence growes weake,
> This new world may be safer being told
> The dangers and diseases of the old. (ll. 81–88)

Lewalski has made theological sense of these opening moves, but reading "The entrie into the worke" is hardly the experience of doctrinal clarification

Lewalski suggests it is; the reader is repeatedly offered a position from which to interpret Elizabeth Drury's death only to be presented with an alternative perspective.[38] What follows is a simplification of the twists and turns of Donne's argument. By the time we reach the statement of motive for the poem we have been told something like this: the virtuous remember Elizabeth, but when she died the connection between matter and spirit in the world was lost; but then the world (the virtuous?) reconsidered that "all" (not just the virtuous?) would emulate Elizabeth's virtue in an effort "to see her" (ll. 16–18); but this was an illusion, the world is sick; even worse, it has no "sense and memory"; but then it appears to have sense and memory but fears to say that Elizabeth has died. There is nothing to be done since the world is not just sick but dead; but maybe something can be gained from an anatomy; but who would read it, since the world is dead? But "there's a kind of world remaining still" (l. 67) that grows from the carcass of the dead world, and although the creatures of this new world are immune to "hom-borne intrinsique harme" (l. 80), they can, like Adam and Eve, be tempted from without, so I will inform them about the evils of the outside (i.e., the old) world (which is, apparently, not dead but sick).

The "entrie" presents an anatomy of motive that eventually delivers a coherent explanation for the work; in the process of constructing a motive, however, the motive repeatedly threatens to slip away. This anatomy of motive encapsulates the double movement of Donne's entire project: the work of closure, the construction of a coherent subject position, requires act after act of division—body/soul, old world/new world. The "entrie into the worke" of anatomy, then, combines the project of constructing the "Idea of a Woman" with the anatomical work of dissecting the world.[39]

The work of both construction and anatomy depends upon a system of correspondences that, it is claimed, has broken down. This disparity in the work has the effect of foregrounding in the way of Renaissance paradoxes the fictional, constructed status of its argument. Opening lines move rapidly between political, sacred, and medical analogies to represent Elizabeth Drury's death as a royal progress, the death of Christ ("in that great earth-quake languished"), and convulsions ("And so the world had fits"). As many commentators have pointed out, this kind of shifting establishes from the outset the microcosm-macrocosm analogy upon which the poem depends (see, for example, Manley's gloss on line 11). But if we slow down the montage, we can also observe slight eccentricities or irregularities that stick out around the sides of the superimposed images and help us to register the work of invention that Hall praised in his introduction. These discrepancies, to speak in Donnean terms, are microcosmic versions of the failure of representation, of the great disparity between the girl and the effects ascribed to her in the poem, the disparity which it is the ideological project of the poem to close up.

Here at the beginning of the poem disjunctions occur in the medical analogy, which in turn corresponds to the earthquake but becomes so involved as to disrupt rather than clarify any analogical system being created. Manley's brilliant scholarly gloss on the "common Bath of teares" of blood in line 12 suggests a telescoped connection with Christ's bloody sweat of Gethsemane and his suffering on the cross: "the world in its agony feels itself deserted by God and at the same time the realization of its own guilt causes it to weep a sweat of blood" (126). At this point Donne has established a number of correspondences: Elizabeth's death is like the end of the Queen's progress; her death is like the death of Christ; the effect of her death on the world is like Christ's agony in the garden and like Christ's death on the cross. But the telescoping produces a distortion in the typology, since the guilty world and the suffering Christ do not quite correspond. The image pulls away slightly from the typological frame. Similarly, a little later the world's fits of joy and mourning at the death of Elizabeth seem to Manley "to suggest the central paradox of Christianity, the *felix culpa*" (127); but, as Manley also notes, the allusion is marked by "considerable ambiguity." Indeed, the fits of joy are shortly exposed as a mistake: "So thou, sicke world, mistak'st thy self to bee / Well, when alas, thou'rt in a Letargee" (ll. 23–24).

The analogy with original sin is explored further in a difficult passage that prepares for the work on naming to follow:

> Her death did wound, and tame thee than, and than
> Thou mightst haue better spar'd the Sunne, or Man;
> That wound was deepe, but 'tis more misery,
> That thou hast lost thy sense and memory. (ll. 25–28)

Both Manley and Lewalski regard the passage as one of the poem's recapitulations of the effects of original sin, traditionally represented as a wound.[40] In this reading, "than" [then], could refer to a sliding time covering the moment of the original Fall and the occasion of Elizabeth's death and, more immediately, to the time before the "Letargee" that followed hard upon the time of her death, as recounted in the preceding lines. The passage encourages associations with original sin and its effects only to insist on a difference in degree concerning the effects; a poststructuralist fate worse than death has overtaken the comatose world: "thou art speechlesse growne. / Thou hast forgot thy name" (ll. 30–31).

Lewalski identifies this name as the primal goodness of the world, here "as recapitulated in Elizabeth Drury"; Manley characterizes the entire passage (ll. 25–42) as "a symbolic action that names her" as the Word—"the soul's ability to speak and call upon God."[41] Both identifications can find abundant support in the text and contexts of the poem (for the latter, see especially Lewalski's study). I want to emphasize not the specific content of the name but the act of naming, of representing Elizabeth, as a means of constructing the speaking/reading subject of the poem. Again, we only know we have a soul by virtue of performing the name or soul of the girl, which "defin'd thee, gaue thee forme and frame" (l. 37).

It is suggestive that Donne represents the naming of the world through the girl in a two-stage conceit that evokes secular and sacred power:

> For as a child kept from the Font, vntill
> A Prince, expected long, come to fulfill
> The Ceremonies, thou vnnam'd hadst laid,
> Had not her comming, thee her Palace made. (ll. 33–36)

W. Milgate and Manley are surely correct in explaining these lines as "a variation of the traditional idea of the soul as a prince in the prison of the body" and as an acknowledgment that "we are not only given our own names in baptism, we are also regenerated into Christ's name."[42] But again, there is a telescoping here that forces the two parts of the correspondence together. The first half draws upon the intersection of an act of courtship with a religious rite in which the analogy of sacred and secular power is particularly ambivalent. In the second half, the child rather straightforwardly, as "primal goodness" or Logos or soul or grace, takes up residence in the world-house and makes it a "Palace." To unpack this comparison and the relationship between its two parts, I must digress to consider briefly the issue of sacraments in the sixteenth and seventeenth centuries.

Controversies over the sacraments, over the precise relationship between the rites and what Richard Hooker terms "the substance" of the sacraments, were constructed around such complicated relationships, indeed, around the whole problem of representation. Hooker's summary of the orthodox Anglican position expresses the extreme complexity of the issue:

> For we take not baptism nor the eucharist for bare *resemblances* or memorials of things absent, neither for *naked signs* and testimonials assuring us of grace received before, but (as they are indeed and in verity) for means effectual whereby God when we take the sacraments delivereth into our hands that grace available unto eternal life, which grace the sacraments represent or signify.[43]

The sacraments are, according to this formulation, an extremely complex and reflexive system of representation: sacraments are both the "means effectual" of delivering grace and the representation of that process of delivering grace. To be sure, Hooker's argument is not focussed on literary theory, but it nonetheless raises one of the crucial problems of literary theory—the grounds of representation.

Hooker is answering Puritan challenges to sacramentalism at the levels both of their necessity for salvation and of the necessities in their administration (i.e., what is essential and what accessory).[44] Donne, of course, is not debating these points, but his baptismal conceit is pulled apart by the controversial discourse over things essential and things accessory in the sacraments. Both Donne's and Hooker's texts are marked by a slippage in their account of the act of signification which seems central to the concept of a sacrament. In the case of the sacrament of baptism this slippage takes on a special force, since one of the functions of the sacrament, in addition to representation of the grace conferred, is to name, to attach a signifier to the person receiving the sacrament.

Hooker distinguishes between "the inward grace of sacraments" and their "outward form," but both this inward grace and "outward substance" are necessary for the sacrament to be effectual: "Hereupon it groweth, that many times there are three things said to make up the substance of a sacrament, namely, the grace which is thereby offered, the element which shadoweth or signifieth grace, and the word which expresseth what is done by the element" (2: 260). Writing of baptism specifically, Hooker explains that "all other orders, rites, prayers, lessons, sermons, actions, and their circumstances whatsoever, they are to the outward substance of baptism but things accessory." And,

> considering that such ordinances have been made to adorn the sacrament, not the sacrament to depend on them; seeing also that they are not of the substance of baptism, and that baptism is far more necessary than any such incident rite or solemnity ordained for the better administration thereof; if the case be such as permitteth not baptism to have the decent complements of baptism, better it were to enjoy the body without his furniture, than to wait for this till the opportunity of that for which we desire it be lost. (2: 261–62)

Here we might pause to take the force of Donne's conceit, which imagines "a child kept from the Font" until what could only theologically be considered an accessory to the sacrament is present to "fulfill / The Ceremonies." Donne's use of the term "ceremonies" here raises one of the flags carried by Hooker in his battle with the Puritans. The value and function of such accessories to the sacrament are treated at great length by Hooker. Even though such rites are not of the substance (inward or outward) of baptism, they are not to be discarded. Hooker spends many chapters defending, for example, signing the cross at baptismal celebrations, a practice that serves "for a sign of remembrance to put us in mind of our duty" (2: 319); signing, that is, is an act of signification that supports the larger form of the sacrament whereby grace is represented. The sacrament of baptism, for Hooker, is an extremely complex network of essential and accessory significations that is matched by his own discourse on the subject: a clean distinction between essential and nonessential elements is followed up by prodigious scholarship and strenuous argumentation largely devoted to defense of the nonessential.

Donne's conceit proceeds in two stages aligned with the accessory and essential features of baptism. In the first half, as already suggested, the girl takes the place of the Prince, an important accessory in an imagined courtly christening. In the second half, she assumes the place of an essential element of the sacrament; according to Lewalski, she would correspond to something like Hooker's essential grace, the regenerate Christian soul. At the same time, the royal dimension of the figure is reinforced by the "Palace made" of the world by her habitation. The prince living in this palace must be Christ, as distinguished from the Prince who is awaited "to fulfill / The Ceremonies." Or it may be that the passage works as an historical allegory, baptism representing the coming of Christ, in turn representing the coming of Elizabeth—a reading supported by the confusing temporal scheme of lines 39–42. In either case, the vehicle of Donne's figure remains the sacrament of baptism, the divinely authorized process of naming or representing ourselves, which, as a sacrament, is nonetheless caught up in the paradox of representation as outlined above. It is both the "means effectual whereby God when we take the sacraments delivereth into our hands that grace available unto eternal life" and the representation of that process of delivering grace.

To put it another way, Donne's highly reflexive figure of naming is a microcosm of the general ideological action of the Anniversaries. The Elizabeth of the first half of the analogy is different from the Elizabeth of the second half. This difference is what Lewalski terms the "symbolic mode." But we also need to be aware that Donne's two-stage figure is a quintessentially ideological construction. Eve Kosofsky Sedgwick has written lucidly on this process:

> The ideological formation . . . permits a criss-crossing of agency, temporality, and space. It is important that ideology in this sense, even when its form is flatly declarative ("A man's home is his castle"), is always at least implicitly narrative, and that, in order for the reweaving of ideology to be truly invisible, the narrative is necessarily chiasmic in structure: that is, that the subject of the beginning of the narrative [accessory Prince] is different from the subject at the end [essential grace; Christ], and that the two subjects cross each other in a rhetorical figure that conceals their discontinuity.[45]

But such discontinuities were not completely concealed in Donne's time, as evidenced by the religious controversies over accessory and essential elements in the sacraments and by the resistance of some of Donne's readers to his move from Elizabeth Drury to the Idea of a Woman.

Elizabeth Drury, then, names the world. But if she is the Word, as Manley suggests, she is *accessible* only as a text, a representation of the Word that is open to interpretation.[46] This interpretive debate over the Anniversaries, like the controversies over sacramental ceremonies and sacramental essence alluded to in Donne's figure of christening, is also a struggle for control over representation. The subjects of and in these controversial discourses are imbricated in the cultural project of representation, which is also the

121

project of the Anniversaries. The Anniversaries represent Elizabeth Drury as the sacraments represent grace—the relationship between signifier and signified is not one of "bare *resemblances* or memorials of things absent"; more is at stake than "bare *resemblances*." The delivery, to borrow Hooker's term, of Elizabeth ("that rich soule") to the reader is at stake; that is to say we the readers are in question, the question being whether we "have one [a rich soule]."

But problems and contradictions in representation produce Elizabeth as an unstable subject of discourse, itself productive of a controversy of interpretation. Readings that settle upon an interpretative key—whether it be the regenerate soul, Wisdom, or the Blessed Virgin—are responding to the poems' representational challenge, but by reading the poems in terms of the ideology produced, I believe they read them upside down, misrepresenting Donne's *work on* ideology rather in the manner of Marx's famous image of ideology as a *camera obscura.*[47] The work of the poem, its production of ideology, is misrepresented as its product. But even the product of the Anniversaries refuses to stand still. We have, thanks to the work of scholars as diverse as Lewalski and Marotti, a choice of ideologies with which to fix the poems to their period, ideologies that, in the work of the two scholars mentioned, produce Elizabeth Drury, John Donne, and scholars as subjects: Elizabeth the regenerate soul, John Donne the coterie poet, and two quite distinct historical scholars. The disparities between these subject-positions testifies to the interrogative power of Donne's text.[48]

"Motion in Corruption"

As their individual titles—"An Anatomy of the World" and "Of the Progres of the Soule"—suggest, the Anniversaries are poems of process or movement. "An Anatomy of the World" locates the subject of the poem (that is, Donne, Elizabeth Drury, and readers) somewhere between death and life. Early in the "Anatomy" Donne seems to back down from the claims of the master conceit of the poem—that the world is dead, its soul having departed:

> For there's a kind of world remaining still,
> Though shee which did inanimate and fill
> The world, be gone, yet in this last long night,
> Her Ghost doth walke. (ll. 67–70)

This curious condition of being both dead and alive is repeated in one of the most spectacular passages in Donne at the opening of the Second Anniversary:

> Or as sometimes in a beheaded man,
> Though at two Red seas, which freely ran,
> One from the Trunke, another from the Head,

> His soule be saild, to her eternall bed,
> His eies will twinckle, and his tongue will roll,
> As though he beckned, and cal'd back his Soul,
> He graspes his hands, and he puls up his feet,
> And seemes to reach, and to step forth to meet
> His soule;
>   . . .
> So strugles this dead world, now shee is gone;
> For there is motion in corruption. ("Of the Progres of the Soule,"
> ll. 10–21)

Donne pronounces the world dead, but then refuses to allow it to stay dead, breeding "new creatures" "from the carcasse of the old world." We might expect these creatures bred by twilight's influence to be revolting and fleshly (Manley cites Hamlet's sun, breeding maggots in a dead dog); instead we get something more like Eliot's "Lilacs out of the dead land, mixing / Memory and desire"—"So many weedlesse Paradises" (l. 82).

This scene of Donne's ideological work is the twilit place of abjection, the world as a wasting corpse, the limiting body that we wish to cast off ("ab-jacere"). This condition has been related to the signifying process by Julia Kristeva in *Powers of Horror.*[49] For Kristeva the abject is that which must be expelled in order to take up a stable position in the symbolic order. As Elizabeth Grosz summarizes, "Abjection is a reaction to the recognition of the impossible but necessary transcendence of the subject's corporeality, and the impure, defiling elements of its uncontrollable materiality"; thus, "Abjection is the underside of the symbolic. . . . It is an insistence on the subject's necessary relation to death, to animality, and to materiality, being the subject's recognition and refusal of its corporeality."[50] I will later discuss how Donne, like Kristeva, locates the abject on the side of the feminine, but for now I want merely to use Kristeva's analysis to highlight the interdependence of Donne's projects of constructing an Idea of a Woman and anatomizing the corpse of the world. The production of Elizabeth as an "Idea of a Woman" is dependent upon both the "recognition and refusal" of the body.

In addition to its manifestations in the breeding cadaver, the ghost, and the animate beheaded man, this abjection is most apparent in the First Anniversary's discourse of the body; it is a discourse of the abject—of rottenness, decay, sickness, disease, maiming, infection, disproportion, disfigurement, ugliness, monstrosity, atomization, to use Donne's vocabulary. The famous idealized body of "eloquent blood" in "The Progres of the Soule" (ll. 244–46) issues from revulsion at limitations of the flesh and impurities of ordinary bodies revealed by the "Anatomy." This purified body stands opposed to the abject bodies of the beheaded man, the ghost of Elizabeth, and most of all the putrifying yet paradoxically generative corpse of the dead world.[51]

The subject of the Anniversaries is constructed in the intermediate space opened up by Donne's anatomy of the dead world and his projection of a world to come—the world haunted by Elizabeth's ghost, the horror show of the beheaded man at the opening of the Second Anniversary: "motion in corruption." Both poems oscillate between a language of loss and the language of recuperation, or rather they generate a language of plenitude from a language of loss and desire. This paradox is what Hall identifies as the curious experience of reading the poem: one feels empowered by Donne's account of powerlessness. Or, I should say, someone feels empowered, but not everyone. The Anniversaries work to the degree that the reader can enjoy their recuperative display of desire, and this display, I want to argue, is gendered masculine.

The Father, the Daughter, and the Poet

Arthur Marotti is the only critic I know of who has suggested, even in passing, a psychoanalytic approach to the Anniversaries. Viewing the poems in light of Donne's political failure, he argues that they are "about loss and the need for recovery" and that their satiric scorn and idealization are "stances suitable to one responding strongly to narcissistic injury."[52] Marotti's biographical take on Donne understandably leads him to consider narcissism with respect to the individual John Donne, but I believe he has also touched upon an important feature of the culture of patronage to which the Anniversaries contribute.

In his paper "On Narcissism: An Introduction" Freud distinguishes between "object-libido" and "ego-libido" or narcissism and tracks the survival of the latter into such adult forms as parental overvaluation of children and the lover's overvaluation of the beloved.[53] In the case of the Anniversaries, parental overvaluation seems joined to another revival of narcissism which Freud treats at length in the paper, the formation of an ego ideal: "This ideal ego is now the target of the self-love which was enjoyed in childhood by the actual ego. The subject's narcissism makes its appearance displaced on to this new ideal ego, which, like the infantile ego, finds itself possessed of every perfection that is of value" (SE 14: 94).[54] Paradoxically, satisfaction of this revived ego-libido is bound up with surveillance and harsh judgment of the ego; Freud suggests that "what we call our conscience [later to be named the superego] has the required characteristics" of "a special psychical agency which performs the task of seeing that narcissistic satisfaction from the ego ideal is ensured and which, with this end in view, constantly watches the actual ego and measures it by that ideal" (SE 14: 95). This aspect of the operation of the ego ideal leads Freud, in a concluding paragraph, to suggest a link between psychological and social processes: "In addition to its individual side, this ideal has a social side; it is also the common ideal of a family, a class or a nation" (SE 14: 101). According to Freud's theory, then, Donne's combination of satire and praise in the Anniversaries could be seen as narcissistic in several directions. The harsh judgment of the world and corresponding construction of "the Idea of a Woman and not as she was" could recuperate a lost self-regard for Donne; for Donne's patron, the father of Elizabeth Drury; and for a society that appears to be in decline.

I mentioned Elizabeth's father and Donne's patron, Robert Drury, but not Lady Drury, and it remains for me to explain why I read the Anniversaries, poems that commemorate the loss of a daughter and celebrate the Idea of a Woman, as poems that call the reader to a masculine subject-position. Narcissism and "what we call our conscience" play key roles in this argument. Freud discusses both of them as distinguishing features of melancholia, a type of response to loss privileged in the Renaissance (and, according to Giorgio Agamben, exemplified in Donne). Freud's analysis of this condition can help to explain several features of Donne's performance in the Anniversaries. I do not wish to claim that melancholy is the key to the mythology of the poems, but rather to suggest how Donne's work of recuperation and our own efforts at interpreting the poems are bound up with what Juliana Schiesari has discussed as a gendered "symbolics of loss."[55] The search for the symbolic identity of Donne's "shee" mimics Donne's own quest for a lost and transcendent object of desire. Scholar and poet are united in their melancholy, the mark of great *men*.

Freud's "Mourning and Melancholia" reads in places like a commentary on the critical history of the Anniversaries. He notes that both mourning and melancholy may be reactions "to the loss of a loved object." But, "in yet other cases [the cases that interest Freud] one feels justified in maintaining the belief that a loss of this kind has occurred, but one cannot see clearly what it is that has been lost." That is, we might know "*whom* he has lost but not *what* he has lost in him" (SE 14: 244–45). As Schiesari points out, this distinction "refocuses attention not on the lost *object* but on the loss, on the 'what' of the lost object, whose thingness points back to the *subject* of the loss (not the 'whom' that is lost in mourning but the 'who' that presents himself as losing in melancholia)."[56] In terms of criticism of the Anniversaries, this translates into the work of discovering *what* (Wisdom, the regenerate soul, etc.), not whom (the Elizabeth Drury Donne never saw), is lost. More important still, this shift of focus from the whom that is lost to the one who presents himself as loser is related to the fundamental distinction Freud draws between melancholia and mourning on the basis of narcissism. Where the "work of mourning" consists of the gradual detachment of the libido from the lost object, leaving the ego "free and uninhibited again," melancholia involves the importation of the lost object along with "the shadow of the object" (the mysterious "what" that the melancholic lost in the object) into the ego by means of "an *identification* of the ego with the abandoned object" (SE 14: 249). Such narcissistic identification explains the melancholic's harsh self-criticism, the "impoverishment of his ego on a grand scale" (SE 14: 246). As Schiesari explains, "this shadow thus draws apart a portion of the ego into an identification with the lost object, over and against which the remaining portion of the ego can rage to assuage the narcissistic wound of its abandonment."[57] By means of this economy of loss, the melancholic recuperates his loss in the form of moral superiority (SE 14: 257). Finally, the ostentatious display of loss functions, Schiesari points out, like a fetish in both affirming and denying loss: "the melancholic display of loss paradoxically increases the value (hence accumulating to the gain) of the subject of loss. . . . In other words, the greater the loss, the greater the wisdom or 'truth' claimed by the loser, who then profits from this turn of psychic events by gaining from the loss."[58]

As indicated earlier, I do not so much wish to press this psychoanalytic interpretation on John Donne's psyche as to suggest a narcissistic dynamics at work in the cultural production of Elizabeth Drury which we know as the Anniversaries. Such an understanding thickens the description of Donne's writings as a product of a culture of patronage, a description that always threatens to reduce writing to a bid for support or an embittered reaction to failure to receive support. What interests me is the mutually sustaining relationship between client and patron—a relationship not entirely explained by economics, on the one hand, and the important cultural work of recuperation performed by the poems, on the other.[59]

As R. C. Bald's *Donne and the Drurys* and his biography of Donne make clear, Donne and Robert Drury had in common the experience of "unsuccessfully seeking public employment overseas." The Drurys had also lost both their children, the firstborn Dorothy having died at age four in 1597 and Elizabeth just before turning fifteen in 1610. (The Donnes, on the other hand, had by this time six children, the seventh arriving January 31, 1611.) These are real losses. Although we have evidence of deplorable attitudes towards female children in the period,[60] there are equally compelling signs of a deep investment in relations between father and daughters. As Boose notes, "because a daughter was the least economically useful member of a patrilineal and primogenitural institution, social historians tracing evidence such as this have perhaps been overhasty to infer that she was likewise the least cherished."[61] Cherish is probably not the word to use here, but Shakespeare's plays and Donne's Anniversaries are two massive pieces of evidence for the importance placed on paternal possession of the daughter. Some of the investments in daughters can be felt now that feminist historians and cultural critics have begun to recover the daughter, heretofore a nearly invisible figure in anthropological studies of the family. Boose's discussion of the father-daughter relationship in terms of exogamous exchange and the incest taboo focusses on the father's loss and returns us to the theme of narcissism:

although the daughter was clearly regarded as legal property inside the family, she has never been a commodity to be bartered in the same way as an ox or an ass. She is explicitly a *sexual* property acquired not by economic transaction but from the father's sexual expenditure and his own family bloodline—which makes the father's loss of her a distinctively personal loss of himself.[62]

Boose is concerned with the loss of the daughter to another man in marriage or to "the world of paternal institution" outside the father's house, but her main point—the "distinctively personal loss of himself" that is bound up with the loss of a daughter—would seem to hold for the loss of a daughter to death (and, ultimately, to the definitive world of paternal institution) as well.

It is, so far as I know, an unchallenged assumption among commentators that the Anniversaries have virtually nothing to do with the "real" Elizabeth Drury.[63] I believe the ease with which Elizabeth has been dismissed needs to be examined. What I have been suggesting is 1) that the extravagance of the Anniversaries might in fact resonate to the felt loss of Robert Drury; 2) that the loss of a daughter can be seen as a defining instance of the narcissistic loss described by Freud;[64] and 3) that the *display* of such loss participates in a tradition of melancholy writing specifically dedicated to recuperating male loss.

As I implied earlier, nearly every major reading of the Anniversaries could be cited in support of the theory of narcissistic loss in two respects: the readings explicate the poems in literary terms that correspond with Freud's analysis of melancholia; and the readings themselves, like Freud's essay, declare their solidarity with the tradition of melancholy genius by recovering the hitherto lost moral truth of the poems and by adopting their rhetoric of superlatives—for example, Tayler's claim that they are "the two greatest poems written between *The Fairie Queene* and *Paradise Lost*."[65] Nearly everyone agrees that Donne is not mourning the loss of Elizabeth Drury (the who), that Elizabeth is "a kind of counterpart image for the self, a symbol" (Earl Miner), "a *symbol* of virtue that may fitly represent the Image and Likeness of God in man" (Louis Martz), "a poetic symbol" of the "Image and Likeness of God in Man" (Barbara Lewalski)—all corresponding to Freud's mysterious "*what* he has lost in him" (or, in this case, her; SE 14: 245).[66] Recent studies that forego a symbolic approach tend to be more explicit, if inadvertent, in advancing the thesis of narcissistic loss; in addition to Marotti, there is Docherty, who self-admittedly "comes very close to arguing that the poet is in fact none other than Elizabeth Drury," and Tayler, who concludes his study with a set of mirrorings—"Poet is poem is subject is reader."[67]

These scholar critics follow the lead of Donne and his harbinger. The melancholy equation of loss and gain, "wherein a kind of satisfaction is gleaned in the idealization of loss *as* loss, in the perpetuation and even capitalization of that sense of loss,"[68] is announced in the first lines (if not in the title) of Hall's "To the Praise of the Dead, and the Anatomy" and is carried through both prefatory poems: "Wel dy'de the world, that we might live to see / This world of wit, in his Anatomee." In "The Harbinger to the Progres" Hall quite explicitly presents the capitalization of loss as literary "immortalitie":

> So while thou mak'st her soules Hy progresse knowne
> Thou mak'st a noble progresse of thine owne,
> From this worlds carcasse having mounted hie
> To that pure life of Immortalitie. (ll. 27–30)

What is perhaps not so obvious is the degree to which the project of recuperation depends upon an emptying of Elizabeth's corporeal womanhood. This theme is sounded in "A Funerall Elegie," published with the first edition of the "Anatomy" but probably written before it,[69] where a description of Elizabeth's ethereal body—elaborated in famous lines in the Second Anniversary which I have already mentioned (ll. 241–46)—prepares for the following remarks upon Elizabeth's fortunate escape from marriage; the comparison is with the assignment of a place to newly-discovered stars:

> So the world studied whose this peece should be,
>> Till she can be no bodies else, nor shee:
> But like a Lampe of Balsamum, desir'd
>> Rather t'adorne, then last, shee soon expir'd;
> Cloth'd in her Virgin white integrity;
>> For mariage, though it doe not staine, doth dye.
> To scape th'infirmities which waite upone
>> Woman, shee went away, before sh'was one. ("A Funerall Elegie," ll. 71–78)

As Docherty also notes, it is important for Donne that the deceased was a girl of fourteen, before, as Donne remarked of another woman in his "Epithalamion Made at Lincoln's Inn," she had the chance to marry and "put on perfection, and a womans name." In psychoanalytic terms, Donne seems here to capture something of what Freud treated in his essay "On Narcissism" as an aspect of woman's difference. Freud observes that some women display a self-contentment and inaccessibility which resemble the child's charming narcissism. In her close critical reading of Freud's writings on women's difference, Sarah Kofman summarizes:

> What is attractive, what accounts for all the charm of this narcissistic woman, is not so much her beauty . . . ; what is attractive in woman is that she has managed to preserve what man has lost, that original narcissism for which he is eternally nostalgic. It may thus be said that man envies and seeks that narcissistic woman as the lost paradise of childhood (or what he fantasizes as such).[70]

If this idea of a woman stands in for what Donne has lost, the corporeal, sexual, married woman is identified with the original experience of loss in Donne's misogynistic account of the Fall, which occurs in the section of the "Anatomy" on the "dangers and diseases of the old" world. "We are borne ruinous" (l. 95): the sickness of the world is immediately linked to women through a joke on the birthing process that makes mothers appear partly to blame for it. This leads easily enough to the epigram, the "first mariage was our funerall" (l. 105), and the further elaboration that "singly, one by one, they kill us now" (l. 107). In place of the opposition between regenerate souls and the old world of sin, Donne here presents the original sin and its consequence of death as caused by woman's frustration of even "Gods purpose." The speaker is thus aligning himself and the reader with a subject position gendered as masculine. The loss or lack represented by Elizabeth Drury's death is traced back to the "One woman" who, "at one blow, then kill'd us all" (l. 106). As Manley notes in his commentary, this is usually said of Adam; Donne's substitution of Eve allows him to generate two paradoxes that bear upon the "Anatomy" as a whole. Although the woman is made the agent of man's original sin, man now happily gives himself over to dying: "We do delightfully our selves allow / To that consumption" (l. 108–9). The phrasing is very subtle here: the word "allow" preserves some male pride; women are still the active party in sex— "they kill us now" (l. 107). From here it is a short step to the commonplace that orgasm shortens life: "We kill our selves, to propagate our kinde" (l. 110).

Marotti describes these passages as "comic antifeminism" and refers to the claim about orgasms as "a flimsy folk belief."[71] I find nothing in the texts or contexts of the Anniversaries to support a "comic" interpretation of these lines. On the question of orgasm, the research of Thomas Laqueur would suggest that this view had a currency that went beyond the folk.[72] The paradox of reproduction that underlies the belief has, in fact, proven to be remarkably durable, turning up in Freud as the victory of species over individual and in Lacan as the statement "that the living being, by being subject to sex, has fallen under the blow of individual death."[73] In the "Anatomy" itself, Donne devotes the next two subsections to wittily expatiating on the not so flimsy commonplace in terms of reduced life spans and "smaleness of stature."

Of course, the overriding reason for replacing Adam with Eve is the symmetry achieved by balancing Eve's sin against Elizabeth Drury's innocence. Donne empties Eve of her sin, or the same thing—her womanhood—to produce Elizabeth as the Other Woman, or the Woman as Other—soul of the world—the knowledge of which becomes the guarantee that he exists (i.e., that he has a soul). To return to the opening lines of the "Anatomy,"

> When that rich soule which to her Heaven is gone,
> Whom all they celebrate, who know they have one,
> (For who is sure he hath a soule, unlesse

> It see, and Iudge, and follow worthinesse,
> And by Deedes praise it? He who doth not this,
> May lodge an In-mate soule, but tis not his.) (ll. 1–6)

This sense of self entails membership in an elite—those who "see, and Iudge, and follow worthinesse." As Schiesari points out, such a "difference from the common *vulgus* is the sign of the melancholic's virtue and intellect," particularly as the melancholy man was revised by Ficino into "one whose quest for knowledge is inspired by an eros that fuels his desire for a relationship with the transcendent."[74] But more important here is the interpellation of the reader as an elite soul mate through a process of mirroring, also narcissistic in structure, whereby the reader sees himself in the poem, which itself mirrors the rich soul: as Hall puts it, "Admired match! where strives in mutuall grace / The cunning Pencill, and the comely face" ("To the Praise of the Dead, and the Anatomy," ll. 17–18).[75]

In his brilliant essay on "The Articulation of the Ego in the English Renaissance," William Kerrigan proposes "that there is a form of narcissism, as well as a form of the imaginary anatomy, peculiar to Renaissance literature."[76] In terms obviously relevant to Donne's Anniversaries, he remarks that "the anatomy of the [Renaissance] ego might coincide, through language, with the structures and textures of the cosmos—a (relatively) benevolent narcissism that helps to explain the pronounced integrity of Renaissance literature, its disaffinity with fragmentation" (303). But this cosmic ego risked dispersion: "the Donne of the Anniversaries . . . dilated the snug human world outward into the potential diffusions of the cosmos," and ultimately, with the coming of the new cosmology, "anthropomorphism was exposed as a solely interior phenomenon" (300, 301). If this is the historical moment of the Anniversaries, its turn toward interiority, I suggest, is also supported by narcissistic identifications, the mutual admiration society of Elizabeth Drury, Donne, Hall, and all "who know they have one" ("Anatomy," l. 2).

In that phrase I hear "all who know they have the phallus." By "one," of course, Donne means a soul, but this soul is carefully separated from female qualities in Donne's construction of the Idea of a Woman.[77] The knowledge that one has a soul, emphasized at the outset, is dependent on the denigration of the corporeal woman. The Anniversaries can then recover narcissistic loss by constructing the woman as a powerful Other capable of securing for the speaker and reader a position of wholeness and self-knowledge.[78] Janel Mueller has recently noted, with understatement, that this project "often take[s] us a great distance from any recognizable female presence."[79] And as "Aire and Angels" demonstrates, this elevation of the woman to the place of the Other entails a countermovement to restore a position of male dominance. Elizabeth Drury is mirrored by Donne and the reader. "Poet is poem is subject is reader."

This position requires an escape from Eve, both as lover and mother. Thus in the Second Anniversary, Donne, apparently in imitation of Christ,[80] celebrates the Virgin "more for being good, / Then for her interest, of mother-hood" (ll. 343–44). More interesting still is his inversion at the opening of the "Progres":

> Immortal Mayd, who though thou wouldst refuse
> The name of Mother, be vnto my Muse,
> A Father since her chast Ambition is,
> Yearely to bring forth such a child as this.
> These Hymnes may worke on future wits, and so
> May great Grand-children of thy praises grow. (ll. 33–38)

This fascinating sequence encapsulates the process of male loss and recuperation that powers the Anniversaries. Donne at once wills the maid into fatherhood and becomes himself a kind of mother of "hymnes" that will inseminate "future wits." The restoration of loss that is the work of "The Progres of the Soule" is represented here as a patriarchal transmission, a tradition, of "hims" of praise.[81]

Donne's "shee" covers an absence at the center of the poem. Donne fills it in with a variety of impossibilities—regenerate soul, Wisdom, and Queen Elizabeth are a few that have been suggested. But the point seems to be that none of them can stick because the loss that Donne keeps gesturing toward cannot be represented; as Donne writes in the First Anniversary, "ruine," in the form of woman, "labour'd to frustrate / Euen Gods purpose" (ll. 99–101), and "The world did in her Cradle take a fall" (l. 196). There was and is, it appears, no paradise other than the paradise within. It is always tempting to present Donne as a titanic subjectivity at work, on the order of that which could eclipse the sun with a wink, or of Kerrigan's anthropomorphism as "interior phenomenon." But the argument I have tried to advance here is something like the inverse: not a subject at work but work towards producing a subject.

At the outset of the Second Anniversary Donne remarks upon this processual aspect of the poems: "Yet in this Deluge, grosse and generall, / Thou seest mee striue for life" (ll. 30–31). In this respect I find the Anniversaries to resemble what Julia Kristeva terms "works in progress": "Art is the possibility of fashioning narcissism and of subtilizing the ideal. . . . A life, a work of art: are these not 'works in progress' only in as much as capable of self-depreciation and of resubmitting themselves to the flames which are, without distinction, the flames of language and of love?"[82] The striving of the Anniversaries is away from corporeality, women, and especially mothers toward an object of desire nominally female—"shee"—but actually, to repeat

Mueller's phrase, "a great distance from any recognizable female presence." It is a rewriting into a religious symbolic (the Lacanian symbolic order, that is, not Lewalski's symbolic mode) of what Kristeva calls the "semiotic *chora*"— "the place where the subject is both generated and negated, the place where his unity succumbs before the process of charges and stases that produce him."[83] Kristeva cites the virgin birth as a foundational example of this process in the Christian symbolic: "In asserting that 'in the beginning was the Word', Christians must have found such a postulate sufficiently hard to believe and, for whatever it was worth, they added its compensation, its permanent lining: the maternal receptacle, purified as it might be by the virginal fantasy."[84] In this context Jonson's oft-quoted criticism, "that he told Mr Donne, if it had been written of ye Virgin Marie it had been something,"[85] is sharpened to disclose the severity of Donne's masculine bias; Elizabeth Drury died a pubescent virgin, and that, Donne says, is all to the good.

Such a denial of the material origins of the subject, the cost of a successful entrance into the symbolic order, can leave the subject, as John Lechte writes, "at the level of a static, fetishized version of language."[86] Donne's repetitive, ritualized use of the signifier "shee" works like the fetish both to display and deny loss. He even seems to acknowledge this aspect of his work as a type of "mis-devotion" at the close of the Second Anniversary, where he alludes to the fact that he wrote the poem while attending Sir Robert Drury in France:

> Here in a place, where mis-devotion frames
> A thousand praiers to saints, whose very names
> The ancient Church knew not, Heaven knowes not yet,
> And where, what lawes of poetry admit,
> Lawes of religion, have at least the same,
> Immortal Maid, I might invoque thy name.
> Could any Saint provoke that appetite,
> Thou here shouldst make mee a french convertite. (ll. 511–18)

Donne immediately corrects himself; there is finally only one, paternal Word:

> But thou wouldst not; nor wouldst thou be content,
> To take this, for my second yeeres true Rent,
> Did this Coine beare any other stampe, then his,
> That gave thee power to doe, me, to say this. (ll. 519–22)

This move, as it were, pulls the cover off Donne's object of desire, his "shee," to disclose it as a stand-in for male loss.[87] "Shee" is the site of men's discourse on loss and recuperation. These and the following lines create a homology between secular and divine "power," "will," and "Autority"—between Sir Robert Drury and God:

> his [Sir Robert's, God's] will is, that to posteritee,
> Thou shouldest for life, and death, a patterne bee
> And that the world should notice have of this,
> The purpose and th'Autority is his. (ll. 523–26)

In this unexpected allusion to the client-patron relationship ("my second yeeres true Rent") Donne both acknowledges and restores Sir Robert's loss and his own lack: "I ame / The Trumpet, at whose voice the people came" (ll. 527–28).

Donne's progress of the soul and Julia Kristeva's "work in progress" move toward opposed ends—his to a point of stability, a transcendental signifier, hers toward motility, openness, heterogeneity. But what characterizes both is motion, a foregrounding of the signifying process. In *Revolution in Poetic Language* Kristeva asks:

> In short, isn't art the fetish *par excellence,* one that badly camouflages its archaeology? At its base, isn't there a belief, ultimately maintained, that the mother is phallic, that the ego—never precisely identified—will never separate from her, and that no symbol is strong enough to sever this dependence?

Kristeva goes on to complicate what at first sounds like a rhetorical question. Although "the poetic function . . . converges with fetishism," she writes, "it is not . . . identical to it. What distinguishes the poetic function from the fetishist mechanism is that it maintains a *signification.*" That is, the text "is not a *substitute* but a sign."[88] The kinesthetics of the Anniversaries, whether "motion in corruption" or stringing of beads and stars and "little bones of necke, and backe" ("Progres," l. 212), "maintains a signification" despite efforts to use them as a substitute for a lost Renaissance, to restore their lost meaning, their lost Renaissance context, once and for all.[89] But such scholarly labors of restoration are only complicitous with Donne's working toward a final, religious "Proclamation," a man's Idea of a Woman, one that depends on not knowing her "as she was."

❖ F I V E

The Subject of Devotion

Constructing Inwardness

DONNE'S HOLY SONNETS have figured prominently in the critical tradition as sites of early modern subjectivity. The sometimes violent and hyperbolic rhetoric of these poems has generally been read as an expression of Donne's personality and/or religious conflicts brought about by personal struggles with doctrinal issues.[1] More recently, Stanley Fish has both continued and challenged this tradition of reading the Holy Sonnets. In "diagnosing" Donne as a literary bulimic, Fish depends upon some idea of an essential Donne available to examination. Fish seems to emphasize this point when he writes that "Donne is sick and his poetry is sick; but he and it are sick in ways that are interestingly related to the contemporary critical scene."[2] On the other hand, as one might expect, Fish's argument in the essay is anti-essentialist to a fault. There is no essential Donnean self: "in the story that Donne's poems repeatedly enact, the skillful rhetorician always ends up becoming the victim/casualty of his own skill. . . . The stronger he is, the more force-full, the more taken up by the desire for mastery, the less he is anything like 'himself.' " The "monarch of wit" is actually the subject of wit, for he can never control "the (verbal) forces he sets in motion."[3] Fish is persuasive, but his own arguments are, like Donne's, necessarily self-consuming. Donne, Fish says, articulates an ongoing dilemma in the "contemporary critical scene," yet Fish himself must write as if this were not the case. Otherwise, his own masculine persuasive force, which constructs Donne as a study in the impossibility of self-fashioning, must be swallowed up by the same crisis of nonidentity. To put it another way, one can say of Fish's diagnosis of the bulimic Donne that it takes one to know one.

134

Fish's essay, like my own discussion of subjectivity and the Holy Sonnets, participates in an ongoing debate about inwardness and subjectivity in the Renaissance and Reformation. An obvious starting point is Stephen Greenblatt's argument in *Renaissance Self-Fashioning* for domination and negation as modes for producing subjectivity; his formula—"*power over sexuality produces inwardness*"—for producing the submissive form of subjectivity found in Wyatt's penitential psalms is clearly relevant to some of Donne's best-known devotional poems.[4] As Alan Sinfield points out, however, Greenblatt's early formulation of a Protestant subjectivity "presents power and ideology as too unified in their impetus and effects." According to Sinfield, "the protestant subject arises, not in the accomplishment of domination or negation, but in the *thwarting* of harmony, cogency, common sense."[5] This critique of Greenblatt is part of a larger concern in Sinfield's book to acknowledge "a complex awareness of interiority" in Renaissance texts while not mistaking this inwardness for a unitary, autonomous self; what Sinfield means to register is the powerful "subjectivity effects" produced by Renaissance dramatic characters.[6] In a similar attempt to reclaim interiority as a category of analysis in Renaissance theater, Katharine Eisaman Maus helpfully differentiates between the philosophical and historical arguments that frequently become intertwined in recent critiques of the subject. Like Sinfield, Maus insists that recognition of a concept of interiority in Renaissance discourse does not commit one to the thesis of a transhistorical essential self, adding the point that even this notion of the self is multivalent. Seeking "to refine and advance a historically self-conscious discussion of subjectivity in the early modern period," she uses the distinction between public and private in legal discourse in order "to analyze some of the ways the distinction *matters*— asking 'How does the existence of such categories help shape thought and behavior?' "[7]

Although my analysis of the Holy Sonnets shares Maus's concern with effects, I believe that, in the case of devotional writing, analysis and evaluation of these effects entails some attention to a version of the distinction between public and private that I would call the distinction between a subject and a subjectivity. How does subjection produce subjectivity? Perhaps Althusser's formulation of religious ideology makes my question clearer: if, as he claims, "the interpellation of individuals as subjects presupposes the 'existence' of a Unique and central Other Subject, in whose Name the religious ideology interpellates all individuals as subjects,"[8] how does it happen that the precise nature and sincerity of the subject's relation to the Other Subject (i.e., inwardness, subjectivity) becomes the center of concern? How does the interpellated individual change places with the "Unique and Central Other Subject"? This is a historical question in both senses that have been operative in this book: it is a question about "subjectivity in the early modern period" but also a question about what Foucault calls the "history of the present," what I have been calling the subject of Donne. The Holy Sonnets, I argue, contribute to a larger ideological project of creating inwardness which is continued and aestheticized in the critical project of interpretation. This argument broadly supports Fish's critique of the monarchical tradition of Donne. The contradictions produced by the poems do, I believe, create an *effect* of inwardness that is often assumed to be the *cause* of the sonnets. Fish's description of Donne's rhetorical dilemma can double as a description of such a "subjectivity-effect."[9] I propose to examine, then, the process by which Donne's devotional poems are constructed as sites of subjectivity and its crisis: specifically, how the reading of the Holy Sonnets produces the subject of devotion as a secular, literary form of subjectivity and its discontents.

Anne Ferry has presented the most compelling argument for a "modern" sense of inwardness in the Holy Sonnets; Donne's sonnets paradoxically represent a continuous inwardness that "passes show," that escapes language, "not because he deliberately cloaks it but because inward and outward spheres are in themselves radically distinct and widely distanced."[10] This understanding of an inner life, Ferry insists, is *literary* in origin, first voiced in the opening sonnet of *Astrophil and Stella* as the distinction between matter and form, imitated by Shakespeare in the sonnets and *Hamlet,* and by Donne in the Holy Sonnets.

Ferry's traditional form and influence study interestingly parallels Joel Fineman's Lacanian analysis of Shakespeare's sonnets: although their theoretical perspectives and literary histories differ, both critics derive what Fineman calls "the literary effect of a subject" from a paradoxical relationship of the subject to language. Fineman insists that Shakespeare's sonnets to the Dark Lady invent a new literary subjectivity by replacing a visionary poetics of identity with a verbal poetics of difference, and that various structuralist and poststructuralist theories of the subject derive from "the Renaissance invention of the literary subject."[11] Both Ferry and Fineman wish to make historical points about the occurrence of interiority in the early modern period (Ferry says it is rare; Fineman argues that it appears decisively in Shakespeare). Fineman, however, understands this construction of the Renaissance literary subject as an ideological project imbricated both with other Renaissance discourses and with the discourse of literary theory itself; in a brief introduction to a work in progress at the time of his death he pointed to "an identifiable complicity that links, by means of an unspoken necessity, Renaissance textuality, sexuality, and ideology one to each of the two others, in a link or collation the historical stability and specificity of which at least raises the possibility that it is Renaissance textuality, as such, that predicates a particular system of sexuality and ideology." In the same essay, he critiques the (admittedly Shakespearean) complicity of Shakespeare critics with this ideological construct of the literary subject "precisely because it begs the question of the subject": "such criticism, whatever its explicit ideological intentions, not only responds to but also capitulates to the historical hegemony of Shakespearean characterology."[12]

In this book I have argued that a similar hegemony has governed Donne criticism. In the critical tradition of the Holy Sonnets, it has produced readings that converge on the question of Donne's character, in particular on interrelated questions of Donne's theological position, self-presentation, and sincerity. If, as Fineman claims, Shakespeare's invention of literary subjectivity "characteristically generates what are taken to be Shakespeare's deeply realized, psychologistically authentic, dramatic personae,"[13] then Donne and readers of Donne's Holy Sonnets might be regarded as some of Shakespeare's greatest characters.

In the introduction to her edition of the *Divine Poems*, Helen Gardner portrays this character, and in the process she is herself produced as the divided subject of the Holy Sonnets. She writes that "his [Donne's] language has the ring of a living voice," though she is quite aware that this is the literary creation of "the illusion of a present experience." "The almost histrionic note" is the product of "the meditation's deliberate stimulation of emotion," but Donne's "choice of subjects and his whole-hearted use of the method are symptoms of a condition of mind very different from" that of his other devotional poetry. In the end, her generic and rhetorical analyses of Donne's effects run up against something like the Lacanian unrepresentable Real: "This dramatic language has a magic that is unanalysable."[14]

Other readers find and enact similar divisions in the sonnets. I have already referred to Anne Ferry's thesis that the Holy Sonnets paradoxically express Donne's "sense that what is grounded inward in his heart is at a distance from language used to describe it, which cannot render it truly."[15] Arthur Marotti finds a similar conflict when he notes that "The self in performance and the self in humble devotion seem . . . to be intractably, if creatively, at odds throughout the holy sonnets." Marotti's reading seems to take both sides in the sincerity debate: the poems "enact personally and socially the contradictory attitudes of assertion and submission that were intrinsic to Donne's temperament, but that were heightened by the desperateness of his ambition in the early Jacobean period."[16] At times, Marotti seems to be saying that the Holy Sonnets express Donne's ambivalences, while in other instances he argues for Donne as "master of a discourse within which individuals from all social strata were theologically leveled."[17] Richard Strier presents the division in theological terms: "Donne's deep inability to accept the paradoxical conception of a regenerate Christian as simultaneously 'righteous and a sinner,' " betrays a fundamental "uncertainty about the status of the self vis-à-vis God."[18] Such uncertainty might be embraced by a postmodern reader as a politically correct position vis-à-vis God, but A. L. French, in a tenacious psychological study, senses that Donne is *using* uncertainty not to expose a religious predicament but "to evade that predicament."[19] Donne is dishonest, although French ultimately performs the Donnean trick of making this dishonesty into "a kind of honesty":

> And yet what distinguishes the Sonnets from the mass of early seventeenth-century devotional writing is the transparency with which the poetry—though not the poet—reveals irreconcilables *as* unreconciled or even irreconcilable. In fact one has to end with a curious paradox: that while from one point of view the Sonnets are continuously dishonest, from another what makes them so startling is that it is impossible to read them intelligently without feeling that the transparency noted above is a kind of honesty.[20]

Here text and author are detached from one another only to allow textuality itself to become the bearer of authenticity: poetry is personified and held to be true unto its own self. French seems to have been edging toward a recognition of what Fineman or Sinfield call the subjectivity-effect, though his conclusion seems to me to retreat into a mystification of the poetic word.[21]

In brief, interpretation of Donne's Holy Sonnets has participated in the work of constructing inwardness that is also the work of the poems. The benefits produced by this collaboration are great, both in the area of literary studies and in a more general discourse of human values. I value both the critical tradition and the kinds of conflicts that critics have associated with Donne's subjectivity (or subjectivity-effects) in the poems. But what Ferry and Fineman in particular seem to insist on is the literary constitution of this subjectivity. And while both aim to historicize this invention in the sense of tracing its origins, both also find it operative in the history of the present. Fineman, however, seems to me to go farther towards a critique; the ongoing literariness of subjectivity needs to be interrogated, he implies, in order to break the hegemony of Shakespeare's gendered, heterosexual, perjured eye/I.

To attempt a reading of Shakespeare's sonnets or the Holy Sonnets without "begging the question of the subject" is, to a degree, to attempt the impossible, as we have observed in Fish's reading of Donne. Recent work on the concept of the subject, however, has emphasized the heterogeneity of ideological formations. As Paul Smith notes, "the interpellation of the 'subject' into oppressed positions is not complete and monolithic; rather, interpellation also produces contradiction and negativity." These features of ideology allow the critic "to try to locate within the 'subject' a *process,* or a tension which is the product of its having been called upon to adopt multifarious subject-positions."[22] In his work on "the reformation subject" Sinfield has similarly emphasized contradiction and conflict.[23] The inwardness of the Holy Sonnets is not, for example, entirely the product of the sonnet tradition, whether defined by Ferry or Fineman. The subjectivity-effect of the poems arises from a variety of discourses that offer the critic places for intervention in the ideological process of producing the literary subject. I believe such interventions also allow us to get beyond a mystification of the poetic construction of inwardness,

138

and thereby to ponder the possible and changing political values of literary subjectivity.

"The Secrecy of Man"

Ferry does not include judicial and political discourse in her review of the grammar of the "inward language" of the sixteenth and seventeenth centuries. Presumably, she would find this discourse lacking the sense of a continuous inner life which she identifies as the mark of a modern notion of self. However, the work of Maus and others on the construction of what we might call thought crimes in the official discourses of witchcraft and treason trials strongly suggests that these ideological discourses played a key role in the development of early modern notions of inwardness.[24]

Both official and minority discourses on the recusant subject, for example, produce concepts of inwardness out of ideological conflict. The confessional controversies between Protestant officialdom and its Catholic opposition depended in great measure on a distinction between secular and spiritual loyalties that were typically represented as outward and inward states of being. The studies of Joel Hurstfield, John Bossy, Arnold Pritchard, Peter Holmes and others have disclosed the many contradictions that Catholics were forced to manage or evade in order to assume a subject-position within the Elizabethan picture.[25] However, many of the recusant documents used by these historians can be shown to imitate or improvise upon arguments and styles of argument found in the government's discourse on its Catholic subjects. The symbiotic discourse of this religio-political controversy offers one means of conceiving of the possibilities and limits of the subject in Elizabethan terms. On the one hand, these texts, pro- and anti-Catholic, represent a subject estranged or divided by conflicting loyalties. On the other, they are often informed by what might be called an imaginary subject unified by its total identification with power. The contradiction between these two subject positions produces a new discourse of inwardness.

Elizabethan commonplace portrayed the Queen as one "not liking to make windows into men's hearts."[26] This benign version of rule represents a subject divided by public and private loyalties. Both the official language of antipapist propaganda and Catholic appeals for toleration are informed by such a notion of the divided subject; more important, both deny the problems created by such a division. Burghley's famous *Execution of Justice in England* (1583), for example, declared that men were executed not for religious beliefs but for their political aspirations:

> And though there are many subjects known in the realm that differ in some opinions of religion from the Church of England and that do also not forbear to profess the same, yet in that they do also profess loyalty and obedience to Her Majesty and offer readily in Her Majesty's defense to impugn and resist

any foreign force, though it should come or be procured from the Pope himself [a bluff later called, as we shall see, by Robert Southwell], none of these sort are for their contrary opinions in religion prosecuted or charged with any crimes or pains of treason, nor yet willingly searched in their consciences for their contrary opinions that savor not of treason.[27]

Joel Hurstfield notes how curiously such extraordinary statements "evaded the central issue at the root of the problem. . . . Men were not free to pursue their religion if they were deprived of the service of a priest: the political intention challenged the religious right."[28] Burghley simultaneously enunciates and re-presses the link between religious and political orders; as Wallace MacCaffrey summarizes, *The Execution* maintained that "reconciliation to the spiritual authority of Rome was in fact a political act" while it remained "resolutely silent about those statutes of the last thirty years which had revolutionized the religious order in England," thereby ignoring the linkage of doctrine and policy in the English Church.[29] Cardinal Allen's response to Burghley, *A True, Sincere and Modest Defense of English Catholics* (1584), was a mirror image of *The Execution,* urging a separation of spiritual and political allegiances and arguing that the English mission had only the *spiritual* goal of reconciling Catholics to the Holy Church. MacCaffrey is again instructive on this mirroring: "The Treasurer [Burghley] insists on ignoring the doctrinal content of the Elizabethan settlement while the Cardinal refuses to admit any link between the pastoral ministrations of the seminarians and the political intentions of the Papacy towards England."[30] As resolutely as Burghley, Allen upholds a division of loyalties while eliding the undeniable historical relationship between the spiritual and temporal orders.

Participants in the Catholic controversy were concerned, then, with defining the position of the subject, and as the historians mentioned above have shown, their texts are disturbed by inconsistencies and silences. Robert Southwell's reply to the Proclamation of 1591, *An Humble Supplication to Her Maiestie,* discloses the contradictions that had to be managed by both professedly loyal Jesuits and the government that persecuted them, thus displaying as well the interdependence of Catholic and official discourses of the subject. The Proclamation had charged the Jesuit missionaries with not being what they seem. Southwell easily counters the charge that the priests are simply malcontents, but the priest represented in the *Supplication* remains a radically divided subject of power. Southwell defends disguise, "sith we cannot reforme the'inconvenience till your Maiestie think it good to license vs without danger to exercise our Functions."[31] Yet his citation of David's example, an example that Hamlet might have invoked, curiously begs the question being disputed: "*David* vpon iust cause feigned himself madd" (9). The justice of his "cause," "the wynning of soules" (9), is precisely what cannot be allowed by the government, despite its official position of not wishing to look into the subject's heart; were Southwell successful in his cause England would be comprised of fundamentally divided subjects like Southwell—professedly willing to offer their bodies in service to the queen but secretly loyal to a faith embodied in a competing institution. It is clear that the *hiddenness* of this commitment was as disturbing as its focus in the Catholic Church. As Carol Weiner has demonstrated, Englishmen commonly feared that Catholics— priests and laypeople—were dissemblers, to the paradoxical extent that Catholics who recanted and conformed were regarded as more dangerous than recusants.[32] This fear was explicitly stated during Southwell's well-publicized interrogation on the matter of equivocation by the lord chief justice, Sir John Popham, and the attorney general, Sir Edward Coke. Southwell argued that to take away equivocation, here narrowly construed to mean mental reservation, would be to "take away the government of all states, both ecclesiastical and temporal, yea, and the secrecy of man." Chief Justice Popham replied that "if this doctrine should be allowed, it would supplant all Justice, for we are men, and no Gods, and can judge but according to their outward actions and speeches, and not according to their secret and inward intentions."[33]

The chief justice's point is in fact foregrounded in the *Supplication* itself by Southwell's extended account of the Babington affair, an account that could hardly have succeeded in allaying the regime's fears of treachery. Southwell's claim that Robert Poolie, Gilbert Gifford, and others were double agents of Walsingham turns against these men the government's own formulaic charges against Catholic priests, including "masking . . . [of] secret intentions vnder the face of Religion," angling "with golden hookes," and resorting to noble houses "in privie sort" (18–19). Southwell has, we recall, defended playing a double part "vpon iust cause" and endorsed a flexible presentation of self whereby "we . . . frame our behavior and attyre to the necessity of our daies" (9). Popham's difficulty with this notion of identity is multiplied when both government agents and those they are seeking to entrap play double parts, as seems to have been the case with William Parry, whom the government regarded as a violent Catholic but who, according to Southwell, "neuer in life or action professed himself to be a Catholique" (17). The truth about Parry, as Lacey Baldwin Smith notes, is never likely to be known.[34]

The weakness of the loyalist argument was ironically most fully revealed in the intra-Catholic struggle known as the Archpriest or Appellant Controversy. The Appellants, secular priests who continued Southwell's attempt to reconcile religious and political loyalties, opposed radical Jesuits like Robert Persons, who resolved the dilemma of the Catholic subject by rejecting the existing political order as corrupt and advocating a reformation identified with the restoration of Catholicism. These radicals, the Appellants argued, had perverted the Catholic mission from its original spiritual object and were therefore the cause of royal persecution.[35] Moreover, as Arnold Pritchard has noted, the radicals' insistence that religious allegiance was the fundamental fact that united or divided people "threatened to break down the stable, traditional, hierarchical, social and political order" assumed by Southwell and the Appellants.[36] Persons's notion of the Catholic subject united by a single commitment is, of course, utopian in its dependence on an imaginary restoration of the Catholic Church in England, but it does serve to highlight the problem of the Catholic loyalist who wants to serve two masters even as each master makes it impossible to serve the other.[37] The loyalist's position betwixt and between is imaged in Southwell's response in the *Supplication* to the notorious "bloody question" of which side the Catholic would take if the Pope invaded England: "What army soever should come against you [Queen Elizabeth], we will rather yeald our brests to be broached by our Cuntrie swords, then vse our swords to th'effusion of our Cuntries bloud" (35).[38] This statement epitomizes the recusant discourse I have been examining, representing again the annihilation of the subject in the act of maintaining separate commitments. And in the indirection of Southwell's hypothetical response—is his commitment to the Queen active or passive? what exactly will he do during the invasion?—we encounter an aspect of the equivocality that so maddened Justice Popham and that underlay English fear of the Jesuit.

It is tempting to claim equivocation to be something like a master figure in the problematizing of the Elizabethan subject, but such a claim must be accompanied by a full awareness of its consequences. As Steven Mullaney has pointed out, equivocal discourse not only "presents authority with a considerable dilemma," but also always threatens to overtake the subject who uses it.[39] If Jesuit equivocation in the sense of mental reservation has the commonsense purpose of evading authority, it can also, in its undecidability and resistance to ideological closure, decenter the subject—in Bossy's words, "the danger was that the disguise would absorb the personality."[40] Southwell's response to the bloody question might be seen as a defensive move, but it might also be held to figure the contradictions of the ideological double bind in which the Catholic loyalist found himself. Southwell's equivocations do not, I suggest, simply cover a coherent inner life distinct from the experience of subjection but, rather, figure a radically divided subject who is "trying," as R. C. Bald wrote of Southwell and other loyalists, "to reconcile the irreconcilable."[41] What cannot enter discourse except as equivocation and paradox are the contradictions contained by the ideology that produces both Southwell and his interrogator Popham as subjects. The "secrecy of Man," Southwell's inwardness, is produced by ideological conflict, on the one hand, and the desire to remain a whole subject, on the other.

Equivocation and the Divided Subject

The problem of determining the truth of an inward condition or belief by means of observation and evidence—a central issue in judicial proceedings against accused traitors and Catholics[42]—is foregrounded in what is perhaps the most explicit treatment of subjectivity in the Holy Sonnets, "If faithfull soules be alike glorified." Since this poem also invokes Donne's Catholic father as witness of his spiritual contest, it affords an especially rich situation for examining the construction of subjectivity.

The poem is organized around three attempts at producing spiritual authenticity, each dependent upon a different certifying spectator. First comes the father:

> If faithfull soules be alike glorifi'd
> As Angels, then my fathers soule doth see,
> And adds this even to full felicitie,
> That valiantly I hels wide mouth o'rstride. ("If faithfull soules,"
> 11.1–4.)

In his commentary on Satire 3 John Carey suggestively notes in passing a connection between this passage, Donne's use of the phrase "thy father's spirit" in his first great religious poem, and the ghost of Old Hamlet ("I am thy father's spirit").[43] Carey's point is not to prove an allusion to Shakespeare but, rather, to emphasize the psychological conflicts in Satire 3 occasioned by the Catholicism of Donne senior. I want to allow here for the particular significance of Donne senior's "old religion" but also for a broader structural resemblance between Hamlet's and Donne's self-fashioning. In the Holy Sonnet, the appearance of Donne's father—overdetermined by familial, confessional, and psychological structures—produces a division in the subject of devotion that is not resolved in the act of devotion. The reference to Donne's father raises questions as to the precise meaning of the heroic spiritual act represented in line 4. Is Donne saying that the x-ray intuition of his glorified father will discern his fidelity to the true Catholic faith? Or, is Donne rather making a *Protestant* claim about his election? In the latter case, the lines carry a beautiful irony, perhaps directed against narrow confessional dogmatists, by enlisting the Catholic John senior as a guarantor of the elect status of his son the apostate.[44]

On a more general level, the quatrain foregrounds the patriarchal structure within which a divided subject of devotion is constructed. The sonnet opens in the "Name-of-the-Father" whereby, according to Lacan, the subject is divided in order to take up a position in language, to become a speaking subject.[45] I find the central concern of the sonnet to be the process of working through this relationship to the father toward a relationship with God that is both like and unlike the original relationship. In his stirring psychoanalysis of Milton's career, William Kerrigan has named and described the structure and resolution of a "sacred complex" that resembles the process I wish to analyze.[46] That is, Donne's dead and glorified father does not seem to be casually called upon to spy into his son's heart; the sonnet works through several oedipal themes on its way to creating a subjectivity-effect.

How to put this without sounding facetious? (Indeed, Donne often places readers in such a dilemma.) But the opening fantasy of the sonnet places Donne in an interesting position: under the omniscient gaze of his father and astride "hels wide mouth." Donne's fantasy seems at once to anticipate and to resist details in Freud's oedipal narrative of the formation of the superego. The unusual, even awkward image of Donne striding over "hels wide mouth" seems to represent both an oedipal sacrifice and a threat of castration. This understanding is strengthened by Donne's obvious identification in this passage with Christ and his victory over the powers of hell, achieved under the approving eye of Almighty God the Father. At the same time the rhetoric of the quatrain resists this resolution in two ways. First, in psychoanalytic terms the relation between ego and superego gets turned around; instead of the ego being rewarded for its sacrifice, it is the superego that seems, impossibly ("adds this even to full felicitie"), to benefit. Thus Donne senior is outdone by Donne junior, an outrageous instance of the "masculine persuasive force" as discussed by Fish. But the quatrain as a whole is also Hamlet-like in its hyperbole and posturing. As Ferry points out, "No appearances could show him as he views himself,"[47] but surely the self-aggrandizing description displays not "his own knowledge of this inward state" but rather delusions of grandeur. Is Donne aware of this delusion? In a sense, "that is the question" put by the poem, and to answer it is to go farther than Donne is able to go, as the middle section of the poem illustrates.

> But if our mindes to these soules be descry'd
> By circumstances, and by signes that be
> Apparent in us, not immediately,
> How shall my mindes white truth to them be try'd?
> They see idolatrous lovers weepe and mourne,
> And vile blasphemous Conjurers to call
> On Jesus name, and Pharisaicall
> Dissemblers feigne devotion. ("If faithfull soules," 11.5–12)

Again like Hamlet, Donne no sooner imagines himself the hero than he falls to questioning the authenticity of his feelings and acts, although this self-criticism is projected onto others in the form of satiric attacks on other insincere devotees. This aggression is also directed at the formerly omniscient spectators: "How shall my mindes white truth to them be try'd?" As Ferry notes, "This is not a plea . . . but a challenge, a defiant boast."[48] Donne turns on the glorified inquisitors, denying them the power to know his "mindes white truth."

> Then turne
> O pensive soule, to God, for he knowes best

> Thy true griefe, for he put it in my breast. ("If faithfull soules,"
> 11.12–14.)

How does the subject "turne" from the heroics and defiance of the major portion of the poem to this quiet insistence on "true grief"? This is not a poem in the manner of Herbert, in which the willful acts of the speaker are subsumed by the divine will. If God is the only judge of authenticity, that authenticity nonetheless remains something fiercely valued and sought by the subject. That is, the poem does not appear to be a catechizing of the reader whereby the speaker's earlier claims are exposed as forms of false piety or devotion.[49] Ferry has commented perceptively on this failure of the couplet to resolve the problem set in the rest of the poem: "the couplet makes a comment upon the preceding lines without negating or cancelling their validity, so that the earlier lines simultaneously reflect on the couplet itself"; thus Donne "offers a resolution less sure than it sounds, more tentative and troubled."[50] Donne's resolution of a sacred complex remains incomplete from a reader's perspective because the claim of a "true grief" is not, by itself, sufficient warrant for distinguishing true and false devotional practice. Ferry, however, does not leave the matter unresolved. Having effectively raised the question of sincerity, she then begs it by positing invisible and unnameable feelings (which she nonetheless names as "the penitence of a sinner" joined by "a sense of his own significance, even impatience at misunderstanding; contempt for less searching honesty than his own; anger against false righteousness"), guaranteed by God, as the "inwardness" that passes show in the sonnet: "No language can present what is in the heart to men so that it can be truly shown as it is seen by God."[51] Ferry limits the functions of language to that of communicating a pre-existing emotion or idea. But, as Donne himself has been asking, how do we know there is anything "in the heart" to communicate? Rather, the poem would seem to be a case of the medium being the message. Fish gets it right here: "the problem with language in these poems is not that it is too weak to do something, but that it is so strong that it does everything, exercising its power to such an extent that nothing, including the agent of that exercise, is left outside its sphere."[52] The feelings and states that Ferry identifies with "inwardness" are all too outwardly on display in the poem. It is the division of the subject across these positions that prompts us to save the appearances and collude with Donne to posit the inward language. But, as Fish argues, Donne's rhetoric prevents us from doing this: inwardness cannot survive its interrogation; verbal *power* is only *verbal* power, maintained at its own expense.

Fish properly corrects those who "put Donne in possession of his poetry and therefore of himself" and create "critical romances of which Donne is the hero."[53] However, Fish's antifoundationalist reading is another critical romance of which Fish the diagnostician is the hero (Donne's bulimia, recall, is "interestingly related to the contemporary critical scene"). Insofar as we grant Fish's claim at the end of his essay that "the very articulation of those dilemmas . . . gives them renewed and devouring life"[54] we restore with one hand the verbal power we have taken away with the other. Like French, Fish preserves an inexhaustible verbal power in the text. Surfeiting and purging, Fish is Donne yet not done.[55]

Donne's sacred complex, like Milton's, is finally empowering. Kerrigan argues that through "a regeneration of the oedipus complex" (the sacred complex), Milton reshapes the self and composes *Paradise Lost.*[56] In the case of "If faithfull soules" a devotional crisis is refigured as an oedipal scene which, in turn, is transformed into the "renewed and devouring life" of a literary text. To put it in a way that sounds self-evident but that should, because it is self-evident, merit the ideological critic's reflection, the Holy Sonnets, or at least some of them, convert devotion into literature.

Terry Eagleton's account of the relation between the ideological and the aesthetic is helpful here. Following Eagleton, I want to say that the sonnets (and readers of the sonnets) "process" ideological conflicts produced by Donne's devotions "under the form of resolving specifically *aesthetic* problems."[57] Eagleton stresses

> the closeness of relation between the "ideological" and the "aesthetic." . . . so that the problem-solving process of the text is never merely a matter of its reference outwards to certain pre-existent ideological cruxes. It is, rather, a matter of the "ideological" presenting itself in the form of the "aesthetic" and *vice versa*—of an aesthetic problem which demands ideological resolution, and so on.[58]

Although Eagleton (faulting Althusser's "consumer-centredness") advocates a "return to the productive process of the text itself,"[59] the "mechanisms of this process" can also be examined in critical discourse on the text. Ferry's subtle study of the sonnet literature of the English Renaissance exemplifies the work of processing ideological conflict in aesthetic terms. Her reading of the Holy Sonnets brilliantly produces Donne's processing of religious conflict as an aesthetic problem in the sonnet tradition. What I think she misses is the critical potential of Donne's processing—his claim of inwardness both saves and weakens the Christian ideology.

A fuller example of Eagleton's cycle of "problem-solving" is Richard Strier's closely-argued essay on the Holy Sonnets, which also reflects on the critical tradition and explicitly raises the question of the relation between ideology and aesthetics. Working from Donne's conflicted relation to Calvinist ideology, Strier argues that some of the Holy Sonnets suffer aesthetically from Donne's irresolution. In a reading of "O my blacke Soule," for example, he notes that Donne presents Catholic and Calvinist alternatives to receiving grace "without either coordination or sequence." The conclusion of the sonnet—"Wash thee in Christs blood, which hath this might / That being red, it dyes red soules to white" (11.13–14)—"is a brilliant poetic solution, but also merely a poetic solution."[60] This flawed aesthetic solution then, again following Eagleton's script, "demands ideological resolution." After a revisionist reading of the most famous Holy Sonnet—"Batter my heart"—Strier examines poems that display psychological and ideological coherence; some of these Strier finds "poetically successful," others less so. This discovery of poetic weakness in otherwise coherent poems leads to a discussion of intentionality: What if the inconsistencies and weaknesses of the poems were intended "to reveal or to dramatize an underlying hysteria" (359, 381)? Strier's answer to this question is nuanced, a close weaving of the aesthetic and ideological that returns us to the issue of sincerity. In Renaissance texts, he believes, "moments of deliberate sophistry or absurdity are generally signaled, . . . often explicitly." Such a text is "If poysonous mineralls," which "may be the greatest of the 1608–10 'Holy Sonnets' " and which "is clear about the nature of its arguments and also about the nature of its desires and fears. It keeps faith with its fears" (381, 382).[61]

The Marlovian irreverence of the octave of this sonnet invites an ideological critique. Although Strier sharply denies the relevance of such an approach to the poem, I believe his reading helps throw into relief the ideological work of the poem. A key early move in Strier's essay is to claim that sometimes the speaker of a poem is the author or "a direct projection of him (or her)" and other times not (358). For the most part, he reads the Holy Sonnets as "direct projections" of Donne's mental states, and this tight relation between author and text is crucial to Strier's rejoinder to critics who see the poems "as not merely serving, through their peculiarities, as a revelation of the (supposed) painfulness of Calvinism, but as intentionally dramatizing this painfulness" (360). Another critically important point is embedded in the parenthetical "supposed"; Strier also argues that such critics operate from a misguided view of Calvinism and the Calvinist God as, in the main, anxiety-producing. Donne's tortuous writhings, evasions, and confusions are therefore mistakenly treated by such critics as the spiritual trials one might expect of a convinced Calvinist. Strier argues, on the other hand, that the bluster, sophistries, and evasions of such sonnets as "Death be not proud," "This is my playes last scene," and "What if this present" are not the outgrowths of Calvinist doctrine but Donne's own, unintended lapses, which lower the aesthetic value of the poems. Whereas Fish sees Donne "always folded back into the dilemmas he articulates," Strier finds this to be so only in inferior poems. In the case of "If poysonous minerals," however, Strier finds ample textual warrant for taking the octave as deliberately fallacious:

> If poysonous mineralls, and if that tree,
> Whose fruit threw death on else immortal us,

> If lecherous goats, if serpents envious
> Cannot be damned; Alas, why should I bee?
> Why should intent or reason, borne in mee,
> Make sinnes, else equall, in mee, more heinous?
> And mercy being easie'and glorious
> To God, in his sterne wrath, why threatens hee? ("If poysonons
> minerals," 11.1–8)

Strier denies any serious ideological conflict in these lines, arguing that Donne's own characterization of them in line 9 as "disputing" reinforces other "textual warrants" of their intentional sophistry. The sestet, according to this reading, makes explicit the self-criticism implied in the far-fetched arguments of the octave; indeed, so strong is Donne's self-criticism in the sestet that he asks for total annihilation in the closing couplet: "That thou remember them, some claim as debt, / I thinke it mercy, if thou wilt forget" (ll. 13–14).

Strier's argument is compelling; particularly in his reading of "If poysonous mineralls" he demonstrates how an orthodox idea can be screwed to such intensity that it becomes unorthodox—a reproduction of ideology that is not identical to ideology. The problems with his reading come down to the "textual warrants" of intentionality and his insistence that the closing lines refer to the speaker's self and not his sins. Some readers will agree, some will not. But arguing from intentionality (deliberate sophistry) seems to me to be, again, begging the question of the subject raised by the poem. What it means to be or have a self—to have intentions, as distinct from being a mineral or a tree or a goat or a serpent—is the question set by the poem. What is "self-evident" or "transparent" to Strier is precisely what the octave seems to be interrogating.

The ideological project of the poem is to use "intent or reason" against itself to create the literary subjectivity represented in the closing paradox. If Strier is right about the deliberate sophistry of the octave, there is still the question of why Donne put it there, textual warrants and all. One possible answer provided by Strier is that framing the protests of the octave as disputations, "perhaps manifesting a Reformation distrust of reason and disgust with the incessantly disputatious self" (383), affords Donne some cover. He regularly "gets away with" outrageous arguments like this in the Songs and Sonnets and Paradoxes and Problems by using the same trick; his one canto epic, *Metempsychosis,* is, as Strier points out, filled with similar disclaimers of seriousness as it delivers its tale of the "progresse of the soule" from the fruit that "threw death on else immortal us" to an ape who attempts rape.[62] This equivocal construction of the self is perhaps most purely articulated in a letter Donne sent to Sir Henry Wotton accompanying a copy of his Paradoxes:

> but indeed they were made rather to deceave tyme then her daughtr truth:
> Although they have beene written in an age when any thing is strong enough

to overthrow her: if they make yo to find better reasons against them they do there office: for they are but swaggerers: quiet enough if yo resist them . . . they are rather alarums to truth to arme her then enemies.[63]

"If poysonous mineralls" internalizes the process described in this letter; the heterodox, "swaggering" octave is countered by an orthodox critique of reason as mere disputatiousness. As Strier notes, however, the closing effect of the poem is not a reinforcement of the orthodox position. Strier writes that "The sense of sin and the fear of God in this poem are so profound that being forgotten replaces being forgiven as the alternative to damnation" (383–84). As I suggested earlier, this reading grounds itself on sincerity; that is, Strier maintains that Donne here does not try to evade his fearful predicament but, rather, follows his fear where it leads him, as it were. Where it leads him, I believe, is to the evasion of evasions; like Marlowe's *Faustus,* which Strier invokes (appropriately) at the end of his argument, Donne's sestet remains in conflict with itself. Most obviously, the antecedent of the pronoun "them" is ambiguous. Strier eliminates the uncertainty by simply asserting that "Line 13 is about persons, not sins, and line 14, to maintain the parallel, must have 'me,' not 'sins,' as the object of 'Thou wilt forget' " (384). But the closing couplet seems to be making two, quite distinct, requests: forget my *sins,* as Gardner would have it, with "Scriptural warrant"; forget *me,* as Strier believes.[64] I want to say 1) that the couplet is an equivoke, a linguistic "solution" to the religious predicament of the subject of divine power; and 2) that the text's equivocal resistance to a unified interpretation creates a "subjectivity effect." I am not suggesting that the lines point to a continuous inner life that cannot be represented in language— Ferry's argument—but, rather, that certain ideological formations have been produced so as to divide the subject and create a kind of gridlock.[65] The ideological struggle between competing religious systems of salvation in the seventeenth century is reproduced as a conflict between "readings" of Donne. Like Justice Popham, the reader finds that the job has shifted from one of making ideological conflicts visible to one of determining and fixing a speaker's intentions. Resistance to such determination is produced not by means of an inwardness that escapes language but by means of an equivocal language that speaks a divided subject.[66]

The Ideology of Devotion

One wants to say that the resistance to closure at the end of the poem is the mark of its "literariness." Strier properly corrects the notion that such indeterminacy is a poetic virtue, a version of what he calls the "Yes, and that's what makes them so great" school of Holy Sonnet criticism.[67] Strier's critique of this viewpoint, however, demystifies this particular instance of literary transcendentalism only to recuperate the privileged place of honor and appreciation for poems "that are truly artistic successes," that is, poems that display the sorts of control over intention, on the one hand, and "real" or "profound" fear, on the other, that Strier regards as marks of literary value (384, 383). Strier ends up begging the question of literariness raised by his earlier quite effective demystification of poetic value. It's no coincidence that Strier is moved to remember Marlowe's Faustus here. The dominant ideology of the poem is literary. Whether one chooses to privilege indeterminacy or "deliberate sophistry" or real fear, the point is that the text produces the effect of subjectivity, an effect that has come to be associated with literariness— again, whether one prefers literature that is open-ended, formally closed, or "real."

I will now turn to a more specific consideration of the process whereby this subjectivity effect is achieved. My argument thus far has opposed the tendency to posit some preliterate, unsymbolized core at the heart of the Holy Sonnets. In what follows I risk the paradox that Donne's text produces a content of the subject that is both outside the text and at the same time the support of the text. The paradox is Lacanian, but before I examine its playing out in the famous "Batter my heart" I would first like to establish a seventeenth-century discursive context for the dilemma that activates Donne's version of the paradox.

The Holy Sonnets participate in a discourse of devotion much analyzed by seventeenth-century scholars during the 1960s and '70s.[68] Although Barbara Lewalski's theory of a "protestant poetics" seems to have carried the day, the broader question of the cultural work of devotion, and specifically poetic devotion, has not been fully discussed. Sinfield's work on the Protestant subject boldly connects Calvinist theology and a social constructionist theory of the individual, identifying the whole Calvinist system "as an instrument for the creation of self-consciousness, of interiority."[69] I would like to suggest that devotional poetry played a particularly important role in this process of creating inwardness. The key to my argument, however, is not the linkage between Calvinism and devotional practice, but rather what might be called the ideology of devotion itself and Donne's interrogation of that ideology.

The ideological function of devotion is perhaps most explicit in the devotional treatises that proliferated in the seventeenth century, before, during, and after the Civil War. One of the first such treatises, Joseph Hall's *Arte of Divine Meditation,* appeared in 1606, a few years before Gardner's suggested date for the earliest Holy Sonnets. In the dedication letter of the 1634 revised edition Hall contrasts polemical religious writing to devotional books:

> For on the one side I perceived the number of Polemicall bookes, rather to breed than end strifes; and those which are doctrinall by reason of their multitude, rather to oppress than satisfie the Reader; wherein, if we write the same things, we are judged tedious; if indifferent, singular. On the other

part, respecting the Reader, I saw the braines of men never more stuffed, their tongues never more stirring, their hearts never more empty, nor their hands more idle.[70]

Works of religious controversy produce conflict and intellectual hyperactivity instead of peace and heartfelt devotion. What is perhaps most striking about Hall's observations is his focus on the reader constructed by the respective discourses of controversy and devotion. Reading religious texts is assumed to have a powerful effect on the reader's spirituality. The reader of controversial prose suffers a sort of "dissociation of sensibility," a split between "stuffed" brain and "empty" heart, "stirring" tongue and "idle" hands. By contrast, as Louis Martz noted long ago, meditation promises an Eliotian fusion of thought and feeling, represented in Hall's treatise by a coordinated, two-part sequence that explores the spiritual topic first intellectually and then emotionally. Meditation, then, brings fullness and unity to the devout subject.

In another dedication to another meditative work, Hall characterizes the split as one between his public work as a churchman and his private meditations on scripture: "All my private studies have gladly vayled to the publike services of my Sovereign Master [i.e., the King]: No sooner could I recover the happinesse of my quiet thoughts, then I renued this my divine task: Wherein I cannot but professe to place so much contentment, as that I wish not any other measure of my life, then it."[71] In the context of the 1647 collected edition of Hall's works from which I have quoted these remarks, however, Hall's *Contemplations upon the Principall Passages of the Holie Storie* carries a Royalist political charge. Hall notes that he has focussed his scriptural meditations on "the Historicall part" of the Old Testament, "For what doth it else but comment upon that, which God hath thought good to say of Kings."[72] In a dedication of this work to Sir Thomas Edwards, treasurer of his majesty's household and of the Privy Council, Hall universalizes "the estate of old Israel" and the king's relation to God: "You shall finde the same hand swaying all Scepters, and you shall meet with such a proportion of dispositions, and occurrences, that you will say, men are still the same, if their names and faces differ."[73] Meditation on the Old Testament, then, affords a transcendental perspective on historical conflicts, a perspective which Hall links to a (presumably Royalist, given Hall's "polemical labor" for Archbishop Laud in the 1640s) resolution of conflicts in the devout soul:

Me thinks *Controversie* is not right in my way to heaven. . . . The favour which my late Polemicall labour hath found (beyond merit) from the Learned, cannot divert my love to those wrangling Studies. How earnestly doth my heart rather wish an universall cessation of these Armes; that all the Professors of the dear Name of Christ might be taken up with nothing but holy and peaceable thoughts of Devotion.[74]

Hall's belief in God's guiding power behind the throne is linked, then, to his promotion of cultivation of a spiritual inwardness that will restore unity and peace to both the spiritual and the political subject.

If Donne was a Royalist, one might expect him to have been of Hall's mind about devotion, but this is clearly not the temper of Donne's poetic meditations.[75] Even if one subscribes to the view of critics who believe the emotionalism of the poems is staged by Donne as a spiritual exercise with a predetermined outcome, the Holy Sonnets are not constructed as pleasant retreats from "the many controversies and tedious disputes of this age" or demonstrations of what Hall called "the slow proficiency of Grace."[76] Their intensity and contradictions, simulated or not, transfer the "wrangling" of doctrinal and ecclesiastical controversy to the site of devotion.[77] In particular, many of the sonnets work, again ironically or not (more on this question later), at exacerbating problems of authority rather than evading or resolving them in meditation. The problem of authority is not constructed in the Holy Sonnets as a Reformation conflict between what John N. King terms "the relative merits of internal and external authority," between an institutionally-sanctioned authority and the individual conscience.[78] In the Holy Sonnets, the conflict is more a case of Calvin's God being placed over against the individual conscience itself. In some of the poems the struggle between this God and his subject produces what I have been calling, following Fineman and Sinfield, a subjectivity-effect.

A Poet Is Being Beaten

> Batter my heart, three-person'd God; for, you
> As yet but knocke, breathe, shine, and seeke to mend;
> That I may rise, and stand, o'erthrow mee,'and bend
> Your force, to breake, blowe, burn and make me new.
> I, like an unsurpt towne, to'another due,
> Labour to'admit you, but Oh, to no end,
> Reason your viccroy in mee, mee should defend,
> But is captiv'd, and proves weake or untrue,
> Yet dearely'I love you, and would be lov'd faine,
> But am betroth'd unto your enemie,
> Divorce mee,'untie, or breake that knot againe,
> Take mee to you, imprison mee, for I
> Except you'enthrall mee, never shall be free,
> Nor ever chast, except you ravish mee.

As noted at the beginning of this chapter, Joel Fineman argued that "the Lacanian subject in particular, and the psychoanalytic subject in general, were epiphenomenal consequences of the Renaissance invention of the literary subject."[79] Although I do not work with his categories of vision and voice, I do want to pursue the general thesis that literary subjectivity is manifested in what Fineman describes in his last essay as "this wrinkle or crease of textuality— what Derrida calls *ecriture,* what Lacan calls the Real, a Real that can be neither specularized nor represented but the marks of which are the condition and consequence of both specularity and representation."[80] The theological and aesthetic weaknesses, as Strier portrays them, of some of the sonnets are symptomatic, in a rather precise sense of the term, of failed interpellation. The rest of this chapter, then, attempts to weave a relationship between literary subjectivity in Donne and some themes in psychoanalysis. Briefly, I argue that "Batter my heart," one of Strier's illustrative cases of theological incoherence, splits the subject of devotion between God (here theorized as the Lacanian Other) and desire (again, following Lacan's ambiguous formula, the desire of the Other[81]). In this poem, Donne is not Donne, he does not give way on his desire; and in this resistance, recorded in the masochistic fantasy of the conclusion, we sense the possibility of a subjectivity that is not wholly captured as a position in the symbolic network of Reformation Christianity.

William Kerrigan asserts that accommodation, the notion that Scripture speaks anthropomorphically to "accommodate" the fallen human intellect, "is the open door between religion and psychoanalysis," and thus his extended analysis of "Batter my heart" provides a helpful starting point for my own reading.[82] Kerrigan takes the sexual violence of the poem seriously, demonstrating how Donne's unpacking of sacred metaphors leads him to the brink of blasphemy in some Holy Sonnets: "Donne could not conceive of God without discovering, somewhere in the folds of his conception, human vice" (360). Kerrigan's reading proceeds along the lines he claims for Donne's poetic strategy: just as he finds Donne "approaching the forbidden, reaching a moment of dangerous anthropomorphism, deflecting that danger, just before the moment appears, with an equation between carnality and virtue," so Kerrigan steps back from danger in his reading of Donne by preserving through a Donnean paradox Donne's religious faith and his poetic power:

> Donne arrived at these moments by permitting the traditional language of devotion to mean what it does mean and opening that language until, having proposed a fallen God, he raised his healing paradox. . . . For whenever his accommodated metaphors spoiled, his humanity had failed, not his God: in deference to this failure he conjured the image of man rectified. At such moments Donne worshipped human evil with the difficult faith that evil was, when predicated of God, perfection. (363)

This closing move, in my view, gives away too much of the critical power generated by Kerrigan's brilliant framing discussion of accommodation and psychoanalysis, where he argues that "The search for salvation, then, is concurrently the search for loving approval from the human characters of a special and uniquely profound kind of fantasy—the devotional life" (347).

Kerrigan too readily dissolves the fantasy of "Batter my heart" into the Christian symbolic. Although he would seem to delay the paradoxical resolution until the last moment, the process begins early in the analysis, when he insists that the poem is controlled throughout by the sacred conceit of the bride and bridegroom. The would-be battered heart is gradually revealed to be a would-be ravished vagina; otherwise, Kerrigan reasons, we must "believe that suddenly and ridiculously, with the phrase 'Yet dearely'I love you,' our speaker changes sex" (353). As Strier has shown, the poem suddenly changes theologies in the second quatrain, so I am hesitant to accept Kerrigan's reasoning on the grounds of sudden change here.[83] More importantly, his argument begs the highly relevant question of the relationship between sex and gender raised by the poem, for one of the grotesqueries, as Kerrigan calls them, revealed by Donne's "fearful accommodations" is the sex-change demanded of heterosexual male believers by the sacred metaphor—demanded but not necessarily yielded by Donne in this poem. The desire of the battered subject of Donne's sonnet is not regulated by a sex-gender system or hetero- or homosexual regimes.[84] This polymorphic quality, I suggest, is a consequence of the sadomasochistic fantasy that inhabits the poem.

The sonnet opens with a beating fantasy, and while I do not insist on a rigidly Freudian reading of the passage, I do want to recall "A Child Is Being Beaten" for two reasons: first, to foreground the sadomasochistic element of the fantasy and thereby to suggest that the bride/bridegroom trope is not by itself sufficient for grasping the accommodated language of sex, power, and pleasure in the sonnet; and second, to highlight the importance of gender-switching to an analysis of the fantasy at the "heart" of Donne's sonnet. Although Freud admits to basing much of his essay on analyses of female patients, he devotes considerable space to reviewing parallels and differences with male instances of the fantasy. As D. N. Rodowick notes, even though Freud attempts to make sharp distinctions between the sexes in his analyses of the fantasy, "the essay is . . . about the difficulty of aligning masculine and feminine identifications with a 'final' sexed subjectivity."[85] For example, Freud claims that while boys consciously fantasize themselves as boys being beaten by women, the boys are nonetheless playing the part of a woman in being beaten (i.e., feminine = passive in this context). Furthermore, Freud goes on to suggest, the "primary" unconscious fantasy here is in the form of "*I am being beaten by my father*," which is a substitute for "*I am loved by my father.*" Thus Freud concludes that "The boy's beating-phantasy is therefore passive from the very beginning, and is derived from a feminine attitude towards his father. . . . *In both cases* [boys and girls] *the beating phantasy has its origin in an incestuous attachment to the father.*" Later, in the conscious fantasy, "the boy evades his homosexuality by repressing and remodelling his unconscious phantasy" by making the beating hetero-sexual.[86]

My aim is not to pinpoint Donne's sexual orientation but, rather the opposite, to underscore, as have numerous recent commentators on Freud's essay, the instability of gender positioning in the sadomasochistic fantasy that serves as the accommodated vehicle for Donne's relation to God in the poem. Indeed, a major limitation of Freud's discussion of the fantasy is the fixed nature of his understanding of identification and pleasure, as exemplified in his strict switching of positions, an understanding reductive in its assumptions about identification in the fantasy and about the consequences for object-choice brought about by identification. In summarizing Parveen Adams's important essay on female masochism, Linda Williams notes how Adams "reworks the beating scenario in Freud's 1919 article . . . to show that identification with any one of the three roles posited by this scenario—beater, beaten, or onlooker—is not dependent on a fixed masculine or feminine identity and the sexual object choice that presumably follows from them. . . . [T]here is no such thing as pure masochistic fusion with the object of identification for male or female masochists," but rather, oscillation, "movement between" identifications.[87]

Walking through Kerrigan's open door between religion and psychoanalysis, then, I find the beating fantasy more accommodating than the bridegroom/bride metaphor as a way of thinking about the conflicts of power, love, and self represented in "Batter my heart." I want to press on both terms in Freud's phrase. First, I mean to consider the *fantasy* in its relation to ideological interpellation, as suggested by Slavoj Žižek in *The Sublime Object of Ideology.* Žižek, critiquing Althusser, insists that interpellation

> never fully succeeds, that there is always a residue, a leftover, a stain of traumatic irrationality and senselessness sticking to it, and that *this leftover, far from hindering the full submission of the subject to the ideological command, is the very condition of it;* it is precisely this non-integrated surplus of senseless traumatism which confers on the Law its unconditional authority: in other words, which—in so far as it escapes ideological sense—sustains what we might call the ideological *jouis-sense,* enjoyment-in-sense (enjoy-meant), proper to ideology.[88]

How does this happen? Žižek captures this leftover or residue by means of the Lacanian theory of fantasy: "the subject (barred S) is trapped by the Other through a paradoxical object-cause of desire in the midst of it (*a*), through this secret supposed to be hidden in the Other" (44). Thus fantasy "constructs the frame enabling us to desire something"; by means of fantasy "*we learn 'how to desire'* " (118). The subject—the Donne of "Batter my heart"—looks for some cause with which to identify in the Other and is trapped by this desire or rather this search for the object-cause of desire which is assumed to be hidden in the Other. This fantasy that the cause of our desire is hidden within the Other is what enables us to mask the Real of our desire. But, Žižek insists, fantasy's masking also "announces" the Real of desire that is not completely assimilated by the ideology:

> The Lacanian thesis is . . . that there is always a hard kernel, a leftover which persists and cannot be reduced to a universal play of illusory mirroring. The difference between Lacan and "naive" realism is that for Lacan, *the only point at which we approach this hard kernel of the Real is indeed the dream.* . . . The only way to break the power of our ideological dream is to confront the Real of our desire which announces itself in this dream. (47–48)

Žižek's Lacanian analysis of ideology concludes that the subject is not simply a position in a network of social relations structured by the external symbolic order. There is the possibility of a "content" outside the Other, the alienating symbolic network, and this is offered by fantasy—in Donne's case the fantasy of being first beaten and then sodomized. The ideological *fantasy* of "Batter my heart," then, offers an opening to a subjectivity-effect that is neither a fixed "subject-position" in the Calvinist symbolic nor a poststructuralist free play of signification.

Second, the sadomasochistic "content" of the fantasy—the *beating*—brings into view a connection between the problems about the self raised by Strier's theological reading and the violence of the poem. Strier's argument about a contradiction between lines 1–4 and 5–8 on the question of the subject's status in relation to God is, in the terms of a beating fantasy, both predictable and deeply meaningful.

> Batter my heart, three-person'd God; for, you
> As yet but knocke, breathe, shine, and seeke to mend;
> That I may rise, and stand, o'erthrow mee,'and bend
> Your force, to breake, blowe, burn and make me new.
> I, like an unsurpt towne, to'another due,
> Labour to'admit you, but Oh, to no end,
> Reason your viceroy in mee, mee should defend,
> But is captiv'd, and proves weake or untrue. ("Batter my heart,"
> 11.1–8)

As Strier points out, the middle section of the poem represents a self "very different from that implied by the opening and closing prayers," one that is "healthy in its dispositions, and merely hampered in their realization" (375). Donne is undecided as to whether his reason, "your viceroy in mee" (l. 7), is "weake or untrue" (l. 8)—that is, impeded by forces beyond its control from defending him against corruption or corrupt in its very constitution. This indecisive shifting corresponds to shifting genders and identifications in the beating fantasy as well as to the classic Freudian ambivalence embedded in it. Something of a change from passivity to activity indeed occurs between the opening quatrain and the representation of the self laboring to admit God in line 6. But this shift is already occurring in terms of gender in the opening scenario, where the passive position of the heart, particularly if it *is* equated to the vagina as Kerrigan wants it, is contradicted by the phallic vision of finally rising and standing.

Donne's clinging to a shred (a "hard kernel") of self-worth in the middle section also suggests that we ought not to limit his identification in the fantasy to the helpless, passive victim of the beating. It may be that among the (forbidden?) pleasures of Calvinism captured in this sonnet are those of identification with the all-powerful punishing father, on the one hand, or the observer of the punishment, on the other, in addition to the obvious identification with the masochistic victim. Recent film criticism, as noted above, has cautioned against an overly restrictive understanding of the pleasures of identification, even when it would seem, as in the cases of sadomasochistic pornography and slasher movies, that the possibilities for multiple identifications are extremely limited.[89] This criticism has also disclosed the crucial link between power and pleasure in such films; as Linda Williams writes, "without a modicum of power, without a little leeway for play within the assigned sexual roles, and without the possibility of some intersubjective give and take and bisexual movement between gender roles, there is no pleasure. For the masochist as well as the sadist, there is no pleasure without some power"[90]—even if, in the case of this poem as in sadomasochistic films, that paradoxical "masochistic power" is exercised in the giving of oneself into the hands of the powerful Other.

What I am getting at here is the "hard kernel" of the fantasy and the pleasures it gives in "Batter my heart." Donne is seeking, desiring something in his Holy Sonnets, and in "Batter my heart" he finds it in a beating fantasy. The type of resolution offered in the fantasy is, however, difficult to pin down. Why does Donne "imagine himself to be a pervert," to borrow a suggestive phrase from Lacan?[91] One approach would be to focus on the something that Donne seeks. What is this something? In Donne's theological language it is grace; in the accommodated language of psychoanalysis (and, I would argue, of "Batter my heart") it is the jouissance of the Other, the lost fullness of being which is assumed to be hidden in the Other. That is, in Lacanian terminology, Donne's fantasy teaches that desire is the desire of the Other. In the Other, one seeks to recover the plenitude (i.e., Paradise) lost in the fall from grace. Donne's beating/rape fantasy offers the prospect of regaining this fullness of being in three ways. Recalling Freud's interpretation of the male fantasy, "I am being beaten by my father" as a substitute for "I am loved by my father," Donne *is* in the fantasy the object of the Other's (God's) desire.[92] Alternatively, Donne fantasizes having the lost object of desire in the form of the grace given by God in the act of beating/raping Donne. Finally, the recuperation might take the form in fantasy of imagining himself to be the Other. I have already referred to Lacan's formulation of this function of fantasy, but the complete passage is quite resonant with respect to Donne's seeking throughout the Holy Sonnets: "To return to phantasy, let us say that the pervert imagines himself to be the Other in order to ensure his *jouissance,* and that it is what the neurotic reveals when he imagines himself to be a pervert—in his case, to assure himself of the existence of the Other."[93]

In this last instance, the sonnet phallicizes the *jouissance* of the Other in the images of the divine hammer of the famous opening lines and the divine penis of the closing rape fantasy.[94] This phallicization is also connected, I believe, to the problems of selfhood treated by Strier in terms of reformation theology. From a Lacanian perspective the recovery of lost *jouissance* is a major cause of cultural activities, but it is highly fraught with danger to the self as well. The unbounded, shattering nature of *jouissance* represents a loss of identity (in psychoanalytic terms, a return to the pre-oedipal infantile position of object of the desire of the mother) as well as a recovery of being.[95] Thus "cultural production . . . embodies an attempt on the one hand to recover the seemingly limitless jouissance of being that is available to the infant in the position of object of the Desire of the Mother and on the other hand to preserve the Name-of-the-Father not only as the instrument of phallic jouissance but also as a defense against being overwhelmed by the limitless jouissance of being."[96] Such a resistance to being overwhelmed is perhaps behind Donne's inconsistent representation of the self in the middle section of the sonnet. More importantly, the phallicization of the *jouissance* of the Other seems crucial to understanding, as Strier writes, "Donne's inability in this period to conceive of divine love in terms of a loving relationship."[97]

I have commented on problems in Donne's phallicization of *jouissance* earlier in this book, in the "overfraught pinnace" of "Aire and Angels," and similar instabilities seem evident in this sonnet. In closing I will turn to a discussion of some of these as they affect the construction of subjectivity in the poem. Writing on male to male sadomasochistic scenarios in heterosexual pornography, Williams remarks that "For the male viewer, identification with either participant in such a scene threatens conventional heterosexual identity perceived as mastery and control".[98] If we transfer this comment to Kerrigan's accommodated scene of the bride and bridegroom, we can see that Donne has effected a similar destabilization in his playing fast and loose with gender and sexuality in the sonnet (does the poem privilege the battered vagina or male to male sodomy?). What is more, Donne's troubles with Calvinism— his uncertainties about the self vis-à-vis God, as Strier puts it—are here represented in terms of a sexual relation, a "perversion," in which power and pleasure converge in an unusual way that destabilizes such "normal" distinctions as pleasure/pain and, in Freudian terms, masculine and feminine sexualities.

Although I do not wish to rule out the multiple identifications offered by "Batter my heart," I do want to focus here on the masochistic side of the poem's fantasy. Masochism gathers up some of the themes of subjectivity and gender discussed earlier in this book, and, I believe, it offers a cogent account of the disturbing power of this sonnet. Both Rodowick and Kaja Silverman see masochism as a possible revolt against inscription in the patriarchal order as crystalized in struggle with oedipal authority, though Silverman is gloomier about the outcome of the revolt and sees it as nihilistic. I say "possible" particularly with respect to Silverman, for in her influential essay on "Masochism and Male Subjectivity" she repeatedly notes the "double nature" of perversion, which "always contains the trace of Oedipus within it . . . and is always organized to some degree by what it subverts."[99] In male subjects, write Silverman, both "moral" masochism, the internalized sense of guilt, and "feminine" masochism, the (male) pathology that positions the suffering subject as a woman, grow out of the normal but impossible oedipal situation of the subject "wanting both to love the father and to be the father, but prevented from doing either" (41).[100] The son must overcome his desire for the father by becoming the father, but, of course, he is also faced with a prohibition in this project (he may not do all that the father does). Moral masochism, "a kind of chamber play for two in which the same actor plays both parts," responds to this dilemma by allowing the subject "to function both as the one who punishes and the one who is punished" for desiring and/or usurping the father (42). As I noted earlier, Donne's sonnet seems to afford this double identification by emphasizing equally the giving and receiving of God's blows. The poem also seems to register the problem with love of the father, which is ingeniously framed as an unsanctioned, "romantic" love blocked by the betrothal "unto your enemie" (ll. 9–10) and needing the radical remedy of divorce; Donne seems to invoke the trope of bride and bridegroom only to mock it with his Romeo and Juliet scenario.

Silverman, summarizing Theodor Reik's *Masochism in Sex and Society,* describes another quality of masochism pertinent to Donne. Reik insists on the element of exhibitionism, a sort of display of loss, in masochism: "the suffering, discomfort, humiliation and disgrace are being shown and so to speak put on display."[101] This is not all that is displayed in masochism, particularly the masochism of male subjects. As Silverman notes, the beating fantasies of Freud's male patients are "subjected to far less censorship and distortion that those recorded by his female patients" (51). In the three phases of the beating fantasies of his female patients, there are numerous substitutions for the subject being beaten, whereas in the two phases he manages to construct for the male fantasies the receiver of the beating remains constant.[102] The male masochist, that is, does not try to dissemble his masochistic desire but instead "flaunts" it. What is being displayed, argues Silverman, is the process of subjectification itself: "he acts out in an insistent and exaggerated way the basic conditions of cultural subjectivity, conditions that are normally disavowed; he loudly proclaims that his meaning comes to him from the Other, prostrates himself before the Gaze even as he solicits it, exhibits his castration for all to see, and revels in the sacrificial basis of the social contract" (51). This variety of demonstrative interpellation crops up now and again in Donne's love poetry, perhaps most tellingly in "A Nocturnall upon S. Lucie's Day," as a trumping of a Petrarchist dialectic of self and other.[103] But the display of "Batter my heart" stands apart from these instances in the love lyrics: even if we admit Kerrigan's controlling metaphor of the bride and bridegroom, the violent sexual act fantasized at the end of the Holy Sonnet and the gender complications entailed by it have no parallels in the Songs and Sonnets. And the other of the Holy Sonnet is manifestly the Other.

What does Donne's demonstration finally demonstrate? Silverman points out that this is often a difficult question. For one thing, Christian masochism "seems to be particularly prone to simulation and masquerade" (44), as Donne seems to acknowledge in "If Faithfull Soules" and "Oh, To Vex Me," and so its ultimate effect is hard to pin down. This question of "sincerity" would seem to take us back to the literary problematic of intentionality, but the violence of the performance in "Batter my heart" prompts another question that encourages us to track the beating and rape fantasy of the sonnet regardless of its authenticity: Why would Donne *want* to mimic such a submission to sexual violence?[104]

I have already discussed this desire in terms of the Lacanian formula of the desire of the Other, but recent studies have rendered different interpretations of the sexual and cultural significance of the operation of this desire in masochism. While cautioning that "masochism in all of its guises is as much a product of the existing symbolic order as a reaction against it" (62), Silverman argues that "[t]he male masochist magnifies the losses and divisions upon which cultural identity is based, refusing to be sutured or recompensed. In short, he radiates a negativity inimical to the social order" (51). This argument puts a radical spin on a conservative psychoanalytic reading of perversion whereby "the pervert is trying to free himself from the paternal universe and the contraints of the law. He wants to dethrone God the Father."[105] Silverman's "heterocosmic" musings are a hedged version of utopian readings of masochism, most notably that of Gilles Deleuze. In masochism, Deleuze argues, the father is replaced by a cold, cruel mother whose beating of the son is actually a beating of the father in the son; out of this transaction is born a "new, sexless man": "what is beaten, humiliated and ridiculed in him is the image and likeness of the father, and the possibility of the father's aggressive return. . . . The masochist thus liberates himself in preparation for a rebirth in which the father will have no part."[106] Deleuze's interpretation would thus seem to draw out the implications of the third and conscious stage of the male beating fantasy constructed by Freud, in which the father of the second, unconscious stage is replaced by the mother (or substitutes in actual masochistic performances) while the male subject takes on the role of a woman. Freud notes "the remarkable thing" about this last phase—"that it has for its content a feminine attitude without a homosexual object choice"; as Silverman remarks, the consequences of this revision of the symbolic order "may be even more socially transforming than eroticism between men—it constitutes a 'feminine' yet heterosexual male subject."[107]

This substitution is, of course, necessarily not part of Donne's beating fantasy in "Batter my heart," and it is just one of the differences between that fantasy and Freud's account that test the limits of a psychoanalytic reading of the sonnet. With respect to Freud's third phase of the fantasy, it must be emphasized that the absence of this substitution in Donne's beating fantasy does not disqualify it as a masochistic and potentially transgressive one. Deleuze's cold and cruel mother is also missing in one of the most detailed and spectacular of the fantasies discussed by Reik in *Masochism in Sex and Society*.[108] What "Batter my heart" shares with other masochistic fantasies is its staging of the entry into patriarchy as a sacrificial drama. If Kerrigan is right about the heart = vagina substitution of the opening line, the sonnet also, like many masochistic fantasies, dramatizes interpellation in terms of a woman's forced subjection to phallic law. The rape fantasy of the concluding lines can be seen in a similar light, so that the "feminine" ideal of chastity, here achieved by means of phallic violence, is equated with the male subject's submission to the phallus. Alternatively—and, again, I do not believe Donne allows us to pin down the gender here, the male subject's achievement of chastity through the violent act of sodomitical rape can be read as a figure of castration; in this masochistic scenario phallic power is both evoked ("you ravish mee") and renounced ("chast"). Whether we regard Donne's beating fantasy as homosexual or heterosexual, its exaggeration of the conditions of interpellation carries at least a potentially negative or critical charge with respect to those terms. This reading is far removed from Deleuze's grand claims for masochism, but it does point to a potentially disruptive, even transgressive effect of the poem.

Perhaps the largest disparity between Donne and Freud has to do with the role of the unconscious in Freud's analysis. Freud admits that what he regards as the "most important and the most momentous," the second phase of the fantasy—verbalized by Freud as "I am being beaten by my father" and constituting the most compelling parallels with Donne's sonnet— is unconscious: "It is never remembered, it has never succeeded in becoming conscious. It is a construction of analysis."[109] But this is not all. In discussing the male version of the fantasy, Freud further reveals 1) that the first stage of the fantasy, which Freud verbalizes as "I am being loved by my father," is a psychoanalytic construction like the second stage, *and* 2) that in both sexes the desire to be loved by the father has been entirely expelled from the psyche, including the unconscious. Freud explains that the beating fantasy represents not so much a *repression* of the original incestuous desire as a *regression* from genital sexuality to anal: in regression, Freud says, "the state of things changes in the unconscious as well"; while the "the masochistic phantasy of being beaten by the father . . . lives on in the unconscious after repression has taken place," this is not the case with "the passive phantasy of being loved by him."[110] Silverman notes the disruptive implications of this effect of regression with respect to the male masochist:

> If no record can be found within his unconscious of the desire to be loved by the father, the male masochist cannot be reconciled to the symbolic order or to his social identity through the revelation that his unconscious is already on the side of harmony and alliance. Indeed, his (barely) repressed desire runs directly counter to any such reconciliation, attesting irrefutably to the violence of the familial and cultural contract. (58)

This is clearly not the case in "Batter my heart," which, as I have noted earlier, openly acknowledges its desire of the Other. Indeed, the contrasts with Freud's three phases of the beating fantasy are quite striking and suggestive. The sonnet can be distinguished according to three "phases" of fantasy which might be rendered by the following statements. I have preserved Freud's declarative constructions while registering in parentheses Donne's optative mood:

1) I am being (want to be) beaten by my Father;
2) I am being (want to be) loved by my Father;
3) I am being (want to be) raped by my Father.

All the contents of the Freudian beating fantasy are here, but Freud's mechanisms of regression and repression, whereby the elements are managed by the psyche, are absent. For example, where Freud unpacks the fantasy to reveal the beating to be *"not only the punishment for the forbidden genital relation, but also the regressive substitute for that relation"* Donne moves straightforwardly from what Freud would call the regressive substitute ("Batter my heart") to a declaration of love ("dearly' I love you") to something like a combination of the two in the fantasy of rape.[111] The poem boldly displays Donne's desire and follows it to its scandalous conclusion. One searches in vain for a distinction between latent and manifest content—Donne represents a psyche that is all surface, no depth. It makes no sense to speak of unconscious phases of fantasy or of changes in the unconscious due to regression because everything in the sonnet seems fully present to consciousness; Donne seems to be fully aware that his wish to be beaten is a wish to be loved.

The comparison with Freud lends support to Stephen Greenblatt's argument about the imperfect fit between psychoanalysis and Renaissance texts. Greenblatt particularly stresses the causal "belatedness" of psychoanalytic readings: "hence the curious effect of a discourse that functions *as if* the psychological categories it invokes were not only simultaneous with but even prior to and themselves causes of the very phenomena of which in actual fact they were the results."[112] This book has been broadly in sympathy with this position; in the case of "Batter my heart," for example, I would argue not that Donne's devotional position is the result of oedipal conflicts but very nearly the reverse—that the devotional subject's interpellation produces psychic conflicts that resemble those analyzed by Freud. What the poem and its fantasy allow us to see is something like the production of a particular form of what Freud, working in a later economy of selfhood, would call the unconscious. This production takes place at a particular historical moment, both in the religious culture and the biography of Donne the son of Catholics who became the famous preaching dean of St. Paul's. Perhaps it is not too much of an exaggeration to say that "Batter my heart" tells of the sacrifice that accompanied that accession to mastery of language.

The argument of this book, however, has not been primarily about historical origins but about the historically variable subjectivity effects of reading Donne's poems. I want to return to Žižek's point about the disruptive effect of fantasy, an effect that seems all too easily contained by the sort of linear historical narrative proposed by Greenblatt's historicist critique.[113] The point, again, is to compare what I have been calling the "beating fantasy" of Donne's sonnet with Freud's account of male masochist fantasy, not to equate the two. If there is an ahistorical move in my use of the term fantasy, my comparison of the fantasies is an attempt to historicize my reading.

Although I have emphasized Donne's apparent lack of a "depth psychology" in the sonnet as a difference from Freud's procedure, this flattening out of the psyche is, as Silverman observes, also a characteristic of Freud's account of male masochism. Freud's "astonishing observation" about the disappearance of the wish to be loved by the father "constitutes a veritable hermeneutic scandal" with respect to the male masochist. By admitting that the fantasy of being loved by the father is entirely a construction of psychoanalysis, Freud has limited the unconscious dimension of the fantasy to that of phase two—being beaten by the father; and this phase is, as Freud suggests, transparently reproduced in the conscious fantasy of the third phase—being beaten by the mother. In effect, the psyche of the male masochist as Freud describes it is, like the psyche of Donne's sonnet, without depth: as Silverman writes, "Here there is no radical divide of manifest from latent content, and no real 'depth' to the psyche. The door to the unconscious need not be picked; it is already slightly ajar, and ready to yield at the slightest pressure" (58). The meanings of both beating fantasies—Donne's in "Batter my heart" and the male fantasy reconstructed by Freud in "A Child Is Being Beaten"—are manifest in the details of the fantasies.

This similarity is matched by an equally important difference. Silverman points out that Freud's male masochist seems irremediably opposed to reconciliation because he has managed to desire not to desire the father. Donne's over-the-top performance of his subjection, on the other hand, hyperbolizes, if anything, the desire for the father in the fantasy of rape. What that fantasy seems to represent, however, is consistent with a psychoanalytic interpretation of masochist fantasy: as Rodowick points out, in the space of what Freud termed the second, unconscious stage of the fantasy, the unconscious, "ruled by the pleasure principle and ungoverned by the principle of noncontradiction, can render an incestuous desire (genital love) and its punishment (beating) as equivalent."[114] In Donne's sonnet this equivalence is expressed in the shocking fantasy of rape, which overlays genital love with the regressive substitute of beating. In his reading of "A Child Is Being Beaten" Jean-Francois Lyotard speculates about the "shattering of the subject" brought on by this conjunction in terms relevant to Donne's concluding image (what Lyotard calls the "thing-presentation"). This image "should simultaneously fulfill the incestuous desire, its interdiction, the sadistic drive and the superimposition of the conglomeration . . . of this cluster of impulsions in the masochistic setting. The subject must be able to recognize himself in the father and in the child; in the beating position and in the position of being beaten. He explodes. . . ."[115]

It is tempting to read "Batter my heart" as an account of such a "shattering of the subject," and, as indicated earlier in this chapter, I do not want to rule out such a split in identification as Lyotard describes. But perhaps the more interesting split here is between the affective force of the image and what Donne *says* it means. He will be made "chast" by the ravishment. The meaning of chastity here is difficult to pin down. The context of the marriage theme of the third quatrain urges a reading of married chastity; Donne the bride will be disciplined and punished to desire only the divine husband/phallus. On the other hand, the more immediate context of line 13 ("Except you'enthrall mee, never shall be free") and the full force of paradox support a reading of chastity as virginity: complete subjection produces autonomy, violation of bodily integrity restores bodily integrity. In this case, it is possible to read in the fantasy a desire not to desire the father, a reading that would place the poem on the side of transgressive readings of male masochism.[116] These two possible readings of chastity suggest a conflict between the desire of the father and the desire not to desire. Finally, chastity implies a mastery of desire, the achievement of "all the attributes, privilege, and authority that patriarchal culture ideally and imaginarily confers on the paternal metaphor."[117] To make the achievement of such power the effect of a paternal rape is, to say the least, a heterodox settlement of the oedipus complex. In this reading, too, Donne's sonnet seems to exhibit what Rodowick describes as the masochist's "utopian drive to imagine scenarios where the subject occupies a position or positions other than those dictated by Oedipal sexuality."[118]

What I have been dealing with here is the problem of Donne's excessive performance of subjectification. This excess or overproduction can also be used to challenge Freud's bedrock contention in "A Child Is Being Beaten" that the beating fantasy originates in a feminine relation to the father, which Freud equates with passivity.[119] Recent work problematizes Freud's notion of passivity, particularly in the case of male masochism. Rodowick suggests that the male masochist "enjoys 'femininity' by magnifying those aspects that erode the phallic ideal"; it is not so much the identification with woman, as Freud argues, that is important as the desire behind this identification— the "renunciation of paternal power and privilege."[120] Similarly, Silverman notes the possibility that "some very unorthodox desires and patterns of identification can be concealed behind what may often be only a masquerade of submission, including ones which are quite incompatible with a subordinate position" (59).

This line of thought suggests the potential for a kind of agency in "feminine masochism" that is reinforced by structural features of this and other fantasies. Silverman remarks on the fantasist's control of the fantasy: "the individual producing the phantasy is his 'own' sexual object. . . . Indeed, the masochistic pervert might be almost said to beat himself" (54).[121] Rodowick goes further to suggest that "[t]he very architecture of phantasy is an unconscious evasion of the demands of patriarchal law"[122]—a utopian reading that depends upon Lyotard's account of fantasy and its production of *jouissance*. Fantasy, Lyotard argues, is never entirely contained by representation (in words or images); in fantasy we encounter "a form in which desire remains engaged." Fantasy produces neither identity nor the annihilation of it but something that oscillates between them—*jouissance*.[123]

Lyotard seems to be using *jouissance* here in the sense of orgasm, and while this meaning is clearly not irrelevant to the poem's fantasy of divine rape, I am not claiming this as the effect of reading the sonnet. But I do want to argue that the work on fantasy by Lyotard, Rodowick, Žižek, and others does speak to the pleasures offered by the poem and, as a consequence, complicates our understanding of the "equivocal process of *subjectification,*" as Montrose phrased it, which has been the focus of this book. Working through the fantasy of a text such as Donne's suggests a complex and subtle relationship between the literary text and ideology, a relationship that seems central to the invention of what Fineman almost redundantly called "literary subjectivity." Understanding the role of fantasy in ideology counteracts the tendency to regard ideology "as a teleological force, fully realizing itself in the forms of the text and in the spectator's apprehension of those forms."[124] Both old and new historicist readings construct "Batter my heart" as a particularly vivid and daring rendering of "desire fulfilled in signs." Reading the sonnet through its fantasy, on the other hand, hints at "the dream of unfulfilled desire."[125] Another divine poem addressed to the Other puts it succinctly: "When thou hast done, thou hast not done, / For, I have more" ("A Hymne to God the Father").

Within the fantasy representing Donne's submission to the divine rod is a desire that produces a deeply conflicted relation to ideology, a struggle between desire and the law. The terms of the submission are, as Silverman emphasizes, given by the culture. But from those terms, the sonnet makes something new—a literary subjectivity which will itself function as a competing ideological formation and which offers the pleasure of its own distinctive ideological fantasy. Quoting Donne to make this point about one of his own poems, I come full circle with the subject of Donne. In my readings I have tried to defer or question such identifications in the interest of exploring their causes and effects—the representations and desires mobilized and circulated by readings of Donne's poems and the various subjectivity effects produced by these readings. In finally relying on one Donne poem to illuminate another, I mean to underscore the connection I have been drawing between his literary practice and our concepts of the subject and subjectivity in the Renaissance and to end this study where I believe many others begin.

Notes

Introduction

1. Elizabeth D. Harvey and Katherine Eisaman Maus, eds., *Soliciting Interpretation: Literary Theory and Seventeenth-Century English Poetry* (Chicago: University of Chicago Press, 1990), xiii.

2. For a recent defense of the Renaissance canon from a deconstructionist position, see Howard Felperin, *The Uses of the Canon: Elizabethan Literature and Contemporary Theory* (Oxford: Clarendon Press, 1990), which includes a chapter on Donne, pp. 79–99.

3. Marotti, *John Donne: Coterie Poet* (Madison: University of Wisconsin Press, 1986); Docherty, *John Donne, Undone* (London and New York: Methuen, 1986); Strier, *Resistant Structures: Particularity, Radicalism, and Renaissance Texts* (Berkeley and Los Angeles: University of California Press, 1995). Another important recent book on Donne and intellectual history is Edward Tayler, *Donne's Idea of a Woman: Structure and Meaning in* The Anniversaries (New York: Columbia University Press, 1991).

4. Docherty, *John Donne, Undone,* 1.

5. Docherty, *John Donne, Undone,* 6.

6. Fish, "Masculine Persuasive Force: Donne and Verbal Power," in Harvey and Maus, *Soliciting Interpretation,* 223.

7. Strier, *Resistant Structures,* 2. 12.

8. Strier, *Resistant Structures,* 7 and Essays (i.e., chapters) 1 and 6.

9. These criticisms inform many of the essays collected in H. Aram Veeser, *The New Historicism* (London and New York: Routledge, 1989).

10. Jonathan Crewe, *Trials of Authorship: Anterior Forms and Poetic Reconstruction from Wyatt to Shakespeare* (Berkeley and Los Angeles: University of California Press, 1990); Liu, "The Power of Formalism: The New Historicism," *ELH* 56 (1989): 755. In another, even more sweeping, essay Liu has related all forms of the new cultural criticism to Romanticism; see "Local Transcendence: Cultural Criticism, Postmodernism, and the Romanticism of Detail," *Representations* 32 (1990): 75–113.

11. Thomas, "The New Historicism and Other Old-Fashioned Topics," in H. Aram Veeser, ed., *The New Historicism* (London and New York: Routledge, 1989), 187. New historicists, of course, grapple with a dilemma or opportunity faced by any historical study. Another classic

formulation is Gadamer's: "To think historically always involves establishing a connection between [the past's] ideas and one's own thinking." *Truth and Method,* trans. William Glen-Doepel (New York: Crossroad, 1975), 358.

12. Thomas, "The New Historicism," 201.

13. Kahn, "Habermas, Machiavelli, and the Humanist Critique of Ideology," *PMLA* 105 (May 1990): 465.

14. Kahn, "Habermas, Machiavelli," 468, 470.

15. Jorge Larrain, *Marxism and Ideology* (New York: Humanities Press, 1983), 92; quoted in Paul Smith, *Discerning the Subject* (Minneapolis: University of Minnesota Press, 1983), 14. Larrain, it should be noted, attacks Althusser's concept of ideology. Louis Althusser's much-discussed theory of interpellation can be found in *Lenin and Philosophy* (New York: Monthly Review Press, 1971), 127–86.

16. Richard Johnson, "What Is Cultural Studies Anyway?" *Social Text* 6 (1987): 77.

17. Bradshaw, *Misrepresentations: Shakespeare and the Materialists* (Ithaca: Cornell University Press, 1993).

18. On this point, see also Louis Montrose, "Professing the Renaissance: The Poetics and Politics of Culture," in Veeser, *The New Historicism,* 15–36.

19. Terry Eagleton, *Criticism and Ideology: A Study in Marxist Literary Theory* (1976; London: Verso, 1978), 69. Since Eagleton's *Criticism and Ideology* figures prominently in my book, this first citation is perhaps the appropriate place to acknowledge that Eagleton's more recent work on ideology and literature has moved away from Althusserian parameters. There are hints of dissatisfaction already in *Criticism and Ideology,* and I have found Paul Smith and Slavoj Žižek, in works cited in this chapter, helpful in articulating my own, similar reservations about structuralist Marxism. I use *Criticism and Ideology* primarily as an alternative to new historicist writing on ideology. For Eagleton's more recent thinking on ideology, see *Ideology: An Introduction* (New York: Verso, 1991).

20. Althusser's thinking on ideology is not everywhere as uniform or totalizing as it has been made to appear. For a view of the complexity of Althusser's thought, see Stuart Hall, "Signification, Representation, Ideology: Althusser and the Post-Structuralist Debates," *Critical Studies in Mass Communication* 2 (June 1985): 91–114.

21. Smith, *Discerning the Subject,* 17.

22. Hodge and Kress, *Social Semiotics* (Ithaca: Cornell University Press, 1988), 106. Hodge and Kress's focus on "relations of power and solidarity" also underlies, though it is not meant to be identical to, my emphasis on power and love in Donne's poetry. For applications of social semiotics to literature, see also Hodge's *Literature as Discourse: Textual Strategies in English and History* (Baltimore: Johns Hopkins University Press, 1990).

23. Greenblatt, *Shakespearian Negotiations: The Circulation of Social Energy in Renaissance England* (Berkeley: University of California Press, 1988); Montrose, "Professing the Renaissance," 21.

24. Eagleton, *Criticism and Ideology,* 88.

25. Eagleton, *Criticism and Ideology,* 97.

26. Eagleton, *Criticism and Ideology,* 98.

27. Eagleton, *Criticism and Ideology,* 101.

28. On rhetoric, see also the conclusion of Eagleton's *Literary Theory* (Minneapolis: University of Minnesota Press, 1983). On formalism as something other than a bugbear, see Tony Bennett, *Formalism and Marxism* (London: Methuen, 1979).

29. Žižek, *The Sublime Object of Ideology* (New York and London: Verso, 1989), 43.

30. Žižek, *Sublime Object,* 43.

31. Carey, *John Donne: Life, Mind, and Art* (New York: Oxford University Press, 1981).

32. Bennett, "Texts in History: The Determinations of Readings and Their Texts," in Derek

Attridge, Geoff Bennington, and Robert Young, eds., *Post-structuralism and the Question of History* (Cambridge: Cambridge University Press, 1987), 70.

33. Marotti's account of the conditions of production, for example, is shaped from Bald's biography, Bateson's concept of metacommunication, and psychoanalytic models of behavior, among other things. For a critique of the "metaphysic of origin," see Bennett, "Texts in History," 68–70.

34. Compare Gadamer: "The idea of the original reader is full of unexamined idealisation" (*Truth and Method,* 263). Marotti's important work on authorship after the Donne book provides grounds for a critique of this metaphysics of origin. See "Shakespeare's Sonnets as Literary Property," in Harvey and Maus, *Soliciting Interpretation,* 143–73, and "John Donne, Author," *Journal of Medieval and Renaissance Studies* 19 (spring 1989): 69–82.

35. Fish, "Masculine Persuasive Force," 250.

36. In *Trials of Authorship,* Crewe distinguishes between a new historicist criticism as "romance" and his form of criticism as "satire." In the following pages I claim that nearly all of the "romantic" aspects of new historicist representation of the Renaissance cited by Crewe are pertinent to Donne's texts: "counterontological innovation, displacement, gender-reversal, theatricality, positional mobility, power-shifting, dispersal, and cosmic remodeling." At the same time, one could go to Donne and Donne criticism for signs of satire in Renaissance representation—again following Crewe, "Not only resistance to radical change and dissolution . . . but a discounting of them, accompanied by a complex problematic of relative immobility, bondage, repetition, and pain" (9). It is the contest between such representations that characterizes Donne's most powerful work.

37. Debora Kuller Shuger has described the dominant culture of Renaissance England as a strenuous process of constructing boundaries in *Habits of Thought in the English Renaissance: Religion, Politics, and the Dominant Culture* (Berkeley and Los Angeles: University of California Press, 1990).

38. The "ultimate formalism" described by Liu in "The Power of Formalism" is related to the bulimia Fish diagnoses in Donne. Fish's Donne is a monarch of textual power: "The object of his desire and of his abhorrence is not food, but words, and more specifically, the power words can exert. Whatever else Donne's poems are, they are preeminently occasions on which this power can be exercised" ("Masculine Persuasive Force," 223).

39. The first phrase is from Thomas M. Greene, "The Poetics of Discovery: A Reading of Donne's Elegy 19," *Yale Journal of Criticism* 2 (1989): 133; on Donne as an absolutist of the bedroom, see Jonathan Goldberg, *James I and the Politics of Literature: Jonson, Shakespeare, Donne and Their Contemporaries* (Baltimore: Johns Hopkins University Press, 1983).

40. On the "anxieties of masculinity," see Mark Breitenberg, *Anxious Masculinity in Early Modern England* (Cambridge: Cambridge University Press, 1996).

41. Fineman, *Shakespeare's Perjured Eye: The Invention of Poetic Subjectivity in the Sonnets* (Berkeley and Los Angeles: University of California Press, 1986).

42. Edward Pechter, "The New Historicism and Its Discontents: Politicizing Renaissance Drama," *PMLA* 102 (1987): 292–303; Liu, "The Power of Formalism."

43. Docherty's study is, I believe, seriously limited by its refusal to engage the critical tradition on Donne except by way of a dismissive preface. In doing so, he inevitably reifies the Donne he wishes to undo, discovering him in deconstruction instead of losing him to the history of interpretation. The last phrase is a near-quotation from Mary Nyquist's brilliant essay, "Fallen Differences, Phallogocentric Discourses: Losing *Paradise Lost* to History," in Attridge, Bennington, and Young, *Post-structuralism and the Question of History,* p. 234.

44. Anthony Low, *The Reinvention of Love: Poetry, Politics and Culture from Sidney to Milton* (Cambridge: Cambridge University Press, 1993), 60.

45. Low, *Reinvention of Love,* 60, 33.

46. Smith explains that his use of the term "discern" derives from conflation and play upon "two rarely used English verbs—'*to cern*' [to accept an inheritance or a patrimony] and '*to cerne*' [to encircle or to enclose]," and thus his aim is to challenge inherited definitions of the unified sovereign subject, on the one hand, and the limiting constructions of the poststructuralist subject, on the other (*Discerning the Subject,* xxx).

Chapter 1

1. Montrose, "The Poetics and Politics of Culture," in H. Aram Veeser, ed., *The New Historicism* (London and New York: Routledge, 1989), 21. Such a formulation of the subject has been challenged both by critics of new historicism (including a good number of critically reflective new historicists) and by literary theorists. New historicism has been labelled Marxist, capitalist, formalist, American, antifeminist, leftist, and rightist, but a common theme of criticism has to do with what is perceived as an emphasis on subjection at the expense of agency. In his comprehensive survey of the concept of the subject Paul Smith has critiqued a variety of totalizing theories of the subject in terms relevant to the new historicism debate. Smith locates within poststructuralism several footholds for a theory of resistance and agency, including prominently its emphasis on the kinds of ideological gaps and fissures I have located in some of Donne's poetry. More broadly, I share with Smith an understanding of subjectification as a *process,* one that, in Smith's words, "is always engaged in a multiform and contradictory series of instances of the 'subject.'" Smith, *Discerning the Subject* (Minneapolis: University of Minnesota Press, 1988), 22.

2. King, *English Reformation Literature: The Tudor Origins of the Protestant Tradition* (Princeton: Princeton University Press, 1982), 84.

3. Weimann, " 'Bifold Authority' in Reformation Discourse: Authorization, Representation, and Early Modern 'Meaning,' " in Jane L. Smarr, ed., *Historical Criticism and the Challenge of Theory* (Urbana: University of Illinois Press, 1993), 168. See also Weimann, *Authority and Representation in Early Modern Discourse,* ed. David Hillman (Baltimore and London: Johns Hopkins University Press, 1996) and Christopher Hill, "The Problem of Authority," in *Collected Essays of Christopher Hill,* Vol. 2: *Religion and Politics in Seventeenth-Century England* (Amherst: University of Massachusetts Press, 1986), 37–50.

4. As noted in the Introduction, I borrow this notion of the literary text as a "*production* of ideology, for which the analogy of a dramatic production is in some ways appropriate," from Terry Eagleton, *Criticism and Ideology: A Study in Marxist Literary Theory* (1976; London: Verso, 1978), 64 ff.

5. Paul de Man, *Allegories of Reading: Figural Language in Rousseau, Nietzche, Rilke, and Proust* (New Haven, Conn.: Yale University Press, 1979), 17.

6. For reviews and critiques of new historicism's appropriation of anthropology, see Vincent P. Pecora, "The Limits of Local Knowledge," in Veeser, *The New Historicism,* 243–76 and Aletta Biersack, "Local Knowledge, Local History: Geertz and Beyond," in Lynn Hunt, ed., *The New Cultural History* (Berkeley and Los Angeles: University of California Press, 1989), 72–96.

7. Dollimore, *Radical Tragedy: Religion, Ideology and Power in the Drama of Shakespeare and His Contemporaries* (Chicago: University of Chicago Press, 1984). My study focuses on Donne, and I do not suggest anything like uniformity in the verse satirists. Clearly the oppositional status and character of these writers is greatly varied—from Marston's wild and sometimes obscene interrogations to Joseph Hall's measured couplets infused with an unusual combination of neoclassical literary theory and Spenserian nostalgia, to mention just two possible poles.

8. Marotti, "John Donne and the Rewards of Patronage," in Guy Fitch Lytle and Stephen Orgel, eds., *Patronage in the Renaissance* (Princeton: Princeton University Press, 1981), 207–34, and *John Donne: Coterie Poet* (Madison: University of Wisconsin Press, 1986); Helgerson,

Self-Crowned Laureates: Spenser, Jonson, Milton and the Literary System (Berkeley and Los Angeles: University of California Press, 1983).

9. Newton, "Donne the Satirist," *Texas Studies in Literature and Language* 16 (1974): 445. Examples of reading the Satires as a sequence include M. Thomas Hester, " 'Zeal' as Satire: The Decorum of Donne's *Satyres*," *Genre* 10 (1977): 173–94; Emory Elliott, "The Narrative and Allusive Unity of Donne's *Satyres*," *Journal of English and German Philology* 75 (1976): 106–16. Studies of Donne's satiric persona include A. F. Bellette, "The Originality of Donne's *Satires*," *University of Toronto Quarterly* 44 (1975): 130–40; John R. Lauritsen, "Donne's *Satyres:* The Drama of Self-Discovery," *SEL* 16 (1976): 117–30; and Howard Erskine-Hill, "Courtiers out of Horace," in A. J. Smith, ed., *John Donne: Essays in Celebration* (London: Methuen, 1972), 273–307. The fullest historico-generic study is M. Thomas Hester, *Kind Pitty and Brave Scorn: John Donne's Satyres* (Durham, N.C.: Duke University Press, 1982).

10. On the seventeenth-century construction of Donne as an author, see Arthur Marotti, "John Donne, Author," *Journal of Medieval and Renaissance Studies* 19 (spring 1989): 69–82.

11. Liu, "The Power of Formalism: The New Historicism," *ELH* 56 (winter 1989): 721–71. In a 1989 MLA talk ("A Historian Looks at New Historicism: What's So Historical about It?") Martha Howell contrasted the text-based, interpretative strategy of new historicists with the historian's interest in what texts *do*. This contrast, and the anxiety it generates, is at the center of Donne's Satires.

12. Liu, "Power of Formalism," 752.

13. LaCapra, *History and Criticism* (Ithaca: Cornell University Press, 1985), 140.

14. Liu, "Power of Formalism," 751, 752, 745.

15. Bateson is quoted in Marotti, *John Donne: Coterie Poet*, 20. Further references to Marotti's book appear within my text.

16. Donne explicitly develops this fantasy in some of his verse and prose letters. In a verse letter to Wotton he writes, "Sir, more then kisses, letters mingle Soules." Donne, *The Satires, Epigrams, and Verse Letters,* ed. W. Milgate (Oxford: Clarendon Press, 1967), 71, l. 1. In a prose letter to Sir Henry Goodyer, he defines the letter as "a kind of extasie, and a departure and suspension of the soul, wch doth then communicate it self to two bodies"; letters function as "sacraments" in "my second religion, friendship." Donne, *Letters to Severall Persons of Honour,* ed. M. Thomas Hester (1651; facsimile rpt. Delmar, N.Y.: Scolar, 1977), 11, 85. Like some of the best-known lyrics, many of Donne's prose letters self-consciously construct a timeless fantasy world in the midst of feverish negotiations for preferment. See also my " 'Friendships Sacraments': John Donne's Familiar Letters," *Studies in Philology* 78 (fall 1981): 409–25.

17. Hodge and Kress, *Social Semiotics* (Ithaca: Cornell University Press, 1988), 6.

18. Strier, *Resistant Structures: Particularity, Radicalism, and Renaissance Texts* (Berkeley and Los Angeles: University of California Press, 1995).

19. Strier, *Resistant Structures*, 2.

20. Strier, *Resistant Structures*, 8.

21. See *Resistant Structures*, 8–9, where Strier defends himself against a form of pluralism, criticized by W. J. T. Mitchell, that sets the critic "above the fray." Strier also advocates close reading of historical documents, an activity he pursues in "The Root and Branch Petition and the Grand Remonstrance: From Diagnosis to Operation," in David L. Smith, Richard Strier, and David Bevington, eds., *The Theatrical City: Culture, Theatre, and Literature in London, 1576–1649* (Cambridge: Cambridge University Press, 1995). My point about a literary textual practice has to do with the shifting position of the reading subject, not with the object of the reading.

22. Strier, *Resistant Structures,* 121.

23. Strier, *Resistant Structures,* 119.

24. In so characterizing the ideological component in the Satires and other poems, I draw, of course, upon post-Althusserian, materialist concepts of ideology discussed in the Introduction, summarized by Jonathan Dollimore as "the condition and grounds of consciousness itself."

Radical Tragedy, 9. Dollimore is certainly right, however, in arguing that a "cognitive" notion of ideology—ideology as "a set of false beliefs capable of correction by perceiving properly" (9)—is "inextricably related" to the materialist version in the Renaissance and that this cognitive view "was indispensable in giving access . . . to the more complex material formulations" (10). Stuart Hall has, to my mind, developed the most supple approach to ideology through his focus on ideological struggle:

> The notion of *the* dominant ideology and *the* subordinated ideology is an inadequate way of representing the complex interplay of different ideological discourses in any modern developed society. Nor is the terrain of ideology constituted as a field of mutually exclusive and internally self-sustaining discursive chains. They contest one another, often drawing on a common, shared repertoire of concepts, rearticulating and disarticulating them within different systems of difference or equivalence.

Hall, "Signification, Representation, Ideology: Althusser and the Post-structuralist Debates," *Critical Studies in Mass Communication* 2 (June 1985): 104. For a useful discussion of Hall's place in the debate over ideology, see Peter Erickson, *Rewriting Shakespeare, Rewriting Ourselves* (Berkeley and Los Angeles: University of California Press, 1991), 17–20.

25. Satire 1, line 3. All references to the Satires are from the Milgate edition.

26. See, for example, the articles by Lauritsen and Bellette. Lauritsen and John Shawcross see the poem as a dialogue of one (see notes in Shawcross's edition of *The Complete Poetry of John Donne* [New York: Anchor Books, 1967]). See also Yvonne Shikany Eddy and Daniel P. Jaeckle, "Donne's 'Satyre I': The Influence of Persius's 'Satire III,' " *SEL* 21 (winter 1981): 111–22.

27. Hester, *John Donne's Satyres,* 20.

28. Marotti argues that Donne rejects only the smooth fantasies of Petrarchism in Satire 2 (*Coterie Poet,* 41). In Satire 1 Donne identifies himself as coarsely attired when "with the Muses I conferre" (l. 47), suggesting the rough and ready "satyr" of Elizabethan satire, so there may be an attempt—parallel to the opposition between his clothing and the humorist's—to distinguish satire from "giddie" poetry.

29. Hester, *John Donne's Satyres,* 18.

30. Milgate confuses me in the explanation for his preferring 1633's "depart'st from mee" to "from hence," found in manuscripts W, O'F, H49, Dob, and Q; "*both* satirist and 'humorist,' " says Milgate, "are departing 'hence' or 'from hence'—i.e., from the poet's chamber into the street; 'from mee' is dramatically more appropriate, more exact, and less harsh" (p. 124). "From mee" *is* better, I think, but only if the speaker of "Come, lets goe" is the humorist, since then the satirist's leaving would be in doubt until the lines (65–66) on his conscience.

31. John Shawcross has challenged the dating of "Satire II" during the Lincoln's Inn days as part of a broader argument for removing the Satires from specific occasions and seeing them instead as retrospective poems, "the products of a thoughtful mind viewing some of the evils of this world." See Shawcross, " 'All Attest His Writs Canonical': The Texts, Meaning and Evaluation of Donne's Satires," in Peter A. Fiore, ed., *Just So Much Honor* (University Park: Pennsylvania State University Press, 1972), 269. Although my reading of the Satires differs sharply from Shawcross's, I am indebted to his comments on an early version of this section.

32. Quoted in Philip J. Finkelpearl, *John Marston of the Middle Temple* (Cambridge: Harvard University Press, 1969), 9.

33. Wilfred R. Prest, *The Inns of Court under Elizabeth I and the Early Stuarts, 1590–1640* (Totowa, N.J.: Rowman & Littlefield, 1972), 41.

34. On "prodigality" and careerism, see Helgerson, *The Elizabethan Prodigals* (Berkeley: University of California Press, 1977). Donne's social and literary activities at the Inns are treated in David Novarr, *The Disinterred Muse: Donne's Texts and Contexts* (Ithaca: Cornell University Press, 1980), 65–84. On the possible relationship between the split at the Inns and developing conflict between Parliament and the Court, see Prest, *The Inns of Court,* 220ff.

35. Whigham, *Ambition and Privilege: The Social Tropes of Elizabethan Courtesy Theory* (Berkeley and Los Angeles: University of California Press, 1984).

36. Whigham, *Ambition and Privilege,* 21–22.

37. Whigham, *Ambition and Privilege,* 21.

38. Marotti argues that in Satire 2 Donne expresses "an aversion to various forms of poetry, an attitude consistent with the harshly unpoetic stance of the formal satirist" (*Coterie Poet,* 40–41). This view overlooks the rhetorical function of the devaluation of poetry, which seems to include satire, "witchcrafts charms" (l. 17).

39. On the trope of devaluation, see Whigham, *Ambition and Privilege,* 120–22. Hester offers a full appreciation of Donne's ironic stance towards the poets in *John Donne's Satyres,* 38–43.

40. See, for example, Joseph Hall, *Virgidemiarum Sixe Bookes,* Satire V. 2 in Arnold Davenport, ed. *The Poems of Joseph Hall* (Liverpool: Liverpool University Press, 1949.). Clayton D. Lein discusses "the strain of lost nobility" in "Theme and Structure in Donne's *Satire II,*" *Comparative Literature* 32 (1980): 130–50. Lawrence Stone notes that "the older nobility showed a surprising readiness both to develop new resources on their own estates and to take a prominent part in industrial, commercial, and colonizing projects." *The Crisis of the Aristocracy 1558–1641* (Oxford: Clarendon Press, 1965), 380.

41. Bouwsma, "Lawyers and Early Modern Culture," *American Historical Review* 78 (1973): 316.

42. H. J. C. Grierson, ed., *The Poems of John Donne* 2 vols. (Oxford: Clarendon Press, 1912), 2: 112. On "Donne and the Ancient Catholic Nobility," see Dennis Flynn, *English Literary Renaissance* 19 (autumn 1989): 305–23 and his "Donne and a *Female* Coterie," *LIT: Literature, Interpretation, Theory* 1 (1989): 127–36. On Donne's Catholicism and the Satires, see also Howard Erskine-Hill, "Courtiers out of Horace," in A. J. Smith, ed., *John Donne: Essays in Celebration* (London: Methuen, 1972), 273–307, and Hester, *John Donne's Satyres,* passim.

43. Strier, *Resistant Structures,* 138.

44. I would also note that Elegy 6 (titled "Recusancy" by Helen Gardner) playfully uses the word "Recusant" to refer to Catholics. It is interesting that this poem also contains an extended passage on a stream, which calmly flows from the spring but "rusheth violently" at the end (ll. 21–34).

45. On this topic see my " 'The secrecy of man': Recusant Discourse and the Elizabethan Subject," *English Literary Renaissance* 19 (autumn 1989): 272–90.

46. Chief Justice Popham's reply to Robert Southwell's defense of mental reservation is exemplary: "if this doctrine should be allowed, it would supplant all justice, for we are men, and no Gods, and can judge but according to their outward actions and speeches, and not according to their secret and inward intentions." Quoted in Pierre Janelle, *Robert Southwell the Writer* (London: Sheed and Ward, 1935). On this point see also Carol Z. Weiner, "The Beleaguered Isle: A Study of Elizabethan and Early Jacobean Anti-Catholicism," *Past and Present* 51 (May 1971): 27–62 and, more recently, Katherine Eisaman Maus, *Inwardness and Theater in the English Renaissance* (Chicago: University of Chicago Press, 1995), especially chap. 2.

47. Docherty, *John Donne, Undone* (London: Methuen, 1986), 201.

48. Strier, *Resistant Structures,* 121. "Impossible Radicalism I" is Strier's ironic title for Essay 6 in his book.

49. "I do not see any criticism of or fetter on the autonomous self here" (Strier, *Resistant Structures,* 163).

50. Strier, *Resistant Structures,* 123.

51. Strier, *Resistant Structures,* 8, 121.

52. I say "seems" because Strier also admits a degree of nervousness and conflict "about its theological radicalism" (*Resistant Structures,* 146).

53. Carey, *John Donne: Life, Mind, and Art* (New York: Oxford University Press, 1981), 28; Docherty, *John Donne, Undone,* 113.

54. Joshua Scodel has also noted the phallocentrism of Donne's quest in "The Medium Is the Message: Donne's 'Satire 3,' 'To Sir Henry Wotton ("Sir, more then kisses"),' and the Ideologies of the Mean," *Modern Philology* 90 (1993): 492–93. Strier also assumes the masculine character of the seeker and suggestively relates Donne's representations of difficulties with religious choice and commitment to "male anxieties about marriage" (139).

55. With respect to this issue of gender and desire in the poem, Ernest Gilman's comments on the gender of Truth are also suggestive. Donne, he argues, seems about to describe an image of Truth as, perhaps, "the kind of personified *Verita* described in Ripa's *Iconologia. . . .* an indomitable nude . . . [that] would convincingly replace the procession of ragged and sullen mistresses who had earlier in the poem embodied the choice of available religions. . . . But the iconographic potential of Donne's 'Truth' fades as he urges us on to the rigors of the climb itself. . . . the female Truth has now, at the end of the quest, become vaguely masculine by virtue of the pun on 'Sunne' and the association of this hill with the Psalmist's 'holy hill of Zion' on which, he says, 'have I set my King' " (Gilman, " 'To adore, or scorne an image': Donne and the Iconoclastic Controversy," *John Donne Journal* 5 [1986]: 63–64). Gilman relates this evocation and retraction of the image of truth to the movement between adoration and scorn in line 76. I would maintain that the gender confusion also figures the subject split by his desire of the Other, the Truth.

My discussion of Satire 3 thus far has drawn on some Lacanian themes related to his notion of the Other. In her often-cited introduction to *Feminine Sexuality: Jacques Lacan and the Ecole Freudienne* (New York: Norton, 1982), Jacqueline Rose notes that woman, truth, and the Lacanian Other can overlap in a manner pertinent to Donne's quest for true religion: "As negative to the man, woman becomes a total object of fantasy (or an object of total fantasy), elevated into the place of the Other and made to stand for its truth. Since the place of the Other is also the place of God, this is the ultimate form of mystification" (50). Donne's turns from the straight allegory of "our Mistresse" to the female truth to the paradoxical "Sunne, dazling, yet plaine to'all eyes" (l. 88), foreground this process of mystification. On this aspect of Lacan's notion of the Other I have found particularly useful Anika Lemaire, *Jacques Lacan* (New York: Routledge, 1977), 157, 169–75; and Kaja Silverman, *The Subject of Semiotics* (New York: Oxford University Press, 1983), chap. 4.

56. Robert C. Elliott, *The Power of Satire: Magic, Ritual, Art* (Princeton: Princeton University Press, 1960), 135.

57. Strier, *Resistant Structures,* 148, 149.

58. Strier, *Resistant Structures,* 148–51.

59. Strier, *Resistant Structures,* 164. I have quoted this phrase somewhat out of context. What Strier says, in concluding his essay, follows: "In terms of intellectual history, Donne can be seen to have shown, in the strongest parts of the third Satire, the perhaps surprising compatibility of three of the most radical notions of the European sixteenth-century; Erasmus's 'philosophy of Christ,' Castillio's vindication of doubt, and Luther's conception of conscience." But the overriding purpose of his essay is, of course, to strongly suggest Donne's affinity with these radical ideas in Satire 3.

60. Weimann, "Discourse, Ideology and the Crisis of Authority in Post-Reformation England," in *The Yearbook of Research in English and American Literature,* vol. 5 (Berlin, New York: De Gruyter, 1987), 136. Strier, *Resistant Structures,* 148.

61. Murray Rosten, *The Soul of Wit* (Oxford: Clarendon Press, 1974), 80.

62. This evocative line is quoted in Janelle, *Robert Southwell,* 81–82.

63. Margaret Ferguson, "Nashe's *The Unfortunate Traveller:* The 'Newes of the Maker' Game," *English Literary Renaissance* 11 (1981): 175. For an extended argument for such purposeful ambiguity, see Annabel Patterson, *Censorship and Interpretation: The Conditions*

of Writing and Reading in Early Modern England (Madison: University of Wisconsin Press, 1984), chap. 2.

64. Steven Mullaney, "Lying Like Truth: Riddle, Representation, and Treason in Renaissance England," *ELH* 47 (1980): 37, 41. John Bossy, a leading social historian of Elizabethan Catholicism, has noted a similar decentering tendency in the Jesuit practice of disguise, suggesting that "the danger was that the disguise would absorb the personality." See "The Character of Elizabethan Catholicism," *Past and Present* 21 (1962): 51–52.

65. See Carey, *John Donne: Life, Mind, and Art,* 26–30.

66. For a useful survey of Elizabethan writing on the problem of secular versus spiritual authority, see Stephen L. Collins, *From Divine Cosmos to Sovereign State: An Intellectual History of Consciousness and the Idea of Order in Renaissance England* (New York: Oxford University Press, 1989), esp. chap. 3. On Catholic loyalism, see Arnold Pritchard, *Catholic Loyalism in Elizabethan England* (Chapel Hill: University of North Carolina Press, 1979).

67. Bald's comment is in his edition of Southwell, *An Humble Supplication to Her Maiestie* (Cambridge: Cambridge University Press, 1953), 64. It is intriguing to think that Donne might have visited Southwell in the Tower of London. On this possibility, see Appendix III of Bald's edition. All references to the pamphlet are from this edition.

68. The problem of the relation between religious and political authority would be vigorously debated by English Catholics several years after Southwell's death, during the so-called Archpriest Controversy. See Pritchard, *Catholic Loyalism,* 192–201 and Peter Holmes, *Resistance and Compromise: The Political Thought of the Elizabethan Catholics* (Cambridge: Cambridge University Press, 1982), 186–204.

69. Weimann, *Authority and Representation,* 60.

70. I borrow this phrase from Weimann, who in turn takes the expression from Christopher Sutton: "Religion is become nothing lesse than Religion, to wit, a matter of meere talk: such politizing is there on all parts, as a man cannot tell, who is who" (quoted in Weimann, *Authority and Representation,* 64).

71. On Protestant theory of state power in relation to this passage, see Strier, *Resistant Structures,* 157–59.

72. Collins, *From Divine Cosmos,* 93. Another revealing comparison might be made between Donne and Robert Persons, a.k.a. R. Doleman. In *A Conference about the Next Succession to the Crown of England* (1594) "Doleman," discussing the relationship of spiritual to secular powers, insists that "there is but one only Religion, that can be found among Christians" but that the king's power is "a power delegate, or a power by Commission from the Commonwealth" (quoted in Collins, *From Divine Cosmos,* 104); thus, the argument runs, believers in the one true religion can replace the king. Donne introduces no commonwealth, a concept also important to Hooker, into his scheme of power. In placing his emphasis on the individual soul rather than the body politic, Donne seems to be using the notion of the "individual" both to evade and focus "anomalies" (Collins's term) in Elizabethan political theory. Again, this move distinguishes him from the radical Persons, as a similar move distinguishes a new historicist investigation from, say, the more "vulgar marxist" analysis of Christopher Hill. James Holstun is suggestive on this aspect of new historicism in "Ranting at the New Historicism," *English Literary Renaissance* 19 (spring 1990): 203–9.

73. Strier, *Resistant Structures,* 159, 158.

74. Strier, *Resistant Structures,* 159.

75. Catherine Belsey, *The Subject of Tragedy: Identity and Difference in Renaissance Drama* (London: Methuen, 1985), 110.

76. Strier has discussed a perhaps related contradiction in Donne's Holy Sonnets concerning grace and human effort in "John Donne Awry and Squint: The 'Holy Sonnets,' 1608–1610," *Modern Philology* 86 (1989): 357–84.

77. Richard Bancroft's *A Sermon Preached at Paul's Cross* (1588) is quoted by Weimann, " 'Bi-fold Authority'," 179.

78. Weimann, " 'Bifold Authority,' " 168. Bancroft, it should be noted, advocates "the meane . . . betwixt both these extremities of trieng nothing and curious trieng of all things" (quoted in Weimann, " 'Bi-fold Authority,' " 180). This is not Donne's solution; though the recommendation to know the boundaries of power might be read as a gesture in the direction of moderation, the poem seems overwhelmingly to promote the idea that radical doubt will result in blessedness. *How* this happens is unclear. Scodel argues that Donne creates a mean of skeptical doubt in "The Medium Is the Message."

79. Strier, *Resistant Structures,* 129. Strier's reading of the stream and flower images differs sharply from mine; he eliminates any disparity between active seeking and passive dwelling by equating Donne's doubt with "dwelling": dwelling "is something one consciously does" (160)—though, of course, flowers are not concious. Indeed, as I have argued, the satire pivots on such contradictions and conundrums in the great hill of truth passage.

80. On the uses and limitations of mystification as a definition of ideology, see Michele Barrett, *The Politics of Truth: From Marx to Foucault* (Stanford: Stanford University Press, 1991).

81. Strier, *Resistant Structures,* 162.

82. Strier, *Resistant Structures,* 161.

83. Louis Althusser, *Lenin and Philosophy and Other Essays* (New York: Monthly Review Press, 1971), 162.

84. It has become standard to point, as Frank Lentricchia does, to Greenblatt's epilogue to *Renaissance Self-Fashioning* as evidence of a closet liberal individualism at the core of the new historicist project (Lentricchia, "Foucault's Legacy: A New Historicism?" in Veeser, *The New Historicism,* 238). What is not mentioned is Greenblatt's discontent with both alternatives—the centered *and* the decentered self. This discomforting ambivalence, it seems to me, is closer to Donne's position.

85. Victor Turner, *The Ritual Process: Structure and Anti-Structure* (Ithaca: Cornell University Press, 1969); Jonathan Crewe, *Trials of Authorship: Anterior Forms and Poetic Reconstruction from Wyatt to Shakespeare* (Berkeley and Los Angeles: University of California Press, 1990), 8–9.

86. See Turner, "Comments and Conclusions," in Barbara Babcock, ed., *The Reversible World: Symbolic Inversion in Art and Society* (Ithaca: Cornell University Press, 1978), 282. The importation of the ritual notion of liminality into literary studies has been critiqued by Richard F. Hardin, " 'Ritual' in Recent Criticism: The Elusive Sense of Community," *PMLA* 98 (1983): esp. 851–52. See also Turner's remarks on this issue in "Comments and Conclusions," 286–87. For a discussion of other "liminal" features of Donne's satirist, see my "Style and Self in Donne's Satires," *Texas Studies in Literature and Language* 24 (summer 1982): 170 ff.

87. In describing the Satires as "productions of ideology" I follow Eagleton's account of the relationship between ideology and the literary text in *Criticism and Ideology,* esp. chap. 3.

88. New historicism's valorization of play has been attacked by Lentricchia as "rigorously aesthetic" ("Foucault's Legacy," 240). My characterization of Donne is probably open to the same charge, although the Renaissance seems to have valorized certain forms of play as well. In any case my point here is that the form of play is operative in new historicist discourse itself. Montrose, "*A Midsummer Night's Dream* and the Shaping Fantasies of Elizabethan Culture: Gender, Power, Form" in Margaret W. Ferguson, Maureen Quilligan, and Nancy Vickers, eds., *Rewriting the Renaissance: The Discourses of Sexual Difference in Early Modern Europe* (Chicago: University of Chicago Press, 1986), 65–87. Crewe has argued that new historicism writes the Renaissance as romance (*Trials of Authorship,* 7–10), but I find its texts, and the dialogical subject produced by them, closer to the carnivalesque Menippean satire recently discussed by Dominick LaCapra as a new model for historical writing. See Dominick LaCapra, *Rethinking Intellectual History:*

Texts, Contexts, Language (Ithaca, N.Y.: Cornell University Press, 1983), 298 ff. and Lloyd S. Kramer, "Literature, Criticism, and Historical Imagination: The Literary Challenge of Hayden White and Dominick LaCapra," in Hunt, *The New Cultural History,* 120–22.

89. Liu, "Power of Formalism," 733.

90. Liu, "Power of Formalism," 732.

91. Milgate reads these lines as "a final hit at the times. . . . no one can accuse the satirist of an offence against any law . . . for all he says is true" (139). But Newton is surely also correct in feeling the effect of the lines to be that of "an evasive maneuver which suggests that he has not really said anything serious at all" ("Donne the Satirist," 434), a reading that also harmonizes with courtly strategies of self-deprecation discussed by Whigham in *Ambition and Privilege.*

92. Liu, "Power of Formalism," 756.

93. See Hester, *John Donne's Satyres,* chap. 4; Erskine-Hill, "Courtiers out of Horace," 282–83.

94. See Bald, *John Donne: A Life* (Oxford: Clarendon Press, 1970), 94.

95. Michel Foucault, *The History of Sexuality,* Volume 1: *An Introduction,* trans. Robert Hurley (New York: Vintage, 1980), 92–93. See also pp. 95–96, where Foucault discusses resistance *within* power).

96. Marotti, *Coterie Poet,* 118.

97. Bossy has commented on "the time-honored fiction of evil counsellors" as a device used by conservative Catholic gentry to deflect criticism from the queen yet also explain her interference in their lives ("Elizabethan Catholicism," 43).

98. On the function of sodomy in satirical discourse of the Renaissance, see Gregory W. Bredbeck, *Sodomy and Interpretation: Marlowe to Milton* (Ithaca: Cornell University Press, 1991), 33–40.

99. See Dollimore, *Radical Tragedy,* chap. 5. Marotti comments on the overlapping of secular and divine courts in Donne's religious poetry, particularly "A Litanie," in *Coterie Poet,* 250.

100. Donne's rhetoric of powerlessness and recusancy, a rhetoric I have also associated with new historicism, at times resembles what Foucault calls the "subjected sovereignty" of humanism: "By humanism I mean the totality of discourse through which Western man is told: 'Even though you don't exercise power you can still be a ruler.' " Foucault's statement in *Language, Counter-Memory, Practice* is quoted by Barrett, *The Politics of Truth,* 147.

101. Weimann, *Authority and Representation,* 67. Weimann's work offers an account of the historical origins of what Foucault called the "politics of truth": "Each society has its regime of truth, its 'general politics' of truth: that is, the types of discourse which it accepts and makes function as true; the mechanisms and instances which enable one to distinguish true and false statements, the means by which each is sanctioned; the techniques and procedures accorded value in the acquisition of truth; the status of those who are charged with saying what counts as true." Michel Foucault, *Power/Knowledge: Selected Interviews and Other Writings, 1972–1977,* ed. Colin Gordon (New York: Pantheon, 1980), 131. The Satires engage many of these questions in the context of *conflicting* regimes of truth produced in the wake of the Reformation.

102. Eagleton, *Criticism and Ideology,* 98.

Chapter 2

1. Dayton Haskin, "New Historical Contexts for Appraising the Donne Revival from A. B. Grosart to Charles Eliot Norton," *ELH* 56 (1989): 869–95. Haskin brilliantly demonstrates how the Revivalists' effacement of the biographical and historical contexts of Donne's writing is deeply political.

2. On the Renaissance move toward an autonomous status for literature, see David Quint, *Origin and Originality in Renaissance Literature: Versions of the Source* (New Haven: Yale University Press, 1983).

3. Marotti, "John Donne and the Rewards of Patronage," in Guy Fitch Lytle and Stephen Orgel, eds., *Patronage in the Renaissance* (Princeton: Princeton University Press, 1981), 213, 220.

4. Marotti, *John Donne: Coterie Poet* (Madison: University of Wisconsin Press, 1986), 165.

5. Hodge and Kress, *Social Semiotics* (Ithaca: Cornell University Press, 1988), 5, 6.

6. Docherty, *John Donne, Undone* (London and New York: Methuen, 1986), 9. Marotti's coterie strikes me as an instance of what Alan Liu terms "person-concept localisms," whereby "local communities become magnified versions of the 'I' in its intersubjective relations." Liu, "Local Transcendence: Cultural Criticism, Postmodernism, and the Romanticism of Detail," *Representations* 32 (fall 1990): 111. The problem, Liu argues, is that "the regional community [here the courtly coterie system] functions as if it were a solidarity of one, as if, in other words, it were immanent with identity" (94).

7. Here I am, of course, invoking the term used by Eve Kosofsky Sedgwick in *Between Men: English Literature and Male Homosocial Desire* (New York: Columbia University Press, 1985).

8. Thomas Laqueur, *Making Sex: Body and Gender from the Greeks to Freud* (Cambridge: Harvard University Press, 1990). See also Stephen Greenblatt's well-known essay on "Fiction and Friction" in *Shakespearean Negotiations: The Circulation of Social Energy in Renaissance England* (Berkeley and Los Angeles: University of California Press, 1988), 66–93.

9. Marotti, "Rewards of Patronage," 220–21; my emphasis.

10. Goldberg, *James I and the Politics of Literature: Jonson, Shakespeare, Donne, and Their Contemporaries* (Baltimore: Johns Hopkins University Press, 1983), xiv, 55, 107, 219.

11. Patterson, "Talking about Power," *John Donne Journal* 2 (1983): 91–106; Alan Sinfield, "Power and Ideology: An Outline Theory and Sidney's *Arcadia*," *ELH* 52 (1985): 259–77; reprinted in *Faultlines: Cultural Materialism and the Politics of Dissident Reading* (Berkeley: University of California Press, 1992), 80–94; David Norbrook, "The Monarch of Wit and the Republic of Letters," in Elizabeth D. Harvey and Katharine Eisaman Maus, eds., *Soliciting Interpretation: Literary Theory and Seventeenth-Century English Poetry* (Chicago: University of Chicago Press, 1990), 3–36. Norbrook points out that "Donne's king cannot stand by himself: as the recurrent sexual puns on that word indicate, he is incomplete without some kind of mutual relationship" (15). Patterson's considered counterstatement to Goldberg's position is in *Censorship and Interpretation: The Conditions of Writing and Reading in Early Modern England* (Madison: University of Wisconsin Press, 1984), where she persuasively argues for a Renaissance "hermeneutics of censorship" that enabled a literary practice of encoding through functional ambiguity. Although my argument explicitly tries to resist this kind of intentionalism, I admit at the outset that it is difficult, if not impossible, ever to do so and that I might be accused of having merely argued that a writer can intend to interrogate his own intention. On the other hand, the writer's (or reader's) mastery of intention can never be assumed to be complete, nor do the intentions of reader and writer necessarily match. Indeed, Donne seems to be struggling or playing games with intentionality in a fair number of the poems discussed in this chapter.

12. Sinfield, *Faultlines*, 94.

13. In support of this approach, I would add that the Renaissance conception of reading as a practice, as an action in which the reader plays a role in the production of meaning, can also promote a shifting relationship between literature and power. Renaissance reading as practice has been brilliantly surveyed and analyzed by Victoria Kahn, *Rhetoric, Prudence, and Skepticism in the Renaissance* (Ithaca: Cornell University Press, 1985).

14. Arnold Stein, *John Donne's Lyrics: The Eloquence of Action* (Minneapolis: University of Minnesota Press, 1962), 106. In what follows I elaborate Stein's notion of "intellectual pleasure" under the influence of Roland Barthes's well-known distinction between *plaisir* and *jouissance* in *The Pleasure of the Text*. Barthes writes that the "text of *jouissance* . . . causes the historical,

cultural, psychological foundations of the reader to vacillate," and I will argue for a similarly disruptive force generated by reading Donne. See Barthes, *The Pleasure of the Text,* trans. Richard Miller (New York: Hill and Wang, 1975), 25. For a recent and suggestive meditation on the *plaisir/jouissance* distinction, see Jane Gallop, *Thinking through the Body* (New York: Columbia University Press, 1988), 119–24.

15. Barbara Babcock, ed., *The Reversible World: Symbolic Inversion in Art and Society* (Ithaca: Cornell University Press, 1978), 14.

16. Victor Turner, "Comments and Conclusions," in Babcock, *The Reversible World,* 282. On liminality in ritual, see Turner, *The Ritual Process: Structure and Anti-Structure* (Chicago: Aldine, 1969). For a critical discussion of the application of the concept of liminality to literature, see Richard F. Hardin, " 'Ritual' in Recent Criticism: The Elusive Sense of Community," *PMLA* 98 (1983): esp. 851–52.

17. Hodge and Kress, *Social Semiotics,* 78.

18. Laqueur, *Making Sex,* 26.

19. Laqueur, *Making Sex,* 124, 128.

20. Louis Montrose, "The Elizabethan Subject and the Spenserian Text," in *Literary Theory/Renaissance Texts,* ed. Patricia Parker and David Quint (Baltimore: Johns Hopkins University Press, 1986), 307, and "*A Midsummer Night's Dream* and the Shaping Fantasies of Elizabethan Culture: Gender, Power, Form," in Margaret W. Ferguson, Maureen Quilligan, and Nancy J. Vickers, eds., *Rewriting the Renaissance: The Discourses of Sexual Difference in Early Modern Europe* (Chicago: University of Chicago Press, 1986), 86.

21. Harth, *Ideology and Culture in Seventeenth-Century France* (Ithaca: Cornell University Press, 1983), 30–31.

22. Stein (*John Donne's Lyrics,* 117–18) suggestively discusses Donne's play with additional religious and philosophical materials, notably the idea of "indifferent" matters in religion and the Stoic notion of *adiaphora.*

23. On the importance of reader response in Renaissance paradox, see A. E. Malloch, "Techniques and Function of Renaissance Paradox," *Studies in Philology* 53 (1956): 191–203; and Rosalie Colie, *Paradoxia Epidemica: The Renaissance Tradition of Paradox* (Princeton: Princeton University Press, 1966), passim.

24. See, for example, Marotti, *Coterie Poet,* 71–82; Clark Hulse, "Stella's Wit: Penelope Rich as Reader of Sidney's Sonnets," in *Rewriting the Renaissance,* 272–86; and, on Petrarchism, Ann Rosalind Jones and Peter Stallybrass, "The Politics of *Astrophil and Stella,*" *Studies in English Literature* 24 (winter 1984): 51–68.

25. On the political implications of Petrarchism, see Marotti, " 'Love is not love': Elizabethan Sonnet Sequences and the Social Order," *ELH* 49 (summer 1982): 396–428; Jones and Stallybrass, "The Politics of *Astrophil and Stella,*"; and Patricia Parker, "Suspended Instruments: Lyric and Power in the Bower of Bliss," in Marjorie Garber, ed., *Cannibals, Witches, and Divorce: Estranging the Renaissance* (Baltimore: Johns Hopkins University Press, 1987), 21–39.

26. Stanley Fish, "Masculine Persuasive Force: Donne and Verbal Power," in *Soliciting Interpretation,* 250.

27. "The Indifferent," line 9, in John Donne, *The Elegies and the Songs and Sonnets,* ed. Helen Gardner (Oxford: Clarendon Press, 1965), 41. All references to this edition are hereafter noted by line number in my text.

28. On this point I am influenced by Janet Adelman, "Fantasies of Maternal Power in *Macbeth,*" in Garber, *Cannibals, Witches, and Divorce,* 90–121.

29. See Laqueur, *Making Sex,* 123–24. The long tradition of the heterosexual threat to manhood is brilliantly explored by James Grantham Turner, *One Flesh: Paradisal Marriage and Sexual Relations in the Age of Milton* (Oxford: Oxford University Press, 1987).

30. Marotti, *Coterie Poet,* 78.

31. This body of work is too voluminous to cite here, but for an overview of studies

pertinent to the problem of romantic love in Shakespeare, see Lynda E. Boose, "The Family in Shakespeare Studies; or—Studies in the Family of Shakespeareans; or—The Politics of Politics," *Renaissance Quarterly* 40 (1987): 707–42. Studies of Shakespeare that have influenced my thinking on Donne in this regard include Boose, "The Father and the Bride in Shakespeare," *PMLA* 97 (1982): 325–47; Peter Erickson, *Patriarchal Structures in Shakespeare's Drama* (Berkeley: University of California Press, 1985); Carol Cook, " 'The Sign and Semblance of Her Honor': Reading Gender Difference in *Much Ado about Nothing*," *PMLA* 101 (1986): 186–202; and especially, Janet Adelman, "Male Bonding in Shakespeare's Comedies," in Coppelia Kahn and Peter Erickson, eds., *Shakespeare's "Rough Magic"* (Newark: University of Delaware Press, 1985), 73–103.

32. On the "intersection and interplay" of structural and psychological determinants, see Valerie Traub, "Jewels, Statues, and Corpses: Containment of Female Erotic Power in Shakespeare's Plays," *Shakespeare Studies* 20 (1988): 215–38.

33. Clay Hunt, *Donne's Poetry: Essays in Literary Analysis* (New Haven: Yale University Press, 1954), 7.

34. On this point, see Lawrence Stone, *The Family, Sex, and Marriage in England, 1500–1800* (New York: Harper and Row, 1977), passim.

35. Goldberg explores the trope of "state secrets," including the politics of Donne's bedroom, in chapter 2 of *James I and the Politics of Literature.* Donne's love lyrics also evidence a particular concern with the arcana of sexual relations, whether they deconstruct such mystifications as do poems examined in this chapter, or reconstruct such mysteries as do poems treated in the next chapter.

36. Turner, "Comments and Conclusions," in Babcock, *The Reversible World,* 294.

37. Wilbur Sanders, *John Donne's Poetry* (Cambridge: Cambridge University Press, 1971), 54–55.

38. Sigmund Freud, "Three Essays on Sexuality," in *The Standard Edition of the Complete Psychological Works of Sigmund Freud,* ed. James Strachey 24 vols. (London: Hogarth Press, 1981), 7: 149, n. 1; hereafter cited as SE. William Kerrigan and Gordon Braden made this footnote the core of their brilliant overview of the Petrarchan tradition in *The Idea of the Renaissance* (Baltimore: Johns Hopkins University Press, 1989), 157–189. Freud also discusses indifference as one of the three opposites of love, in "Instincts and Their Vicissitudes," *SE* 14: 133–40.

39. Kerrigan and Braden, *The Idea of the Renaissance,* 176, 189.

40. Bergmann, *The Anatomy of Loving: The Story of Man's Quest to Know What Love Is* (New York: Columbia University Press, 1987), 179.

41. I owe this observation to my colleague Mark Bracher. See the concluding section of *The Four Fundamental Concepts of Psycho-Analysis,* ed. Jacques-Alain Miller, trans. Alan Sheridan (New York: Norton, 1977) and Bracher's discussion in *Lacan, Discourse, and Social Change: A Psychoanalytic Cultural Criticism* (Ithaca: Cornell University Press, 1993), 95–96.

42. On the unstated, unsettling character of *jouissance,* see Gallop's discussion of Barthes in *Thinking through the Body,* 121–24.

43. Dryden's statement, from his *Essay on Satire,* is quoted from Herbert J. C. Grierson, ed., *The Poems of John Donne* 2 vols. (1912; rpt. Oxford: Oxford University Press, 1968), 2: viii.

44. Donne's definition of paradox is quoted from Evelyn M. Simpson, *A Study of the Prose Works of John Donne* (Oxford: Clarendon Press, 1948), 316. For readings of "Confined Love" as paradox, see Michael McCanles, "Paradox in Donne," *Studies in the Renaissance* 13 (1966): 278–80; Carol Marks Sicherman, "The Mocking Voices of Donne and Marvell," *Bucknell Review* 17 (1969): 32–46; and Silvia Ruffo-Fiore, "Donne's 'Parody' of the Petrarchan Lady," *Comparative Literature Studies* 9 (1972): 392–406.

45. Ann Rosalind Jones, "Surprising Fame: Renaissance Gender Ideologies and Women's Lyric," in Nancy K. Miller, ed., *The Poetics of Gender* (Columbia: Columbia University Press, 1986), 76, 77. On the topic of women's speech, see also Catherine Belsey, *The Subject of Tragedy: Identity and Difference in Renaissance Drama* (London: Methuen, 1985), chap. 6.

46. See McCanles, "Paradox in Donne," 279.

47. On this feature of subversion, see Greenblatt's notorious formulation, which appeared first in "Invisible Bullets: Renaissance Authority and Its Subversion," *Glyph* 8 (1981): 40–61 and then in *Shakespearean Negotiations,* 21–65.

48. Joel Altman, *The Tudor Play of Mind: Rhetorical Inquiry and the Development of Elizabethan Drama* (Berkeley: University of California Press, 1978), 62.

49. See Ian Maclean, *The Renaissance Notion of Woman* (Cambridge: Cambridge University Press, 1980), chap. 3.

50. Greene, "The Poetics of Discovery: A Reading of Donne's Elegy 19," *Yale Journal of Criticism* 2 (1989): 135–36. I subscribe to the "working hypothesis" that controls Greene's reading: "One way to think about a poem or series of poems is to think of it as an attempt by an inchoate self, an unformed, indefinite subject, to formulate itself into being, into coherent selfhood" (129).

51. See, for example, Carey's reading in *Life, Mind & Art,* 104–8, and Achsah Guibbory's " 'Oh, Let Mee Not Serve So': The Politics of Love in Donne's *Elegies,* " *ELH* 57 (1990): 821–23. Guibbory argues convincingly that "Donne's poems embody strong anxiety about transgressions of hierarchical distinctions between the sexes" (826), although she does not discuss Elegy XIX in terms of such an anxiety.

52. Lacan distinguishes penis from phallus. For recent expositions of this aspect of his thought, particularly as it affects feminism, see Elizabeth Grosz, *Jacques Lacan: A Feminist Introduction* (London and New York: Routledge, 1990), 116–22; and Gallop, *Thinking through the Body,* 124–31. Grosz remarks, "It is during the identificatory blurring of self and other that (from the boy's point of view, at least), the penis becomes regarded as a 'detachable' organ. . . . The detachable penis, the penis that the mother once had, prefigures the function of the phallus. It produces the penis as an object of signification, rather than a biological organ" (117).

53. On this equivocal functioning of the penis as an object of signification (i.e., as the phallus), see Grosz, *Jacques Lacan: A Feminist Introduction,* 117.

54. Greene, "The Poetics of Discovery," 136.

55. Guibbory has recently re-read this and other misogynistic elegies as "strategies for reasserting male control in love," subversions of the Petrarchan ideology of Elizabeth's Court (" 'Oh, Let Mee Not Serve So,' " 819).

56. Nancy J. Vickers, "Diana Described: Scattered Woman and Scattered Rhyme," in Elizabeth Abel, ed., *Writing and Sexual Difference* (Chicago: University of Chicago Press, 1982), 95–109.

57. On this point see Marotti, *Coterie Poet,* 50–51, who, mistakenly in my view, relates the economic motive to social climbing.

58. On Petrarch's "visionary poetics," see Joel Fineman, *Shakespeare's Perjured Eye: The Invention of Poetic Subjectivity in the Sonnets* (Berkeley and Los Angeles: University of California Press, 1986).

59. Annette Kuhn, *The Power of the Image: Essays on Representation and Sexuality* (London: Routledge, 1985), 39.

60. Gary Day suggests that "the voyeur's fascination with this object is that it satisfies him that someone else has suffered castration and not he"; again, the project of defining femininity is actually a defense of masculinity. Gary Day, "Looking at Women: Toward a Theory of Porn," in Gary Day and Clive Bloom, eds., *Perspectives on Pornography: Sexuality in Film and Literature* (New York: St. Martin's, 1988), 93.

61. On economics and love poetry, see Raymond Southall, *Literature and the Rise of Capitalism: Critical Essays Mainly on the Sixteenth and Seventeenth Centuries* (London: Lawrence and Wishart, 1973), 21–85. See also Anthony Low's suggestive piece, "Love and Science: Cultural Change in Donne's *Songs and Sonnets," Studies in the Literary Imagination* 22 (1989): 5–16.

62. Freud, of course, refers to homosexuality as an "inversion" in "Three Essays on Sexuality."

63. Gardner, ed., *Elegies and Songs and Sonnets,* xlvi; Grierson, ed., *The Poems of John Donne,* 2: 91; John T. Shawcross, ed., *The Complete Poetry of John Donne* (Garden City, N.Y.: Anchor Books, 1967). Shawcross prints the poem with the elegies, while Grierson places it alone, as an "Heroicall Epistle."

64. Holstun, " 'Will You Rent Our Ancient Love Asunder?': Lesbian Elegy in Donne, Marvell, and Milton," *ELH* 54 (1988): 838; Harvey, "Ventriloquizing Sappho: Ovid, Donne, and the Erotics of the Feminine Voice," *Criticism* (spring 1989): 129, 131.

65. Mueller, "Troping Utopia: Donne's Brief for Lesbianism," in James Grantham Turner, ed., *Sexuality and Gender in Early Modern Europe: Institutions, Texts, Images* (Cambridge: Cambridge University Press, 1993), 182–207; Blank, "Comparing Sappho to Philaenis: John Donne's 'Homopoetics,' " *PMLA* 110 (May 1995): 359.

66. Roof, *A Lure of Knowledge: Lesbian Sexuality and Theory* (New York: Columbia University Press, 1991), 23.

67. Day, "Looking at Women," 94. I need to emphasize that these comments pertain to pornography which is predominantly addressed to a male heterosexual audience. On lesbian pornography addressed to a lesbian audience, see, for example, Terralee Bensinger, "Lesbian Pornography: The Re/Making of (a) Community," *Discourse: Journal for Theoretical Studies in Media and Culture* 15 (fall 1992): 69–93; Lisa Henderson, "Lesbian Pornography: Cultural Transgression and Sexual Demystification," in Sally Munt, ed., *New Lesbian Criticism: Literary and Cultural Readings* (New York: Columbia University Press, 1992), 173–91; and Heather Findlay, "Dyke Porn 101: How to Enjoy (and Defend) Your Porn," *On Our Backs* 10 (Nov.–Dec. 1993): 14–15, 42–43.

68. The printless path traced by fish also appears in "To Sir Henry Wotton" ("Sir, more then kisses, letters mingle Soules"): Donne urges Wotton to "Bee thine owne Palace. . . . And in the worlds sea . . . as / Fishes glide, leaving no print where they passe. . . . Let men dispute, whether thou breathe, or no" (52–58). Donne, *The Satires, Epigrams, and Verse Letters,* ed. W. Milgate (Oxford: Clarendon Press, 1967), 72. Here too the image combines properties of self-sufficiency, wholeness, and invisibility.

69. Day, "Looking at Women," 94–95. Roof also comments on this paradox in conventional pornography's use of lesbian sexuality: "While the project of imaging a phallusless sexuality results in a scene that is in some ways more conventionally portrayed than heterosexual encounters, that lesbian sexuality is forced into a traditionally heterosexual model causes the images to slip away from and break down these conventions" (*A Lure of Knowledge,* 16–17).

70. On this point see Roof, *A Lure of Knowledge,* 23–24.

71. Mueller, "Donne's Brief for Lesbianism," 199; Harvey, "Ventriloquizing Sappho," 131; Holstun, "Lesbian Elegy," 843.

72. Day, "Looking at Women," 91.

73. Valerie Traub notes that "it is not woman's desire for other women, but her usurpation of male prerogatives that incites writers to record and thus reveal the anxieties of their (and our) culture." "The (In)significance of 'Lesbian' Desire in Early Modern England," in Susan Zimmerman, ed., *Erotic Politics: Desire on the Renaissance Stage* (New York: Routledge, 1992), 155–56. I borrow the term "apparitional lesbian" from Terry Castle, *The Apparitional Lesbian: Female Homosexuality and Modern Culture* (New York: Columbia University Press, 1993).

74. Roof, *A Lure of Knowledge,* 23.

75. See note 73.

76. On the "lesbian phallus" and its relation to the Lacanian distinction between *being* and *having* the phallus, the latter identified by Lacan with the masculine position, see Judith Butler, *Bodies That Matter: On the Discursive Limits of "Sex"* (New York: Routledge, 1993), chap. 2.

77. Blank, "Comparing Sappho to Philaenis," 359.

78. Weeks, *Sexuality and Its Discontents: Meanings, Myths and Modern Sexualities* (London: Routledge, 1985), 132.

79. Bennett, *Formalism and Marxism* (London: Methuen, 1979), 173–74. On related theory and practice, see also Terry Eagleton, *Criticism and Ideology: A Study in Marxist Literary Theory* (1976; London: Verso, 1978) and Catherine Belsey, *Critical Practice* (London: Methuen, 1980).

80. On this point see Patterson, *Censorship and Interpretation,* chap. 2 and Margaret Ferguson, "Nashe's *The Unfortunate Traveller:* The 'News of the Maker' Game," *English Literary Renaissance* 11 (1981): 165–82.

81. On paradox and Jacobean ideology, see Goldberg, *James I and the Politics of Literature,* esp. chap. 2.

82. De Lauretis, *Technologies of Gender: Essays on Theory, Film, and Fiction* (Bloomington: Indiana University Press, 1987), 9.

83. De Lauretis, *Technologies of Gender,* 9.

84. Tony Bennett, "Texts in History: The Determinations of Readings and Their Texts," in Derek Attridge, Geoff Bennington, and Robert Young, eds., *Post-structuralism and the Question of History* (Cambridge: Cambridge University Press, 1987), 70.

85. Wiggins, " 'Aire and Angels': Incarnations of Love," *English Literary Renaissance* 12 (1982): 87. Further references to this essay appear in my text.

86. Gardner, *The Business of Criticism* (Oxford: Clarendon Press, 1959), 74–75.

87. Docherty, *John Donne, Undone,* 10–11. Frederic Jameson argues that "ideology is not something which informs or invests symbolic production; rather the aesthetic act is itself ideological, and the production of aesthetic or narrative form is to be seen as an ideological act in its own right, with the function of inventing imaginary or formal 'solutions' to unresolvable social contradictions." *The Political Unconscious: Narrative as a Socially Symbolic Act* (Ithaca: Cornell University Press, 1981), 79.

88. Joan Kelly (-Gadol), "Did Women Have a Renaissance?" rpt. in *Women, History and Theory: The Essays of Joan Kelly* (Chicago: University of Chicago Press, 1984), 44, 45.

89. Gallop, *The Daughter's Seduction: Feminism and Psychoanalysis* (Ithaca: Cornell University Press, 1982), esp. chaps. 2–4. See also the influential introductions of Juliet Mitchell and Jacqueline Rose, eds., *Feminine Sexuality: Jacques Lacan and the Ecole Freudienne* (New York: Norton, 1982). A Renaissance practice of reading that suits Donne's text is the post-humanist rhetoric discussed in Kahn, *Rhetoric, Prudence, and Skepticism in the Renaissance.*

90. Butler, *Bodies That Matter,* 95. This book expands upon and revises her work on gender as performance in *Gender Trouble: Feminism and the Subversion of Identity* (New York: Routledge, 1990).

91. My discussion of the conventions of praise is indebted to Fineman, *Shakespeare's Perjured Eye,* esp. 49–85.

92. West, *Milton and the Angels* (Athens: University of Georgia Press, 1955), 8–9.

93. Gardner, ed., *Elegies and Songs and Sonnets,* 177.

94. Rose, "Introduction II," in Mitchell and Rose, *Feminine Sexuality,* 50. Docherty discusses at length "the problem of women," authority, and the Other in chapter 2 of *John Donne, Undone.*

95. Luce Irigaray, *Speculum of the Other Woman,* trans. Gillian C. Gill (Ithaca: Cornell University Press, 1985), 48.

96. Fineman, *Shakespeare's Perjured Eye,* 23.

97. Irigaray, *Speculum of the Other Woman,* 50.

98. On the Neoplatonic (Plotinian) roots of love as a child of the soul, see Peter Dane, "The Figure of the Pinnace in 'Aire and Angels,' " *Southern Review: Literary and Interdisciplinary Essays* 12 (1979): 200–1.

99. Fineman, *Shakespeare's Perjured Eye,* 5–15.

100. My understanding of the divided subject of the poem resembles Catherine Belsey's formulation in *The Subject of Tragedy.* Renaissance tragedy, she argues, produces "a radical uncertainty . . . by withholding from the spectator the single position from which a single and unified meaning is produced" (29); furthermore, the subject-positions of women characters in these plays are "radically discontinuous" (164), reflecting or reproducing contradictions in the discourse of church and state regarding women (149–60).

101. Redpath, ed., *The Songs and Sonets of John Donne,* 2d ed. (New York: St. Martin's Press, 1983), 198–99.

102. Allen, "Donne and the Ship Metaphor," *Modern Language Notes* 76 (1961): 308–12; Dane, "The Figure of the Pinnace in 'Aire and Angels,'" 195–202.

103. Allen, "Donne and the Ship Metaphor," 312, urges taking "the full Falstaffian connotation of that word [pinnace]." He is referring to *The Merry Wives of Windsor,* I.3.79–80, where, following a Donnean passage on Mistresses Ford and Page as "my East and West Indies," Falstaff dispatches his page: "Hold, sirrah, bear you these letters tightly; / Sail like my pinnace to these golden shores." Raymond Waddington has argued for the punning meaning as primary in " 'All in All': Shakespeare, Milton, Donne, and the Soul-in-Body Topos," *English Literary Renaissance* 20 (1990): 40–68. His reading of the poem differs markedly from my own.

104. An interesting analogue to Donne's pun—pinnace (whore)/penis—is also a topic in classical psychoanalysis. See Otto Fenichel, "The Symbolic Equation: Girl = Phallus," *Psychoanalytic Quarterly* 18 (1949): 303–24; Fenichel analyzes the equation in clinical terms as "a substitute for the phallic exhibition which is inhibited by castration anxiety, and is composed of the two kinds of 'castration denial': 'I keep my penis by acting as though I were in fact a girl,' and 'girls are really no different from myself' " (317). I am struck by the resemblance between this diagnosis and the language of Galenic sexology. Freud distinguishes between having the phallus (the position of the subject of desire) and being the phallus (the position of the object of desire), and Lacan, of course, distinguishes between the penis and the phallus. Donne's overloaded "pinnace" seems to equate the phallus and the penis and to blur the distinction between having it and being it. Donne's sinking is brought on by overvaluing his love object; this overvaluing, Freud argues, is typical of "anaclitic" love, which Elizabeth Grosz describes as "an active, masculine form of love, modelled on loving another who resembles the subject's infantile nurturers" (126). Grosz provides a helpful exposition of the phallus/penis, being/having distinctions in chapter 5 of her book, *Jacques Lacan: A Feminist Introduction.*

105. West, *Milton and the Angels,* 49.

106. Gardner, ed., *Elegies and Songs and Sonnets,* 205.

107. This passage from Henry Lawrence, *Militia Spiritualis, or a Treatise of Angels,* 4th ed. (London, 1652) is quoted by West, *Milton and the Angels,* 55. As West notes, Lawrence's ideas on the topic of angelic substance are derived from Tertullian and are virtually identical with Calvin's.

108. Gardner, ed., *Elegies and Songs and Sonnets,* 205.

109. I take the pronoun "it" in line 24 to refer to "Angell" in line 23. For an excellent summary and commentary on the problem of "it" and subsequent possibilities of meaning for the closing lines of the poem, see Redpath, ed. *The Songs and Sonets,* Appendix V.

110. Gardner, *Business of Criticism,* 72.

111. Or perhaps more accurately, my reading of "Aire and Angels," in Pierre Macherey's words, "brings out a difference within the work by demonstrating that it is other than it is." Macherey's point must be acknowledged as an ideology of reading; "Just such disparitie" as Macherey recommends "will ever bee" the mark of an "ideological" analysis of Donne's poetry. Macherey, *A Theory of Literary Production,* trans. Geoffrey Wall (London: Routledge, 1978), 7.

112. Gardner, *Business of Criticism,* 72.

113. For a critique of traditional historical criticism as "a preemptive appeal to scholarship to settle issues" (5), see Richard Strier, *Resistant Structures: Particularity, Radicalism, and Renaissance Texts* (Berkeley and Los Angeles: University of California Press, 1995), Essay 1 ("Tradition").

114. Gardner, ed., *Elegies and Songs and Sonnets,* 206.

115. Franciscus Georgius, *Problemata in Sacris Scripturis* (Paris, 1574), quoted in Gardner, ed., *Elegies and Songs and Sonnets,* 206.

116. Woodbridge, *Women and the English Renaissance: Literature and the Nature of Womankind, 1540–1620* (Urbana: University of Illinois Press, 1984), 8.

117. Jane Anger, *Her Protection for Women* (London, 1589) in Henderson and McManus, *Half Humankind: Contexts and Texts of the Controversy about Women in England, 1540–1640* (Urbana: University of Illinois Press, 1985), 177.

118. Belsey, *The Subject of Tragedy,* 150.

119. Gouge, *Of Domesticall Duties* (London, 1622), 271.

120. Like many Protestant writers on marriage, Gouge ranks love as the first duty of the husband and subjection as the first duty of the wife. See his tables of "Particular Duties" in *Domesticall Duties,* 168, 350.

121. Belsey, *The Subject of Tragedy,* 199.

122. See Jameson, *The Political Unconscious,* 79.

123. Kristeva, *Tales of Love,* trans. Leon S. Roudiez (New York: Columbia University Press, 1987), 277.

Chapter 3

1. Low, *The Reinvention of Love: Poetry, Politics and Culture from Sidney to Milton* (Cambridge: Cambridge University Press, 1993), 33, xi.

2. Marotti, *John Donne: Coterie Poet* (Madison: University of Wisconsin Press, 1986), 164–65.

3. Sedgwick, *Between Men: English Literature and Male Homosocial Desire* (New York: Columbia University Press, 1985), 15.

4. I wish to note at the outset that my discussion of Donne's relationship to these debates depends upon Foucault's idea of "discursive relations," defined in in *The Archaeology of Knowledge* as "Relations between statements (even if the author is unaware of them; even if the statements do not have the same author; even if the authors were unaware of each other's existence); relations between groups of statements . . . (even if these groups do not concern the same, or even adjacent fields; even if they do not possess the same formal level . . .)." I cite the passage as quoted in Annabel Patterson, "All Donne," in Elizabeth D. Harvey and Katherine Eisaman Maus, eds., *Soliciting Interpretation: Literary Theory and Seventeenth-Century English Poetry* (Chicago: University of Chicago Press, 1990), 42.

5. Haskin, "A History of Donne's 'Canonization' from Izaak Walton to Cleanth Brooks," *JEGP (Journal of English and Germanic Philology)* 92 (1993): 27, 22. Haskin is careful to note, however, that the lack of critical commentary on the poem's possible links to Donne's biography does not preclude the possibility that it was read biographically by members of Donne's coterie (see 24).

6. Haskin, "A History of Donne's 'Canonization,' " 36.

7. Rose, *Expense of Spirit: Love and Sexuality in English Renaissance Drama* (Ithaca: Cornell University Press, 1988), 118.

8. Rose, *Expense of Spirit,* 104.

9. See, especially, Peter Erickson, *Patriarchal Structures in Shakespeare's Drama* (Berkeley: University of California Press, 1985); Janet Adelman, "Male Bonding in Shakespeare's

Comedies," in Peter Erickson and Coppelia Kahn, eds., *Shakespeare's "Rough Magic": Renaissance Essays in Honor of C. L. Barber* (Newark: University of Delaware Press, 1985), 73–103; Gayle Whittier, "The Sublime Androgyne Motif in Three Shakespearean Works," *Journal of Medieval and Renaissance Studies* 19 (1989), 185–210; and Valerie Traub, *Desire and Anxiety: Circulations of Sexuality in Shakespearean Drama* (New York: Routledge, 1992), 93–94. References to Songs and Sonnets are from John Donne, *The Elegies and the Songs and Sonnets*, ed. Helen Gardner (Oxford: Clarendon Press, 1965) and are noted by line number in my text.

10. Sedgwick, *Between Men*, 40.

11. I am following Anika Lemaire's summary of Lacan's concept of the Other in *Jacques Lacan*, trans. David Macey (London: Routledge, 1977), 157 and also B. Benvenuto and R. Kennedy, *The Works of Jacques Lacan: An Introduction* (London: Free Association Books, 1986), 86–87.

12. Rebirth after "death" but not the births. Robert Hodge comments suggestively on the disparity between Donne's echo of biblical phrases (Genesis 2:24; Ephesians 5:31) on marriage—"two being one"—and the actual condition of married life for Ann More and Donne—two having become at least three—at the time Donne probably wrote this poem in *Literature as Discourse* (Baltimore: Johns Hopkins University Press, 1990), 231. Whittier, "The Sublime Androgyne."

13. These passages are discussed as "not only emasculation but . . . a metamorphic—and pejorative—description of the act of love itself" by Leonard Barkan, *The Gods Made Flesh: Metamorphosis and the Pursuit of Paganism* (New Haven: Yale University Press, 1986), 57–58.

14. See Ricks, "Donne after Love," in Elaine Scarry, ed., *Literature and the Body: Essays on Populations and Persons* (Baltimore: Johns Hopkins University Press, 1988), 64.

15. On androgyny, hermaphroditism, and the distinctions between them, see Lauren Silberman, "Mythographic Transformations of Ovid's Hermaphrodite," *Sixteenth-Century Journal* 19 (1988): 643–52; Carla Freccero, "The Other and the Same: The Image of the Hermaphrodite in Rabelais," in Margaret Ferguson et al., eds., *Rewriting the Renaissance: The Discourses of Sexual Difference in Early Modern Europe* (Chicago: University of Chicago Press, 1986), 145–58; and Jerome Schwartz, "Aspects of Androgyny in the Renaissance," in D. Radcliffe-Umstead, ed., *Human Sexuality in the Middle Ages and the Renaissance* (Pittsburgh: Center for Medieval and Renaissance Studies, University of Pittsburgh, 1978), 121–31.

16. On this cultural application of androgyny, see Linda Woodbridge, *Women and the English Renaissance: Literature and the Nature of Womankind, 1540–1620* (Urbana: University of Illinois Press, 1984), 140–41. On the Renaissance distinction between sex and gender, see Constance Jordan, *Renaissance Feminism: Literary Texts and Political Models* (Ithaca: Cornell University Press, 1990), chap. 3.

17. A. R. Cirillo, "The Fair Hermaphrodite: Love-Union in the Poetry of Donne and Spenser," *Studies in English Literature* 9 (1969): 81–95.

18. Turner, *One Flesh: Paradisal Marriage and Sexual Relations in the Age of Milton* (Oxford: Oxford University Press, 1987), 69.

19. Williams quoted in Whittier, "The Sublime Androgyne," 185.

20. On misogyny in the Elegies, see Achsah Guibbory, " 'Oh, Let Mee Not Serve So': The Politics of Love in Donne's *Elegies*," *ELH* 57 (1990): 811–33.

21. See Turner, *One Flesh*, 24–27, for some brilliant comments on Paul's reading of the Genesis story.

22. Silberman notes a fourteenth-century allegorization of Ovid in which Christ, uniting God's masculine nature with humanity's feminine, is the hermaphrodite; this moralization, however, "gives no indication that the metaphysical union of the divine and the human is figured by the carnal union of man and woman" ("Mythographic Transformations," 647).

23. Rose, *Expense of Spirit*, 119.

24. Whately, *A Bride-bush* (London, 1619), 16–17.

25. Empson, "Donne the Space Man," *Kenyon Review* 19 (1957): 337–99; "Donne in the

New Edition," *Critical Quarterly* 8 (1966): 255–80; "Rescuing Donne," in Peter Amadeus Fiore, ed., *Just So Much Honor: Essays Commemorating the Four-Hundredth Anniversary of the Birth of John Donne* (University Park: Pennsylvania State University Press, 1972), 95–148. Norbrook, "The Monarchy of Wit and the Republic of Letters: Donne's Politics," in Harvey and Maus, *Soliciting Interpretation*, 3–36; Low, *Reinvention of Love*, 53–59.

26. On James's discourse of "state secrets" and its relation to Donne's love poetry, see Goldberg, *James I and the Politics of Literature: Jonson, Shakespeare, Donne, and Their Contemporaries* (Baltimore: Johns Hopkins University Press, 1983), chap. 2, esp. 107–12.

27. Marotti reads stanza three as a rare instance of breakdown in coterie communication: "this stanza would probably have perplexed even the most adept member of Donne's coterie audience" (163). But Marotti still grants Donne "a playful control" over his readers; again, Donne's mastery is preserved, and, indeed, the whole point of the poem seems to be an exercise of power. This is close to Stanley Fish's view of Donne's "need first to create a world and then endlessly to manipulate those who are made to inhabit it." Fish, "Masculine Persuasive Force: Donne and Verbal Power," in Harvey and Maus, *Soliciting Interpretation*, 224.

28. Carey, *John Donne: Life, Mind, and Art* (New York: Oxford University Press, 1981), 43. Low, *Reinvention of Love*, 54.

29. Flynn, *Donne and the Ancient Catholic Nobility* (Bloomington and Indianapolis: Indiana University Press, 1995). The indispensable article on the political function of love poetry in the period is Marotti's " 'Love is not love': Elizabethan Sonnet Sequences and the Social Order," *ELH* 49 (1982): 396–428. Marotti, however, tends to argue that love poetry is really a coded political discourse; I mean to suggest something like the opposite—that recusant politics is a means of representing love.

30. For an example of this type of critique, see Robert Persons, *A Temperate Ward-word to the Turbulent and Seditious Wach-word of Sir Francis Hastings* (1599), 5–6.

31. The phrase and the characterization of Persons's tale are borrowed from Christopher Haigh, "From Monopoly to Minority: Catholicism in Early Modern England," *Transactions of the Royal Historical Society,* 5th series, 31 (1981): 129. Other essential reading on this topic includes the foundational work of John Bossy, "The Character of Elizabethan Catholicism," *Past and Present* 21 (1962): 39–59 and *The English Catholic Community, 1570–1850* (London: Darton, Longman and Todd, 1975); Haigh, "The Continuity of Catholicism in the English Reformation," *Past and Present* 93 (1981): 37–69; Arnold Pritchard, *Catholic Loyalism in Elizabethan England* (Chapel Hill: University of North Carolina Press, 1979); and the fullest treatment, Peter Holmes, *Resistance and Compromise: The Political Thought of the Elizabethan Catholics* (Cambridge: Cambridge University Press, 1982).

32. Guibbory, " 'Oh, Let Mee Not Serve So,' " 811. Marotti's general thesis is stated in " 'Love is not Love' " and is applied specifically to Donne in *Coterie Poet.*

33. Holmes, *Resistance and Compromise*, 81.

34. An exception to this principle was Robert Persons's claim in his *A Conference about the Next Succession to the Crown of England* (1594) that the Pope was feudal overlord of England. See Holmes, *Resistance and Compromise*, 155–57, for a discussion of this "highly original" argument.

35. Holmes, *Resistance and Compromise*, 111.

36. Carey, *John Donne: Life, Mind, and Art*, 43, notes the irony of the claims made in the final stanza.

37. Docherty (*John Donne, Undone* [London and New York: Methuen, 1986], 174) notes Donne's maintainance of a male point of view in the lines on resurrection.

38. Southwell, *An Humble Supplication to Her Maiestie*, ed. R. C. Bald (Cambridge: Cambridge University Press, 1953), 3. On the recusants' use of Marian exiles as a historical precedent, see also Persons, *A Ward-word,* 83 and the discussion by Holmes, *Resistance and Compromise*, chap. 6. On Southwell's equivocal use of history in the *Humble Supplication,* see

my " 'The Secrecy of Man': Recusant Discourse and the Elizabethan Subject," *English Literary Renaissance* 19 (1989): 272–90.

39. For a different perspective on Donne's fantasies of future glorification, particularly as they relate to Catholicism, see Low, *Reinvention of Love,* 52–58.

40. "I have been ever kept awake in a meditation of martyrdom, by being derived from such a stock and race as, I believe, no family . . . hath endured and suffered more in their persons and fortunes, for obeying the teachers of Roman doctrine, than it hath done." And, "I used no inordinate haste nor precipitation in binding my conscience to any local religion. I had a longer work to do than many other men, for I was first to blot out certain impressions of the Roman religion, and to wrestle both against the examples and against the reasons, by which some hold was taken, and some anticipations early laid upon my conscience, both by persons who by nature had a power and superiority over my will, and others who by their learning and good life seemes to me justly to claim an interest for the guiding and rectifying of mine understanding in these matters." These passages from the prefatory matter of *Pseudo-Martyr* (1610) are quoted from *John Donne,* ed. John Carey, The Oxford Authors (New York: Oxford University Press, 1990), 190, 191.

41. My quotations from Kristeva's *Revolution in Poetic Language* are taken from *The Kristeva Reader,* ed. Toril Moi (New York: Columbia University Press, 1986), 95, 97, 112.

42. Moi, ed., *The Kristeva Reader,* 120.

43. "An Elegie upon the Death of the Deane of Pauls, Dr. Iohn Donne" (ll. 37–38), in *The Poems of John Donne,* ed. H. J. C. Grierson 2 vols. (Oxford: Clarendon Press, 1912), 1:378–79.

44. Quint, *Origin and Originality in Renaissance Literature: Versions of the Source* (New Haven: Yale University Press, 1983), 219–20. Quint's study centers on the issue of originality, a topic I do not explore here but which certainly has relevance to Donne's work.

45. Tilottama Rajan notes that Donne's reference to an auditor "undermines the speaker's claim for the self-enclosedness of mutual love by conceding within the poem itself an implied reader who has the power to resist or overturn the speaker's argument" in " 'Nothing Sooner Broke': Donne's *Songs and Sonets* as Self-Consuming Artifact," *ELH* 49 (1982): 813. Rajan's readings are directed against "the New Critical adaptation of a Romantic aesthetics," but in making Donne his own deconstructor in both individual poems and the arrangement of the entire collection of Songs and Sonnets they oddly recuperate the ironic and paradoxical Donne of New Criticism.

46. Liu, "The Power of Formalism: The New Historicism," *ELH* 56 (1989): 736–37.

47. In Shakespeare, "spy" appears three times as a noun (*Macbeth* III.i.129, *The Tempest* I.ii.456, *Venus and Adonis* l. 655) and in all instances it has a subversive meaning; in *Macbeth* and *The Tempest* it is explicitly related to usurpation.

48. Rajan, " 'Nothing Sooner Broke,' " 806.

49. On the interplay of rhetoric and aesthetics in defenses, I am influenced by Margaret W. Ferguson, *Trials of Desire: Renaissance Defenses of Poetry* (New Haven: Yale University Press, 1983).

50. David Simpson's *The Academic Postmodern and the Rule of Literature: A Report on Half-Knowledge* (Chicago: University of Chicago Press, 1995) came to my attention too late to be incorporated fully into my argument, but his long-durational historical thesis on the distinctively *literary* mode of modern subjectivity parallels the overarching thesis of my study of Donne. Simpson also traces the movement of literature since the eighteenth century "incrementally gravitating toward the domestic, feminized sphere and away from the public sphere" (100). Donne's urgently masculinist love poetry might be seen as an interesting prelude to the large historical movement Simpson outlines. Simpson's gendering of the literary subject as feminine contrasts with my argument in this and the preceding chapter, though I believe the various inversions and instabilities in many of Donne's love poems evidence a struggle against feminization.

51. Ferguson writes of Sidney's Defense, "it offers a model of that relation between text and reader which consists of a constant turning of master into servant and servant into master. In this turning, at once an exercise of ambition and a contemplation of it, the boundaries between oratory and poetry, play and persuasion, invention and interpretation, are repeatedly drawn and transgressed" (*Trials of Desire,* 162).

52. Liu, "The Power of Formalism," 739. A number of recent critics and theorists have argued that the new historicist focus on subversion has led into an interpretative cul-de-sac. See also James Holstun, "Ranting at the New Historicism," *English Literary Renaissance* 19 (1989): 189–225. Of course, it is always possible for Liu to argue that I am constructing Donne in my own formalist image, and indeed this is his major thesis in the article. The facile response is to claim that he does the same thing with his Romanticism—not, "I would make a Renaissance," but "I would make a Romanticism." (There do seem to be some academic territorial motives in Liu's argument—Romanticism, not the Renaissance is the defining historical moment in his narrative.) The more responsible, but still finally partial, answer is to try to demonstrate that if the Renaissance articulated by new historicists is "a dream academy. . . . where the postmodern intellect fantasizes safely about subversion and transgression against 'the regime of power and knowledge that at once sustains and constrains us' " ("The Power of Formalism," 749) there is also some evidence that the academy is built on a Renaissance foundation. (The inside quotation is from Montrose, "The Elizabethan Subject and the Spenserian Text," in Patricia Parker and David Quint, eds., *Literary Theory/Renaissance Texts* [Baltimore: Johns Hopkins University Press, 1986], 333.) Liu writes, "A New Historicist paradigm holds up to view a historical context on one side, a literary text on the other, and, in between, a connection of pure nothing" ("The Power of Formalism," 743). This is a good description of many of Donne's poems.

53. Greenblatt, *Shakespearean Negotiations: The Circulation of Social Energy in Renaissance England* (Berkeley and Los Angeles: University of California Press, 1988), 18.

54. Greenblatt, *Shakespearean Negotiations,* 12–13. On the significance of the topographical place of the theater in London, see Steven Mullaney, *The Place of the Stage: License, Play, and Power in Renaissance England* (Chicago: University of Chicago Press, 1988).

55. This passage from Bourdieu's *Outline of a Theory of Practice,* trans. Richard Nice (Cambridge: Cambridge University Press, 1977), 177 is quoted in Greenblatt, *Shakespearean Negotiations,* 167.

56. Helgerson, *Self-Crowned Laureates: Spenser, Jonson, Milton, and the Literary System* (Berkeley: University of California Press, 1983), 28. Helgerson allows for generational differences in terms of genre preferences and centers of literary activity, but the thesis concerning poetry as a credential for service seems to be advanced for amateurs of both Sidney's and Donne's generations.

57. Marotti, "John Donne, Author," *Journal of Medieval and Renaissance Studies* 19 (1989): 75.

58. See R. C. Bald, *John Donne: A Life* (Oxford: Clarendon Press, 1970), 241–42.

59. In a review of Marotti's book Anthony Low challenges Marotti's belief that the conditions of production determine meaning; quoting Marotti, Low writes, "Granted that Donne was born into a milieu that defined lyric poetry as 'basically a genre for gentlemen amateurs who regarded their literary "toys" as ephemeral works that were part of a social life that also included dancing, singing, gaming, and civilized conversation,' a culture that thought of individual poems as 'trifles to be transmitted in manuscript within a limited social world and not as literary monuments to be preserved in printed editions for posterity' . . . or, at best, that thought of poems as tools to be used and dropped as a minor means of career advancement; must we now accept such limitations as inevitable and definitive?" "Donne and the New Historicism," *John Donne Journal* 7 (1988): 128. With Low, I would answer, No. Our reasons for so answering differ. Where

Low finds transcendence or transformation of the *conditions of production,* I find the creation of an alternative ideology out of the ideologemes assembled in "The Canonization."

60. Marotti's argument in "John Donne, Author" is paradoxically dependent upon a certain reification of the term "author" in its attempt to historicize Donne the author. The notion of the "canonical author" is highly problematic as Marotti suggests when he mentions Jonson's tendency to see himself, Sidney, and Donne as authors ("John Donne, Author," 79). The question is canonical to whom—a question Donne himself poses in the last lines of Satire 4. In one sense Donne is the first to claim himself as a "canonical author," in "The Canonization," though he seems to mean by that something rather different from what Marotti means.

61. The construction of privacy is also a function of the circulation of the poems. Marotti uses the greater or lesser freedom of circulation of Donne's poetry in manuscript as an index to its degree of privacy; by this measure, the Songs and Sonnets emerge as more private than the Satires and Elegies (*Coterie Poet,* 16–17).

62. Low, *Reinvention of Love,* 51.

63. Janel Mueller, "Women among the Metaphysicals: A Case, Mostly, of Being Donne For," *Modern Philology* 87 (1989): 147. In "The Role of the Lady in Donne's *Songs and Sonets,*" *Studies in English Literature* 23 (1983): 113–29, Ilona Bell has argued that Donne conveys "an empathetic, imaginative, and varied response to the lady's point of view" (113). Although I agree with her sense of "stress and conflict" (118) in the poems, I feel that Bell's aim of defending Donne leads her to misread his struggle to control himself and women as recognition and accommodation of the woman's point of view.

64. On this point see Clark Hulse, "Stella's Wit: Penelope Rich as Reader of Sidney's Sonnets," in Ferguson et al., *Rewriting the Renaissance,* 283–84.

65. J. B. Broadbent, *Poetic Love* (London: Chatto & Windus, 1964), 222.

66. Bell, "The Role of the Lady," 122.

67. Bell, "The Role of the Lady," 120.

68. For another perspective on the reflected images, see Arnold Stein, *John Donne's Lyrics: The Eloquence of Action* (Minneapolis: University of Minnesota Press, 1962), 75–77.

69. The "other" or "Other" has a range of possible meanings in Lacan's formulation, including the image of another person. On this point, see Mark Bracher, *Lacan, Discourse, and Social Change: A Psychoanalytic Cultural Criticism* (Ithaca: Cornell University Press, 1993), 19–21.

70. See Grierson, ed., *Poems,* 2:11.

71. Both Redpath and Gardner find the ending unsatisfactory and suggest that Donne revised. Redpath adopts "the Group I reading ["Love so alike . . ."], since I believe it may represent a revision by Donne, even though not a wholly satisfactory one" (*The Songs and Sonets of John Donne,* 2d ed. [New York: St. Martin's Press, 1983], 231). Gardner writes that "it seems impossible to explain the variants . . . on any other theory than that of the poet's rewriting an unsatisfactory line. Neither version provides a close worthy of the poem's opening. Conditional clauses must always suggest an element of doubt" (*Elegies,* 199).

72. Bell summarizes the range of response to these lines ("The Role of the Lady," 123). It is interesting to note that one of the most moving, exultant readings of the poem, J. B. Broadbent's in *Poetic Love,* does not touch upon the last stanza (see 221–23).

73. Redpath, *Songs and Sonets,* 231.

74. Or as Lacan has it, "One-ness." See Lacan's "God and the Jouissance of The Woman," in Juliet Mitchell and Jacqueline Rose, eds., *Feminine Sexuality: Jacques Lacan and the Ecole Freudienne* (New York: Norton, 1982), 141.

75. Bell, "The Role of the Lady," 123.

76. Blank, "Comparing Sappho to Philaenis: John Donne's 'Homopoetics,' " *PMLA* 110 (May 1995): 359. Blank defines "homopoetics" as "the cultural making of likenesses" (359).

77. Donne uses this proverbial expression to close his elegy "The Comparison." For a different perspective on Donne's appropriation of the proverb, see Fish, "Masculine Persuasive Force," 225–27.

78. See, for example, Barbara Kiefer Lewalski, *Writing Women in Jacobean England* (Cambridge: Harvard University Press, 1993), who writes: "Attention to these women writers will . . . help us recognize that authorship may be the process as well as the product of asserting subjectivity and agency. I believe that for most of them writing itself was a major means of self-definition. In this study I have tried to let several women's voices be heard as they begin a dialogue with the literary tradition, with one another, and with the men shaping politics and culture in Jacobean England" (11).

Chapter 4

1. Tayler, *Donne's Idea of a Woman: Structure and Meaning in* The Anniversaries (New York: Columbia University Press, 1991), 2. Tayler's complaint is a grumpy version of T. S. Eliot's 1931 disclaimer of his earlier views on Donne: "It is impossible for us or for anyone else ever to disentangle how much was genuine affinity, genuine appreciation, and how much was just a *reading into* poets like Donne our own sensibilities" (quoted in John R. Roberts, "John Donne's Poetry: An Assessment of Modern Criticism," *John Donne Journal* 1 [1982]: 56). Unlike Eliot, Tayler is quite certain of his ability to disentangle Donne's from "our own sensibilities."

2. Nicolson, *The Breaking of the Circle: Studies in the Effect of the "New Science" upon Seventeenth-Century Poetry,* rev. ed. (New York and London: Columbia University Press, 1960), 81. Jonson's famous criticism of the poems, and Donne's reply "that he described the Idea of a Woman and not as she was," are recorded in *Conversations with William Drummond of Hawthornden* in Jonson, *Works,* ed. C. H. Herford and Percy Simpson, 11 vols. (Oxford: Clarendon Press, 1925), 1: 133.

3. Martz, *The Poetry of Meditation: A Study in English Religious Literature of the Seventeenth Century* (1954; rev. ed. New Haven: Yale University Press, 1962); Lewalski, *Donne's* Anniversaries *and the Poetry of Praise: The Creation of a Symbolic Mode* (Princeton: Princeton University Press, 1973) and *Protestant Poetics and the Seventeenth-Century Religious Lyric* (Princeton: Princeton University Press, 1979).

4. Thomas Docherty, *John Donne, Undone* (London and New York: Methuen, 1986), 8.

5. Tayler, *Donne's Idea of a Woman,* x.

6. Tayler, *Donne's Idea of a Woman,* 130, 135.

7. Tayler, *Donne's Idea of a Woman,* x.

8. Easthope, *Literary into Cultural Studies* (London and New York: Routledge, 1991), 59. Easthope's argument, I wish to emphasize, is on the side of a historical understanding of the "reader/text relation" that sharply differs from Tayler's historical approach: "a text of literary value can be distinguished from one with merely historical interest by the degree to which its signifiers have actively engaged with new contexts, contexts different ideologically but also different in the protocols of literary reading in which the text is construed. An historical observation, this is a description of how literary value works, not a definition of what it *is*" (58).

9. See especially, Arthur F. Marotti, *John Donne: Coterie Poet* (Madison: University of Wisconsin Press, 1986). Tayler argues that the poems are about "a specifically *human* process of intellectual abstraction" (*Donne's Idea of a Woman,* 18, my italics). Although my argument turns on a crucial qualification of Tayler's "human process," I share his concern with process and with the relationship between speaker, reader, Elizabeth Drury, and the Idea of a Woman.

10. For a different approach to the First Anniversary through the reader, see Kathleen Kelly, "Conversion of the Reader in Donne's 'Anatomy of the World,' " in Claude J. Summers

and Ted-Larry Pebworth, eds., *The Eagle and the Dove: Reassessing John Donne* (Columbia: University of Missouri Press, 1986), 147–56.

11. On the importance of desire in ideology, see Mark Bracher, *Lacan, Discourse, and Social Change: A Psychoanalytic Cultural Criticism* (Ithaca: Cornell University Press, 1993), 19–52, and Slavoj Žižek, *The Sublime Object of Ideology* (New York: Verso, 1989).

12. Tayler, *Donne's Idea of a Woman*, 116.

13. Greenblatt, *Shakespearian Negotiations: The Circulation of Social Energy in Renaissance England* (Berkeley and Los Angeles: University of California Press, 1988), 2–3.

14. Donne's difficulties with reception of the poems are summarized in R. C. Bald, *John Donne: A Life* (Oxford: Clarendon Press, 1970), 242–51.

15. John Donne, *Letters to Severall Persons of Honour (1651)* (Delmar, N.Y.: Scholars' Facsimiles and Reprints, 1977), 75.

16. As noted earlier, Tayler places considerable emphasis on the fit reader of the poems in his conclusion to *Donne's Idea of a Woman*; see esp. 130–35.

17. My characterization of the poems is influenced by Lacan's idea of the Imaginary and Symbolic orders, with "The Anatomy" corresponding to a disintegration of imaginary wholeness in the world's body and "The Progress" corresponding to the identification with a master signifier—the idea of a woman—that fills in for the lack touched upon in "The Anatomy." On the concepts of the imaginary and the symbolic orders I have drawn on Lacan, *Ecrits: A Selection*, trans. Alan Sheridan (New York: Norton, 1977), chaps. 1, 3; *The Seminar of Jacques Lacan, Book I: Freud's Papers on Technique, 1953–54*, ed. Jacques-Alain Miller (New York: Norton, 1988), esp. chap. 11; and such lucid expositions of Lacan's thought as Kaja Silverman, *The Subject of Semiotics* (New York: Oxford University Press, 1983) and Bracher, *Lacan, Discourse, and Social Change*.

18. Greenblatt, *Shakespearean Negotiations*, 5.

19. Exceptions, abbreviated though they are, would include Lindsay A. Mann, "The Typology of Woman in Donne's *Anniversaries*," *Renaissance and Reformation* 11 (1987): 337–50; Ira Clark, " 'How Witty's ruine': The Difficulties of Donne's 'Idea of a Woman' in the First of His *Anniversaries*," *South Atlantic Review* 53 (1988): 19–26; Janel Mueller's paragraph in "Women among the Metaphysicals: A Case, Mostly, of Being Donne For," *Modern Philology* 87 (1989):150–51; and Docherty's discussion in *John Donne, Undone*, 227–31 where the *donna* quickly becomes Donne. Of course, Nicolson notoriously gendered Donne's idea as the "she" and "double shee" in *The Breaking of the Circle*, 65–104.

20. Lynda E. Boose, "The Father's House and the Daughter in It: The Structures of Western Culture's Daughter-Father Relationship," in Boose and Betty S. Flowers, eds., *Daughters and Fathers* (Baltimore: Johns Hopkins University Press, 1989), 20.

21. In "Canonical Texts and Non-Canonical Interpretations: The Neohistoricist Rereading of Donne," *Southern Review* 18 (1985): 235–50, Howard Felperin notes the inevitable slippage between context of production and context of reception in any contextualized reading practice: "This new context is not, as some of them [new historicists] might maintain, discovered as some pre-existing authentic condition, but decidedly constructed and produced, constructed and produced in response to a contemporary climate very different from the one in which the new critics worked to produce their own context" (248). See also Felperin's recent book in which this argument is amplified, *The Uses of the Canon* (Oxford: Clarendon Press, 1990).

22. Marotti, *Coterie Poet*, 245.

23. Donne, *Letters to Severall Persons of Honour (1651)*, 74–75.

24. Donne had also explained in a letter his privately-circulated paradoxes, and at the time he took orders he would interpret his entire career as an coterie writer in another letter that began the durable biographical tradition of Jack Donne and Dr. Donne. Both of these accounts of his own works are primarily aimed at preventing any scandal should they become public, but they

also record a concern for authorial control over the meaning of a text as well as a sense that a writer's works somehow correspond to his "personality."

25. In another letter on the Anniversaries a piqued Donne writes, "If any of those Ladies think that Mistris *Drewry* was not so, let that Lady make herself fit for all those praises in the book, and they shall be hers" (*Letters to Severall Persons of Honour [1651]*, 239).

26. Jonathan V. Crewe, *Unredeemed Rhetoric: Thomas Nashe and the Scandal of Authorship* (Baltimore: Johns Hopkins University Press, 1982), 21.

27. Chartier, *Cultural History: Between Practices and Representations* (Ithaca: Cornell University Press, 1988), 8.

28. Manley's interpretation of the "she" of the poem as Wisdom appears in the introduction to his edition, *John Donne: The Anniversaries* (Baltimore: Johns Hopkins University Press, 1965). Lewalski's idea of the regenerate soul is presented in *Donne's* Anniversaries *and the Poetry of Praise*.

29. Tayler, *Donne's Idea of a Woman*, 12, 16. Tayler reads Donne's "representing" as a pun: "In 'Idea' she re-presents the 'richness' of prelapsarian innocence and virtue" (65). This formulation does not address the use of the term in the subtitle, which states that the work of the Anatomy is the representation of the world's decline, occasioned by Elizabeth Drury's death.

30. Here as well as later in the chapter I use the term "master signifier" in a Lacanian sense. Lacan speaks of a process whereby the subject is called to or actively seeks a mode of being by identification with signifiers. In the discussion of "Aire and Angels" I found Donne to be struggling to maintain an identification with the phallus, Lacan's master signifier *par excellence*. Every culture produces a great, though not unlimited, number of master signifiers—e.g., freedom, power, holiness, even John Donne—by which individuals place themselves within the culture. Everyone has multiple identifications which can produce conflict—as in the case of "Aire and Angels," where Donne's identification as lover comes into conflict with his identification as male. In the Anniversaries, I argue, Donne works on conflicts produced by his identification with a cultural "Idea of Woman." Criticism of the Anniversaries in turn works on conflicts brought about by identification with the signifier "John Donne." Lacan's ideas on identification can be glimpsed in *The Four Fundamental Concepts of Psycho-Analysis*, trans. Alan Sheridan (1977; New York: Norton, 1981) and in unpublished Seminars V (1957–58) and IX (1961–62). I follow the reconstruction of his discourse theory in Bracher, *Lacan, Discourse, and Social Change*, 19–80, and "On the Psychological and Social Functions of Language: Lacan's Theory of the Four Discourses," in Marshall Alcorn, Mark Bracher, Ronald Corthell, and Francois Massardier-Kenney, eds., *Lacanian Theory of Discourse: Subject, Structure, and Society* (New York: New York University Press, 1994), 107–28.

31. On the dangers of assuming a seamless orthodoxy in dominant Renaissance belief systems, see Debora Kuller Shuger, *Habits of Thought in the English Renaissance: Religion, Politics, and the Dominant Culture* (Berkeley and Los Angeles: University of California Press, 1990), who argues for seeing a traditional *mentalité* as "more a thinking than a thought" (16).

32. "To the Praise of the Dead, and the Anatomy," ll. 1–5, in Manley, ed., *John Donne: The Anniversaries*. References to line numbers of poems in this edition and to page numbers of Manley's commentary will appear in my text.

33. Thomas Fuller, *The History of the Worthies of England* (1662), "Leicester-shire," 129. On Hall's prefatory poems, see Leonard Tourney, "Joseph Hall and the Anniversaries," *Papers on Language and Literature* 13 (1977), 25–34.

34. The argument for the absence of affective familial relations is most famously put by Aries in *Centuries of Childhood: A Social History of Family Life*, trans. Robert Baldick (New York: Vintage, 1962). For an interesting counterexample and a bibliography of debate on this issue, see Margaret L. King, "The Death of the Child Valerio Marcello: Paternal Mourning in Renaissance Venice," in Maryanne Cline Horowitz, Anne J. Cruz, and Wendy A. Furman, eds., *Renaissance Rereadings: Intertext and Context* (Urbana: University of Illinois Press, 1988), 205–24.

35. This argument was made long ago by Florence S. Teager, "Patronage of Joseph Hall and John Donne" *Philological Quarterly,* 15 (1936), 412–13. Manley dismisses the idea, stating simply that it is "not very likely. It does not give much credit to Donne's intelligence" (120–21). Drury had been Hall's patron, but their relationship was uneven. Donne was probably aware of Hall's difficulties with Drury, which reached a head in 1608, since it is likely that he met Hall through Donne's sister, who (another interesting twist) was married to one of Hall's enemies. See R. C. Bald, *Donne and the Drurys* (Cambridge: Cambridge University Press, 1959). But even if Donne did know about Hall's stormy relationship with Drury, he could not have been omniscient about Hall's motives in 1611; indeed, most scholarly readers know all about Hall and Drury and, like Manley, dismiss the idea of any hostility. Hall himself could have denied (quite sincerely) any hostility. Finally, it is not clear to what extent Donne was involved with the printing of the First Anniversary or exactly how Hall got involved with the Anniversaries project (perhaps it was through Lady Drury, with whom he remained friendly). Editors Milgate and Manley agree that Donne probably read proofs for the "Anatomy." But the First Anniversary was published by Samuel Macham, who came from Hall's hometown and had published several books by Hall; these facts, together with Hall's relationship with the Drurys (Donne was, of course, in the process of establishing a relationship) make it clear to Milgate "that Hall played a considerable part in the publication of Donne's poems on Elizabeth Drury"; W. Milgate, ed., *The Epithalamions, Anniversaries, and Epicedes* (Oxford: Clarendon Press, 1978), xxxi. Hall, we should remember, was the more eminent of the two writers on the Anniversaries project.

36. On this episode, see Bald, *Donne and the Drurys,* 70.

37. In "The Death of the Child Valerio Marcello," Margaret L. King makes the point that an intense personal investment in the mourning can co-exist with highly conventional forms of a memorial apparently commissioned by the grieving parents (217–20).

38. Lewalski argues that there are three or four audiences implied in the "Anatomy," on the basis of Donne's different uses of the term "world," and she relates these various audiences to the shifting tonalities of the poem. But she also admits that the poem is primarily addressed to those "assum'd unto this Dignitee" (*Donne's* Anniversaries *and the Poetry of Praise,* 240–43). I do not find it easy to identify which audience is being addressed at any particular time.

39. In this respect, the poem imitates the paradoxical movement of other Renaissance anatomies, medical and moral. Devon Hodges notes the "paradoxical doubleness" of an anatomy: "it is a method for revealing order, but it also causes its decay" (*Renaissance Fictions of Anatomy* [Amherst: University of Massachusetts Press, 1985], 6). In a close reading of William Harvey's *Prelectiones* Luke Wilson has tracked the unfolding of this paradox in terms that appear highly relevant to Donne's overall argument in the Anniversaries. It might be said that the purpose of anatomy is to destroy the body in order to save it; the anatomist's dissection aims at a recuperation of the body as a unified structure, "a *structure manifesting intention,* and the intention it manifests, in the Aristotelian terms Harvey adheres to, is that of the soul." In the terms of Donne's analogy, each division of the anatomy of the world is followed up by the refrain of "shee," by a celebration of the world's soul. On the other hand, Donne's anatomy is different from Harvey's in being split between Platonic and Aristotelian notions of the body-soul relation. In the "Anatomy" the soul of his world-body is not an informing principle; soul and body are not imagined as a unity but as quite the opposite, a disjunction. The body of the world is represented as a meaningless ruin; the soul, Elizabeth, can only reinforce our sense of the senselessness of the world-as-body. On the other hand, in this paradoxical work we encounter one of Renaissance literature's most brilliant celebrations of a *body* so informed by soul "one might almost say, her body thought" (l. 246 in "The Progres of the *Soule*"). Wilson, "William Harvey's *Prelectiones:* The Performance of the Body in the Renaissance Theater of Anatomy," *Representations* 17 (winter 1987): 80.

40. Lewalski, *Donne's* Anniversaries *and the Poetry of Praise,* 244–45; Manley, 129–30.

41. Lewalski, *Donne's* Anniversaries *and the Poetry of Praise,* 245; Manley, 128.

42. Milgate, *Epithalamions,* 131; Manley, 130.

43. Hooker, *Of the Laws of Ecclesiastical Polity,* Book V, in W. Speed Hill, ed., *The Folger Edition of the Works of Richard Hooker* 2 vols. (Cambridge, Mass.: Belknap Press, 1977), 2: 247. Further references to the volume and page number of this edition appear in my text.

44. The large implications for signification that stem from these doctrinal disputes have long been and continue to be discussed by "old" historians and "new." Recent studies with literary interest include, John Phillips, *The Reformation of Images: Destruction of Art in England, 1535–1660* (Berkeley and Los Angeles: University of California Press, 1973); Ernest Gilman, *Iconoclasm and Poetry in the English Reformation: Down Went Dagon* (Chicago: University of Chicago Press, 1986); and Greenblatt, "Shakespeare and the Exorcists," in *Shakespearean Negotiations,* 94–128.

45. Sedgwick, *Between Men: English Literature and Male Homosocial Desire* (New York: Columbia University Press, 1985), 14–15.

46. For an excellent treatment of this distinction, see Mary Nyquist, "The Father's Word/ Satan's Wrath," *PMLA* 100 (1985): 187–202.

47. Marx, *The German Ideology,* in *The Marx-Engels Reader,* ed. Robert C. Tucker, 2d ed. (New York: Norton, 1978), 154. For the notion of literature as work on ideology, see Terry Eagleton, *Criticism and Ideology: A Study in Marxist Literary Theory* (1976; London: Verso, 1978) and my introduction.

48. I borrow the notion of an "interrogative text" from Catherine Belsey, *Critical Practice* (London: Methuen, 1980), chap. 4.

49. Kristeva, *Powers of Horror: An Essay on Abjection,* trans. Leon S. Roudiez (New York: Columbia University Press, 1982). Kristeva characterizes the abject as neither object nor subject, but something "in-between, the ambiguous, the composite" (4): "The abject has only one quality of the object—that of being opposed to *I.* If the object, however, through its opposition, settles me within the fragile texture of a desire for meaning, which, as a matter of fact, makes me ceaselessly and infinitely homologous to it, what is *abject,* on the contrary, the jettisoned object, is radically excluded and draws me toward the place where meaning collapses" (1–2). See also chap. 5, " . . . Qui Tollis Peccata Mundi," which relates abjection to Christian relocation of sin in subjectivity.

50. Grosz, "The Body of Signification," in John Fletcher and Andrew Benjamin, eds., *Abjection, Melancholia, and Love: The Work of Julia Kristeva* (London and New York: Routledge, 1990), 87 88, 89.

51. As Elizabeth Grosz remarks, "The corpse signifies the supervalence of the body, the body's recalcitrance to consciousness, reason or will. It poses a danger to the ego in so far as it questions its stability and its tangible grasp on and control over itself" ("The Body of Signification," 92).

52. Marotti, *Coterie Poet,* 236.

53. Freud, "On Narcissism: An Introduction," in *The Standard Edition of the Complete Psychological Works of Sigmund Freud,* trans. James Strachey, 24 vols. (London: Hogarth Press, 1953–74): "If we look at the attitude of affectionate parents towards their children, we have to recognize that it is a revival and reproduction of their own narcissism, which they have long since abandoned" (14: 91). References to this edition will appear with the abbreviation SE in my text.

54. Freud uses the terms "ego ideal" and "ideal ego" interchangeably. In Lacan's reworking of this passage in Freud, the two terms are distinguished according to Lacan's theory of the imaginary (ideal ego) and the symbolic (ego ideal) orders. See *The Seminar of Jacques Lacan, Book I,* 118–42.

55. Schiesari, *The Gendering of Melancholia: Feminism, Psychoanalysis, and the Symbolics of Loss in Renaissance Literature* (Ithaca and London: Cornell University Press, 1992). Although she does not discuss Donne in her book, Schiesari (110) quotes Giorgio Agamben's study of melancholy, *Stanze: La parola e il fantasma nella cultura occidentale:* "A second epidemic is in Elizabethan England: the exemplary case is that of John Donne" (*Stanze,* 16). My discussion of

Freud's "Mourning and Melancholia" is indebted to Schiesari's brilliant chapter, "The Gendering of Freud's 'Mourning and Melancholia.' "

56. Schiesari, *The Gendering of Melancholia,* 43.

57. Schiesari, *The Gendering of Melancholia,* 47.

58. Schiesari, *The Gendering of Melancholia,* 47, 52–53.

59. For an analysis of the discursive interdependence of suitors and patrons, see Frank Whigham, "The Rhetoric of Elizabethan Suitors' Letters," *PMLA* 96 (Oct. 1981): 864–82.

60. For a summary of attitudes towards female offspring in the period, see King, *Women of the Renaissance* (Chicago: University of Chicago Press, 1991), 1–80.

61. Boose, "The Father's House," 45.

62. Boose, "The Father's House," 46. See also Boose's article, "The Father and the Bride in Shakespeare," *PMLA* 97 (1982): 325–47.

63. In her suggestive feminist reading Elizabeth Harvey comments on the ideological significance of Elizabeth Drury's absence from the poems: "That Donne never knew the person he was elegizing and that his depiction of her remains so idealized as to lack any human specificity at all enhances his ability to usurp her speechlessness, her absence, and to colonize her dead spirit, as it were." *Ventriloquized Voices: Feminist Theory and Renaissance Texts* (New York: Routledge, 1992), 114. Harvey interestingly brings another Kristevan text—"Stabat Mater"—to the poems in order to elucidate Donne's treatment of virginity and motherhood. Her approach to the Donnean "voice" as "a construction that takes place within a cultural and historical matrix" (78) parallels in some respects my notion of a "subject of Donne." Although I emphasize masculinity rather than maternity in relation both to the originating culture of patronage and to the ongoing cultural effect of the poems, I believe our readings are compatible.

64. In this instance the mysterious "what" that is lost in the object and that Freud says is "withdrawn from consciousness" (SE 14: 245) would be that which is forbidden by the incest taboo.

65. Tayler, *Donne's Idea of a Woman,* ix.

66. As quoted in Tayler's convenient gathering of "symbolic readings" in *Donne's Idea of a Woman,* 12–13. The statements are taken from Miner, *The Metaphysical Mode from Donne to Cowley* (Princeton: Princeton University Press, 1969); Martz, *The Poetry of Meditation;* and Lewalski, *Donne's* Anniversaries *and the Poetry of Praise.*

67. Docherty, *John Donne, Undone,* 229; Tayler, *Donne's Idea of a Woman,* ix, 135. Docherty's argument is more complex than Tayler makes it out to be, but it is still ironic that Tayler debunks Docherty for claiming much the same thing Tayler ends up asserting at the close of his book.

68. Schiesari, *The Gendering of Melancholia,* 52.

69. See Bald, *A Life,* 240 and Tayler's reconstruction of the cynic's "worst-case" composition history in *Donne's Idea of a Woman,* 5–7.

70. Sarah Kofman, *The Enigma of Woman: Woman in Freud's Writings,* trans. Catherine Porter (Ithaca: Cornell University Press, 1985), 52. Also pertinent to Donne's poetic argument here is Freud's suggestion that the man's overvaluation of the love object is in some cases occasioned by an attempt to regain a plenitude that, again following Freud's characterization of feminine sexuality, would make the man lovable (Freud repeatedly stresses the difference between masculine love, which is active in its aim to love, and feminine love, which is passive in its aim to be loved). In the instance of the Anniversaries Donne's attempt to "follow worthinesse" as represented in the soul of Elizabeth Drury will make Donne lovable in the eyes of both Robert Drury and the Eternal Father.

71. Marotti, *Coterie Poet,* 239. For two serious, yet quite different, treatments of Donne's misogyny see Christopher Ricks, "Donne after Love," in Elaine Scarry, ed., *Literature and the Body: Essays on Populations and Persons* (Baltimore: Johns Hopkins University Press, 1988),

33–69; and Achsah Guibbory, " 'Oh, Let Mee Not Serve So': The Politics of Love in Donne's *Elegies," ELH* 57 (1990): 811–32.

72. Laqueur, *Making Sex: Body and Gender from the Greeks to Freud* (Cambridge: Harvard University Press, 1990).

73. On Freud and Lacan see Juliet Mitchell and Jacqueline Rose, eds., *Feminine Sexuality: Jacques Lacan and the Ecole Freudienne* (New York: Norton, 1982), 35; and Lacan, *The Four Fundamental Concepts,* 205.

74. Schiesari, *The Gendering of Melancholia,* 115. The apparently paradoxical combination of this enhanced sense of self and self-loathing is also explained by Freud's analysis of narcissistic loss. The identification of part of the ego with the lost object produces a split in the ego "in which hate and love contend with each other; the one seeks to detach the libido from the object, the other to maintain this position of the libido against the assault"; this ambivalence "is represented to consciousness as a conflict between one part of the ego and the critical agency," and "the ego may enjoy in this the satisfaction of knowing itself as the better of the two, as superior to the object" (SE 14: 256, 257).

75. As Elizabeth Grosz points out, Lacan's famous theory of the mirror stage "can be interpreted as his attempt to fill in the genesis of the narcissistic ego"; "the mirror stage initiates the child into the two-person structure of imaginary identifications, orienting it forever towards identification with and dependence on (human) images and representations for its own forms or outline." See Grosz, *Jacques Lacan: A Feminist Introduction* (London and New York: Routledge, 1990), 31, 48.

76. Kerrigan, *The Literary Freud: Mechanisms of Defense and the Poetic Will,* ed. Joseph H. Smith, M.D., Psychiatry and the Humanities Vol. 4 (New Haven: Yale University Press, 1980), 289. Other references to Kerrigan's chapter appear in my text.

77. Schiesari writes of the Renaissance melancholic: "The sense of loss privileges a male subject as historically sensitive or lyrically sentient. *He* is the one privileged to understand and to speak the loss of God in a philosophical register that reinstates God's omnipotence, the loss of textual authority through a proliferation of citations that seeks to reclaim that authority, the loss of a phallus refound by the very discourse that mourns that loss *insofar as that mourning is marked by a masculine prerogative" (The Gendering of Melancholia,* 256). There is also a *class* dimension to this tradition: "melancholy is equivalent to spiritual grandeur and characteristic of certain men in whom is displayed a nobility of line and a nobility of spirit" (258–59).

78. Lacan's formulation in *Encore* seems apropos: "For the soul to come into being, she, the woman, is differentiated from it . . . called woman and defamed." For this passage and for a discussion of the elevation of woman to the place of the Other I am here again drawing on Jacqueline Rose, "Introduction II," in Mitchell and Rose, *Feminine Sexuality,* 48–49, 50.

79. Mueller, "Women among the Metaphysicals," 149.

80. See Manley's note (193), which cites Luke 11: 27–28.

81. Manley (176) points out the pun ("hims") in line 37. Ira Clark also comments on these lines and relates them to Donne's larger misogynistic argument (" 'How Witty's ruine,' " 23). For a rich discussion of maternity and the Anniversaries, see Harvey, *Ventriloquized Voices,* chap. 3.

82. Quoted from a discussion paper by Kristeva on *"Histoires d'amour—Love Stories"* for the Institute of Contemporary Arts, in John Lechte, "Art, Love, and Melancholy in the Work of Julia Kristeva," in Fletcher and Benjamin, *Abjection, Melancholia and Love,* 25.

83. *The Kristeva Reader,* ed. Toril Moi (New York: Columbia University Press, 1986), 95. This passage and Kristeva's extended discussion of "the signifying process" as constituted by the two "modalities" of the semiotic and the symbolic is found in *Revolution in Poetic Language,* trans. Margaret Waller (New York: Columbia University Press, 1984). I am following also Elizabeth Grosz's discussion of religious discourse as a "recoding" of the semiotic in

symbolic terms in her critique of Kristeva, "The Body of Signification," in Fletcher and Benjamin, *Abjection, Melancholia, and Love,* 99.

84. Quoted by Grosz, "The Body of Signification," 99, from Kristeva, *Tales of Love,* trans. Leon S. Roudiez (New York: Columbia University Press, 1987), 251.

85. Jonson, *Works,* Herford and Simpson, eds., 1: 133.

86. Lechte, "Art, Love, and Melancholy," 27.

87. See Rose, "Introduction II," in Mitchell and Rose, *Feminine Sexuality,* 49: "In relation to the man, woman comes to stand for both difference and loss." See also Schiesari, *The Gendering of Melancholia,* 111–12. It is curious that Donne uses the image of the coin impressed with the King's seal, which recollects the Aristotelian account of procreation as male form impressed on female matter and momentarily feminizes Donne and foregrounds the client-patron relationship out of which the Anniversaries arose. Both nuances make it possible to read the paternal "stampe" to refer to God and Sir Robert.

88. *The Kristeva Reader,* 115–16.

89. In Lacanian terms, the *objet a,* the lost object of desire that would restore the feeling of plenitude, always eludes symbolization. On the object *a,* see Bracher, *Lacan, Discourse, and Social Change,* 40–45.

Chapter 5

1. For a suggestive psychological reading, see A. L. French, "The Psychopathology of the 'Holy Sonnets,'" *Critical Review* 13 (1970): 111–24. Notable doctrinal approaches include John Stachniewski, "John Donne: The Despair of the 'Holy Sonnets,'" *ELH* 48 (1981): 677–705 and Richard Strier, "John Donne Awry and Squint: The 'Holy Sonnets,'" *Modern Philology* (1989): 357–84.

2. Fish, "Masculine Persuasive Force: Donne and Verbal Power," in Elizabeth D. Harvey and Katharine Eisaman Maus, eds., *Soliciting Interpretation: Literary Theory and Seventeenth-Century English Poetry* (Chicago: University of Chicago Press, 1990), 223.

3. Fish, "Masculine Persuasive Force," 250, 251.

4. Greenblatt, *Renaissance Self-Fashioning: From More to Shakespeare* (Chicago: University of Chicago Press, 1981), 125.

5. Sinfield, *Faultlines: Cultural Materialism and the Politics of Dissident Reading* (Berkeley: University of California Press, 1992), 173–74. Greenblatt critiques his own earlier work in the first chapter of *Shakespearean Negotiations: The Circulation of Social Energy in Renaissance England* (Berkeley: University of California Press, 1988).

6. Sinfield, *Faultlines,* 61, 65.

7. Maus, "Proof and Consequences: Inwardness and Its Exposure in the English Renaissance," *Representations* 34 (spring 1991): 30, 31. Maus's article has been incorporated into a larger argument concerning new historicist and materialist work on subjectivity in *Inwardness and Theater in the English Renaissance* (Chicago: University of Chicago Press, 1995).

8. Louis Althusser, *Lenin and Philosophy and Other Essays,* trans. Ben Brewster (New York: Monthly Review Press, 1971), 178–79.

9. For the notion of subjectivity-effects, I draw here and elsewhere in this chapter on Sinfield, *Faultlines,* esp. chaps. 3 and 7, and on the work of Joel Fineman, *Shakespeare's Perjured Eye* (Berkeley and Los Angeles: University of California Press, 1986), "Shakespeare's Ear," *Representations* 28 (fall 1989): 6–13, and *The Subjectivity Effect in Western Literary Tradition: Essays toward the Release of Shakespeare's Will* (Cambridge, Mass.: MIT Press, 1991).

10. Ferry, *The "Inward" Language: Sonnets of Wyatt, Sidney, Shakespeare, and Donne* (Chicago: University of Chicago Press, 1983), 249. It should be emphasized that Ferry's main concern in her book is to demonstrate the *rarity* of references in the early modern period to inwardness in the sense of a state that cannot be represented completely.

11. I am drawing here on Fineman's own summary of his work in his 1989 article on "Shakespeare's Ear," 6–8. The article is reprinted in his *The Subjectivity Effect,* 222–31.

12. See Fineman, "Shakespeare's Ear," 11, 7.

13. Fineman, "Shakespeare's 'Perjur'd Eye,' " in Stephen Greenblatt, ed., *Representing the English Renaissance* (Berkeley: University of California Press, 1988), 154.

14. Gardner, ed., *The Divine Poems,* 2d ed. (Oxford: Clarendon Press, 1978), xxxi, xxxii. Passages from the Holy Sonnets are quoted in my text from this edition.

15. Ferry, *The "Inward" Language,* 243.

16. Marotti, *John Donne: Coterie Poet* (Madison: University of Wisconsin Press, 1986), 257, 253.

17. Marotti, *Coterie Poet,* 260.

18. Strier, "John Donne Awry and Squint," 374.

19. French, "The Psychopathology of the 'Holy Sonnets,' " 113.

20. French, "The Psychopathology of the 'Holy Sonnets,' " 124.

21. French's turnaround at the end of his essay resembles Foucault's account of rescuing the author through the concept of *ecriture,* in "What Is an Author?" *Language, Counter-Memory, and Practice,* ed. Donald Bouchard (Ithaca: Cornell University Press, 1977), 119–20.

22. Smith, *Discerning the Subject* (Minneapolis: University of Minnesota Press, 1988), 152, 157.

23. See Sinfield, *Faultlines,* 174.

24. In addition to Maus's work already mentioned see also Elizabeth Hanson, "Torture and Truth in Renaissance England," *Representations* 34 (spring 1991): 53–84: "In the Catholic accounts [of treason trials], the lie perpetrated by governmental torturers was to treat a realm of experience that the victims increasingly defined as interior, private, and subjective *as though* it were external reality" (55).

25. Hurstfield, *Freedom, Corruption and Government in Elizabethan England* (London: Jonathan Cape, 1973); Bossy, *The English Catholic Community, 1570–1850* (London: Darnton, Longman, and Todd, 1975); Pritchard, *Catholic Loyalism in Elizabethan England* (Chapel Hill: University of North Carolina Press, 1979); Peter Holmes, *Resistance and Compromise: The Political Thought of Elizabethan Catholics* (Cambridge: Cambridge University Press, 1982). Christopher Haigh offers critical overviews in "From Monopoly to Minority: Catholicism in Early Modern England," *Transactions of the Royal Historical Society,* 5th Series, 31 (1981): 129–47 and "The Continuity of Catholicism in the English Reformation," *Past and Present* 93 (1981): 37–69.

26. On the commonplace and its origins, see Conyers Read, *Lord Burghley and Queen Elizabeth* (New York: Knopf, 1960), 565, n. 49. For a pertinent discussion of its relevance to the question of inwardness, see Maus, *Inwardness and Theater,* 82–85.

27. *The Execution of Justice in England by William Cecil and A True, Sincere, and Modest Defense of English Catholics by William Allen,* ed. Robert M. Kingdon (Ithaca: Cornell University Press, 1965), 9–10.

28. Hurstfield, *Freedom, Corruption, and Government,* 89–90.

29. MacCaffrey, *Queen Elizabeth and the Making of Policy, 1572–1588* (Princeton: Princeton University Press, 1981), 136, 137.

30. MacCaffrey, *Queen Elizabeth and the Making of Policy,* 138. In *Treason in Tudor England: Politics and Paranoia* (Princeton: Princeton University Press, 1986), Lacey Baldwin Smith has explored at length the curious interrelationship of rebellious behavior and "normal" Tudor politics, concluding that "If Tudor plotting appears 'feckless, scarcely concealed, and bizarre,' the infantilism must be judged and explained in terms of the larger political world whence it sprang and which manifested the same childishness, absurdity, suspiciousness and apparent irrationality" (33).

31. Southwell, *An Humble Supplication to Her Maiestie,* ed. R. C. Bald (Cambridge:

Cambridge University Press, 1953), 8–9. References to the *Humble Supplication* are from this edition and appear in my text.

32. Weiner, "The Beleaguered Isle: A Study of Elizabethan and Early Jacobean Anti-Catholicism," *Past and Present* 51 (1971): 38.

33. This exchange is quoted in Pierre Janelle, *Robert Southwell the Writer* (London, 1935), 81–82.

34. Smith, *Treason in Tudor England*, 17.

35. Bossy, "The Character of Elizabethan Catholicism," *Past and Present* 21 (1962): 53.

36. Pritchard, *Catholic Loyalism*, 198.

37. On this paradox of the Appellant position, see Pritchard, *Catholic Loyalism*, 190 and Maus, *Inwardness and the Theater*, 81.

38. This is the reading of Bald's copy text, MS Petyt 538.36 in the Library of the Inner Temple. The 1600 octavo reads, "we will rather yield our breasts to be broached by our enemies' swords, than use our swords to the effusion of our country blood" (quoted and modernized by Pritchard, *Catholic Loyalism,* 69). This version is also equivocal, patriotic in (apparently, although not certainly?) naming the invaders as "our enemies" and ambivalent in its commitments to the English cause.

39. Steven Mullaney, "Lying Like Truth: Riddle, Representation, and Treason in Renaissance England," *ELH* 47 (1980): 37, 41.

40. Bossy, "The Character of Elizabethan Catholicism," 51–52.

41. Bald, *John Donne: A Life* (Oxford: Clarendon Press, 1970), 66. Bald also discusses the possibility that Donne attended as a boy a meeting of Jesuits that included Southwell in the Tower of London to discuss the issue of addressing Elizabeth as "sacred" in the *Humble Supplication* (63–64).

42. See Maus, *Inwardness and the Theater:* "The authorities and the heretic collide in their assessment of the facts—facts which, it became increasingly clear in the course of the sixteenth century, are not subject to universally acknowledged proof or disproof" (77).

43. Carey, *John Donne: Life, Mind, and Art* (New York: Oxford University Press, 1980), 28.

44. In a letter to his friend Sir Henry Goodyer written during the period of composition of the Holy Sonnets, Donne supports Goodyer in "that sound true opinion, that in all Christian professions there is way to salvation." Quoted in John Carey, ed., *John Donne*, The Oxford Authors (New York: Oxford University Press, 1990), 196.

45. See Lacan, *Ecrits: A Selection*, trans. Alan Sheridan (New York: Norton, 1977): "It is in the *name of the father* that we must recognize the support of the symbolic function which, from the dawn of history, has identified his person with the figure of the law" (67); and "the symbolic Father is, in so far as he signifies this Law, the dead Father" (199).

46. Kerrigan, *The Sacred Complex: On the Psychogenesis of* Paradise Lost (Cambridge: Harvard University Press, 1983).

47. Ferry, *The "Inward" Language*, 236.

48. Ferry, *The "Inward" Language*, 236.

49. See Stanley Fish, *The Living Temple: George Herbert and Catechizing* (Berkeley: University of California Press, 1979).

50. Ferry, *The "Inward" Language*," 237.

51. Ferry, *The "Inward" Language*," 237.

52. Fish, "Masculine Persuasive Force," 249.

53. Fish, "Masculine Persuasive Force," 250.

54. Fish, "Masculine Persuasive Force," 251.

55. Donne's pun on his own name ("A Hymne to God the Father") has, I admit, been overworked. I would suggest, nonetheless, that the frequency of puns on *Fish's* name in contemporary critical discourse uncannily underwrites the identification with Donne. It goes without saying

that Fish's confession of his negative response to Donne is also an invitation to a psychoanalytic account of his relation to Donne.

56. Kerrigan, *Sacred Complex,* 73 et passim.

57. Eagleton, *Criticism and Ideology: A Study in Marxist Literary Theory* (1976; London: Verso, 1978), 88.

58. Eagleton, *Criticism and Ideology,* 88.

59. Eagleton, *Criticism and Ideology,* 86.

60. Strier, "John Donne Awry and Squint," 372. Further references to this article are noted in my text.

61. Although Strier opens the article by declaring his intention of taking "the psychological states portrayed in the 'Holy Sonnets' as biographically anchored and informative" (358), he, like French, whom he criticizes, personifies the poems by ascribing authenticity to the literary text.

62. On Donne's equivocations in *Metempsychosis,* see my "Donne's *Metempsychosis:* An 'Alarum to Truth,' " *SEL* 21 (1981): 97–110.

63. Printed in Evelyn M. Simpson, *A Study of the Prose Works of John Donne* (Oxford: Clarendon Press, 1948), 316.

64. In her edition Gardner also uses a passage from Donne's sermons to support a reading of "sins" as the antecedent of "them" (69); Barbara Lewalski is between Gardner and Strier in opting for the *sinful* self in her *Protestant Poetics and the Seventeenth-Century Religious Lyric* (Princeton: Princeton University Press, 1979), 270.

65. Here I follow Eagleton, who argues that the text produces ideological discourse—in this case, the Protestant doctrine of election—in such a way as to display disorder: "the relative coherence of ideological categories is revealed under the form of a concealment—revealed by the very *incoherence* of the text, by the significant disarray into which it is thrown in its efforts to operate its materials in the interests of a 'solution' " (*Criticism and Ideology,* 86).

66. Compare Sinfield, *Faultlines,* 161. Sinfield stresses the *Protestant* character of this subject. I believe the recusant experience sometimes worked in a similar way, so that it is a mistake to insist on a Protestant invention of inwardness. Agency, what you *do* with your resistance or contradictions, would seem to have a denominational identity, but Protestants did not hold a monopoly on contradiction and interiority in early modern England.

67. This equation of unresolved conflict and poetic brilliance is indeed a staple in criticism of the Holy Sonnets; in a recent study Anthony Low writes that Donne's "efforts to resolve his psychological conflicts, to accommodate his aggressive personality to a passive devotional stance based on an ancient system of religious metaphor, repeatedly fail. But the issue of his struggle is strong, admirable poetry." *The Reinvention of Love: Poetry, Politics and Culture from Sidney to Milton* (Cambridge: Cambridge University Press, 1993), 85.

68. See especially Louis M. Martz, *The Poetry of Meditation: A Study in English Religious Literature of the Seventeenth Century,* rev. ed. (New Haven: Yale University Press, 1962) and *The Paradise Within: Studies in Vaughan, Traherne, and Milton* (New Haven: Yale University Press, 1964); U. Milo Kaufmann, The Pilgrim's Progress *and Traditions in Puritan Meditation* (New Haven: Yale University Press, 1966); and Barbara K. Lewalski, *Protestant Poetics and the Seventeenth-Century Religious Lyric* (Princeton: Princeton University Press, 1979).

69. Sinfield, *Faultlines,* 159.

70. Hall, *The Arte of Divine Meditation* (1640 ed.), in *The Works of Joseph Hall* (London, 1647), 91. Compare Isaac Ambrose in *Prima, Media, and Ultima* (1659): "I have purposely omitted the many controversies and tedious conflicts of this age: for my part, I see little edifying in them; nay, is not the fat and marrow of Christian religion lost by them?" Ambrose, *Works* (Dundee: Hanry Galbraith and Co., 1759), b^r.

71. Hall, *Contemplations upon the Principall Passages of the Holy Storie,* vol. 4 (London, 1618), in *Works,* 1258.

72. Hall, *Works,* 1258.

73. Hall, *Works,* 1041.

74. Hall, *Works,* 1065.

75. For a strong counterstatement to the standard view of a Royalist Donne, see David Norbrook, "The Monarchy of Wit and the Republic of Letters: Donne's Politics," in Harvey and Maus, *Soliciting Interpretation,* 3–36.

76. The first phrase is from Ambrose, *Prima, Media, and Ultima,* in *Works,* b^r. Hall's phrase is from *Susurrium cum Deo. Soliloquies, or Holy Self-Conferences of the Devout Soul* (London, 1651), 58. For a critique of ironic and persona-based interpretations of the Holy Sonnets, see Stachniewski, "The Despair of the 'Holy Sonnets.' "

77. Donne's struggles with doctrinal issues in the Holy Sonnets have been explored at length from a variety of perspectives. For recent discussions see the articles by Stachniewski and Strier and chapter 7 of Sinfield's *Faultlines.*

78. King, *English Reformation Literature: The Tudor Origins of the Protestant Tradition* (Princeton: Princeton University Press, 1982), 84.

79. Fineman, "Shakespeare's Ear," 8.

80. Fineman, "Shakespeare's Ear," 9.

81. On the Lacanian Other in ideology, see Slavoj Žižek, *Enjoy Your Symptom! Jacques Lacan in Hollywood and Out* (New York: Routledge, 1992), 39–40. See also Anika Lemaire's summary of Lacan's developing thought on the Other in *Jacques Lacan,* trans. David Macey (New York: Routledge & Kegan Paul, 1977), 157. On the desire of the Other, see Lacan, *Four Fundamental Concepts of Psycho-Analysis,* ed. Jacques-Alain Miller, trans. Alan Sheridan (New York: Norton, 1981), 235–36; and the exposition by Mark Bracher, *Lacan, Discourse, and Social Change* (Ithaca: Cornell University Press, 1993), 19–21.

82. Kerrigan, "The Fearful Accommodations of John Donne," *English Literary Renaissance* 4 (1974): 346. References to this article will appear in my text. As noted earlier in this chapter, A. L. French's "The Psychopathology of Donne's Holy Sonnets" is another hard look at the psychological conflicts of the poems; like Kerrigan, French only at the last moment remystifies the poems.

83. See Strier, "John Donne Awry and Squint," 369.

84. Arthur Marotti reads the rape fantasy at the close of the poem as a homoerotic one and suggestively relates the homosexual theme to the patronage system and a rewriting of Petrarchan erotics (*Coterie Poet,* 259–60). Richard Rambuss finds "Donne imagining and embracing a limit experience with his God in terms of a homosexual bondage and rape fantasy." See Rambuss, "Pleasure and Devotion: The Body of Jesus and Seventeenth-Century Religious Lyric," in Jonathan Goldberg, ed., *Queering the Renaissance* (Durham and London: Duke University Press, 1994), 273. I believe it is a mistake to pin the desire down to either hetero- or homosexual choices. On this point of "homosexual" or "heterosexual" regulation of desire, see Jonathan Goldberg, *Sodometries: Renaissance Texts, Modern Sexualities* (Stanford: Stanford University Press, 1992), esp. chap. 2.

85. Rodowick, *The Difficulty of Difference: Psychoanalysis, Sexual Difference, and Film Theory* (New York: Routledge, 1991), x. I am indebted to the discussion of Freud's essay in chap. 4 of Rodowick's book.

86. Freud, "A Child Is Being Beaten," in *The Standard Edition of the Complete Psychological Works of Sigmund Freud,* trans. and ed. James Strachey, 24 vols. (London: Hogarth Press, 1955), 17: 198, 199. Hereafter abbreviated as SE.

87. Williams, "Power, Pleasure, and Perversion: Sadomasochistic Film Pornography," *Representations* 27 (summer 1989): 55, summarizing Parveen Adams, "Per Os(cillation)," *Camera Obscura* 17 (1988): 17–18, 28.

88. Žižek, *The Sublime Object of Ideology* (London: Verso, 1989), 43–44. Further references to this book appear in my text.

89. In addition to Williams's article, "Power, Pleasure, and Perversion," see her book *Hard Core: Power, Pleasure, and the "Frenzy of the Visible"* (Berkeley: University of California Press, 1989); Carol Clover, "Her Body, Himself: Gender in the Slasher Film," *Representations* 20 (fall 1987): 187–228; and Bracher, *Lacan, Discourse, and Social Change,* chap. 3.

90. Williams, "Power, Pleasure, and Perversion," 61.

91. Lacan, *Ecrits,* 322.

92. Freud, "A Child Is Being Beaten," 17: 197.

93. Lacan, *Ecrits,* 322.

94. My discussion of phallicization of the *jouissance* of the Other is indebted to an unpublished portion of a paper by Mark Bracher on "Culture as Phallicization of the Jouissance of the Other." For a playful version of the phallicization of (in this case) feminine *jouissance,* see "Divine Hammer" on the compact disk *Last Splash* by The Breeders, an alternative rock band fronted by twin sisters Kim and Kelly Deal.

95. For a different, object-relations perspective on this struggle for male identity which also underlines the importance of fantasy, see Janet Adelman's brilliant study of *Hamlet* in *Suffocating Mothers: Fantasies of Maternal Origin in Shakespeare's Plays, "Hamlet" to "The Tempest"* (New York: Routledge, 1992).

96. Bracher, "Culture as Phallicization," 16.

97. Strier, "John Donne Awry and Squint," 380.

98. Williams, "Power, Pleasure, and Perversion," 58.

99. Kaja Silverman, "Masochism and Male Subjectivity," *Camera Obscura* 17 (1988): 32. References to this essay appear in my text. This essay is incorporated in Silverman's *Male Subjectivity at the Margins* (New York: Routledge, 1992).

100. As Silverman points out, pathological masochism in males is actually what Freud terms "feminine masochism" in "The Economic Problem of Masochism." Freud implies as much when he says he will limit his discussion of feminine masochism to male patients (Freud, "The Economic Problem of Masochism" in SE 19: 161). A similar slippage occurs in "A Child Is Being Beaten," where Freud discusses primarily female cases but, as Silverman notes, "manages to articulate the masochistic desire he attributes to them only through recourse to one of his male patients, who speaks what they are unable to" ("Masochism and Male Subjectivity," 47). In "A Child" Freud notes of his male patients that "in their masochistic phantasies, as well as in the performances they go through for their realizations, they invariably transfer themselves into the part of a woman; that is to say, their masochistic attitude coincides with a *feminine* one" (SE 17: 197). Silverman offers a cultural explanation for the apparent anomaly of a disorder termed "feminine" occurring primarily in men: "Although masochism is a centrally structuring element of both male and female subjectivity, it is only in the latter that it can be safely acknowledged. It is an accepted—indeed a requisite—element of 'normal' female subjectivity, providing a crucial mechanism for eroticizing lack and subordination. The male subject, on the contrary, cannot avow his masochism without calling into question his identification with the masculine position, and aligning himself with femininity. All this is just another way of saying that what is acceptable for the female subject is pathological for the male" ("Masochism and Male Subjectivity," 36).

101. Reik, *Masochism in Sex and Society,* trans. Margaret H. Beigel and Gertrud M. Kurth (New York: Grove Press, 1962), 72, quoted in Silverman, "Masochism and Male Subjectivity," 43. Silverman points out that Reik's examples of Christian identification with the crucified Christ, "the very picture of divestiture and loss," suggest a potential in Christian masochism of challenge to "phallic values" and that "Christianity also redefines the paternal legacy," since "it is after all through the assumption of his place within the holy family that Christ comes to be installed in a suffering and castrated position" (44).

102. Indeed, in the case of males the crucial unconscious second phase of the fantasy, which is the fantasy of "Batter my heart" and which takes the form "I am being beaten by my father,"

is brought to consciousness by the substitution of the mother for the father, and this phase in male patients becomes the means whereby Freud constructs phase 2 of the female fantasy. On this point see Silverman, "Masochism and Male Subjectivity," 51.

103. See also "The Paradox," "The Expiration," "Negative Love," "The Dampe," "The Funerall," "The Will, "The Broken Heart," and "Loves Exchange."

104. Silverman remarks in passing that "[t]his talent for mimicry may lie at the bottom of all masochism" ("Masochism and Male Subjectivity," 44), a comment with considerable implications for students of literature.

105. This statement is quoted by Silverman from "a book which consistently comes down on the side of the father" ("Masochism and Male Subjectivity," 33) by Janine Chasseguet-Smirgel, *Creativity and Perversion* (London: Free Association Books, 1984), 12.

106. Deleuze, *Masochism: An Interpretation of Coldness and Cruelty*, trans. Jean McNeil (New York: George Braziller, 1971), 21, 58. I follow Silverman's reading of this work. Other important "utopian" studies include Rodowick, *The Difficulty of Difference*, 66–94; Leo Bersani, *The Freudian Body* (New York: Columbia University Press, 1986); and Jean-Francois Lyotard, "Fiscourse Digure: The Utopia Behind the Scenes of the Phantasy," trans. Mary Lydon, *Theatre Journal* 35 (Oct. 1983): 333–57.

107. Freud, "A Child Is Being Beaten," SE 17: 197, 199; Silverman, "Masochism and Male Subjectivity," 57.

108. For a description and discussion of this "Moloch" fantasy, see Silverman, "Masochism and Male Subjectivity," 51–55.

109. Freud, "A Child Is Being Beaten," SE 17: 185.

110. Freud, "A Child Is Being Beaten," SE 17: 199–200.

111. Freud, "A Child Is Being Beaten," SE 17: 189; italics appear in Strachey's translation.

112. Greenblatt, "Psychoanalysis and Renaissance Culture," in Patricia Parker and David Quint, eds., *Literary Theory/Renaissance Texts* (Baltimore: Johns Hopkins University Press, 1986), 221.

113. Greenblatt's account of causality in the essay on "Psychoanalysis and Renaissance Culture" strikes me as quite different from his critical practice of new historicism. For a critique of Greenblatt's privileging of historicism in this essay see David Lee Miller, "The Death of the Modern: Gender and Desire in Marlowe's 'Hero and Leander,' " *South Atlantic Quarterly* 88 (fall 1989): 758–61.

114. Rodowick, *The Difficulty of Difference*, 79.

115. Lyotard, "Fiscourse Digure," 351.

116. On the "desire to abolish the desire for the father's love" in male masochism, see Rodowick, *Difficulty of Difference*, 87.

117. Rodowick, *Difficulty of Difference*, 73.

118. Rodowick, *Difficulty of Difference*, 86.

119. "The boy's beating-phantasy is therefore passive from the very beginning, and is derived from a feminine [i.e., passive] attitude towards his father" (Freud, "A Child Is Being Beaten," SE 17: 198).

120. Rodowick, *Difficulty of Difference*, 88, 87.

121. Silverman also notes, however, that the terms of this agency "have already been culturally dictated to him. Here as elsewhere, perversion reflects what it undermines" ("Masochism and Male Subjectivity," 55).

122. Rodowick, *Difficulty of Difference*, 72.

123. Lyotard, "Fiscourse Digure," 354, 355. I am here indebted to Rodowick's reading of Lyotard. Lyotard's description of *jouissance* as a compromise between life and death parallels in some respects the Renaissance commonplace of orgasm as a little death: "*Jouissance* is not death,

but like death, at the same time that it discharges tension, it brings obscurity: the annihilation of representation, and the annihilation of words: silence" (355).

124. Rodowick, *Difficulty of Difference,* 94. Lyotard describes the form of fantasy as "*form in the grip of transgression*—but . . . also, potentially at least, *the transgression of form*" (354).

125. The phrases are Rodowick's, *Difficulty of Difference,* 94.

Bibliography

Adelman, Janet. "Male Bonding in Shakespeare's Comedies." *Shakespeare's "Rough Magic":
Renaissance Essays in Honor of C. L. Barber.* Ed. Coppelia Kahn and Peter Erickson.
Newark: University of Delaware Press, 1985. 73–103.

———. "Fantasies of Maternal Power in *Macbeth." Cannibals, Witches, and Divorce: Estranging
the Renaissance.* Ed. Marjorie Garber. Baltimore: Johns Hopkins University Press, 1987.
90–121.

———. *Suffocating Mothers: Fantasies of Maternal Origin in Shakespeare's Plays, "Hamlet"
to "The Tempest."* New York: Routledge, 1992.

Allen, Don Cameron. "Donne and the Ship Metaphor." *Modern Language Notes* 76 (1961):
308–12.

Althusser, Louis. "Ideology and Ideological State Apparatuses." *Lenin and Philosophy and Other
Essays.* Trans. Ben Brewster. New York: Monthly Review Press, 1971. 127–86.

Altman, Joel. *The Tudor Play of Mind: Rhetorical Inquiry and the Development of Elizabethan
Drama.* Berkeley: University of California Press, 1978.

Ambrose, Isaac. *Works.* Dundee: Henry Galbraith and Company, 1759.

Aries, Phillipe. *Centuries of Childhood: A Social History of Family Life.* Trans. Robert Baldick.
New York: Vintage, 1962.

Babcock, Barbara, ed. *The Reversible World: Symbolic Inversion in Art and Society.* Ithaca:
Cornell University Press, 1978.

Bald, R. C. *Donne and the Drurys.* Cambridge: Cambridge University Press, 1959.

———. *John Donne: A Life.* Oxford: Clarendon Press, 1970.

Barken, Leonard. *The Gods Made Flesh: Metamorphosis and the Pursuit of Paganism.* New
Haven: Yale University Press, 1986.

Barrett, Michele. *The Politics of Truth: From Marx to Foucault.* Stanford: Stanford University
Press, 1991.

Barthes, Roland. *The Pleasure of the Text.* Trans. Richard Miller. New York: Hill and Wang,
1975.

Bell, Ilona. "The Role of the Lady in Donne's Songs and Sonnets." *SEL* 23 (1983): 113–29.

Bellette, A. F. "The Originality of Donne's *Satires." University of Toronto Quarterly* 44 (1975):
130–40.

Belsey, Catherine. *Critical Practice.* London: Methuen, 1980.

————. *The Subject of Tragedy: Identity and Difference in Renaissance Drama.* London: Methuen, 1985.

Bennet, Tony. *Formalism and Marxism.* London: Methuen, 1979.

————. "Texts in History: The Determinations of Readings and Their Texts." *Post-structuralism and the Question of History.* Ed. Derek Attridge, Geoff Bennington, and Robert Young. Cambridge: Cambridge University Press, 1987. 63–81.

Bensinger, Terralee. "Lesbian Pornography: The Re/Making of (a) Community." *Discourse: A Journal for Theoretical Studies in Media and Culture* 15 (1992): 69–93.

Benvenito, B., and R. Kennedy. *The Works of Jacques Lacan: An Introduction.* London: Free Association Books, 1986.

Bergmann, Martin S. *The Anatomy of Loving: The Story of Man's Quest to Know What Love Is.* New York: Columbia University Press, 1987.

Bersani, Leo. *The Freudian Body.* New York: Columbia University Press, 1986.

Biersack, Aletta. "Local Knowledge, Local History: Geertz and Beyond." *The New Cultural History.* Ed. Lynn Hunt. Berkeley and Los Angeles: University of California Press, 1989. 72–96.

Blank, Paula. "Comparing Sappho to Philaenis: John Donne's 'Homopoetics.'" *PMLA* 110 (1995): 358–68.

Boose, Lynda. "The Father and the Bride in Shakespeare." *PMLA* 97 (1982): 325–47.

————. "The Family in Shakespeare Studies: or—Studies in the Family of Shakespeareans; or—The Politics of Politics." *Renaissance Quarterly* 40 (1987): 707–42.

————. "The Father's House and the Daughter in It: The Structures of Western Culture's Daughter-Father Relationship." *Daughters and Fathers.* Ed. Boose and Betty S. Flowers. Baltimore: Johns Hopkins University Press, 1989. 19–74.

Bossy, John. "The Character of Elizabethan Catholicism." *Past and Present* 21 (1962): 39–59.

————. *The English Catholic Community, 1570–1850.* London: Darton, Longman and Todd, 1975.

Bouwsma, William J. "Lawyers and Early Modern Culture." *American Historical Review* 78 (1973): 303–27.

Bracher, Mark. *Lacan, Discourse, and Social Change: A Psychoanalytic Cultural Criticism.* Ithaca: Cornell University Press, 1993.

————. "On the Psychological and Social Functions of Language: Lacan's Theory of the Four Discourses." *Lacanian Theory of Discourse: Subject, Structure, and Society.* Ed. Bracher et al. New York: New York University Press, 1994. 107–28.

————. "Culture as Phallicization of the Jouissance of the Other." Unpublished Manuscript.

Bradshaw, Graham. *Misrepresentations: Shakespeare and the Materialists.* Ithaca: Cornell University Press, 1993.

Bredbeck, Gregory W. *Sodomy and Interpretation: Marlowe to Milton.* Ithaca: Cornell University Press, 1991.

Breeders, The. "Divine Hammer." *Last Splash.* New York and Beverley Hills: Electra, 1993.

Breitenberg, Mark. *Anxious Masculinity in Early Modern England.* Cambridge: Cambridge University Press, 1996.

Broadbent, J. B. *Poetic Love.* London: Chatto and Windus, 1964.

Butler, Judith. *Gender Trouble: Feminism and the Subversion of Identity.* New York: Routledge, 1990.

————. *Bodies That Matter: On the Discursive Limits of "Sex."* New York: Routledge, 1993.

Carey, John. *John Donne: Life, Mind, and Art.* New York: Oxford University Press, 1981.

Castle, Terry. *The Apparitional Lesbian: Female Homosexuality and Modern Culture.* New York: Columbia University Press, 1993.

Chartier, Roger. *Cultural History: Between Practices and Representations.* Ithaca: Cornell University Press, 1988.

Cirillo, A. R. "The Fair Hermaphrodite: Love-Union in the Poetry of Donne and Spenser." *SEL* 9 (1969): 81–95.

Clark, Ira. " 'How Witty's ruine': The Difficulties of Donne's 'Idea of a Woman' in the First of His Anniversaries." *South Atlantic Review* 53 (1988): 19–26.

Clover, Carol. "Her Body, Himself: Gender in the Slasher Film." *Representations* 20 (1987): 187–228.

Colie, Rosalie. *Paradoxia Epidemica: The Renaissance Tradition of Paradox.* Princeton: Princeton University Press, 1966.

Collins, Stephen L. *From Divine Cosmos to Sovereign State: An Intellectual History of Consciousness and the Idea of Order in Renaissance England.* New York: Oxford University Press, 1989.

Cook, Carol. " 'The Sign and Semblance of Her Honor': Reading Gender Difference in *Much Ado about Nothing.*" *PMLA* 101 (1986): 186–202.

Corthell, Ronald J. " 'Friendships Sacraments': John Donne's Familiar Letters." *Studies in Philology* 78 (fall 1981): 409–25.

———. "Donne's Metempsychosis: An 'Alarum to Truth.' " *SEL* 21 (1981): 97–110.

———. "Style and Self in Donne's Satires." *Texas Studies in Literature and Language* 24 (summer 1982): 155–82.

———. " 'The secrecy of man': Recusant Discourse and the Elizabethan Subject." *ELR* 19 (autumn 1989): 272–90.

Crewe, Jonathan. *Unredeemed Rhetoric: Thomas Nashe and the Scandal of Authorship.* Baltimore: Johns Hopkins University Press, 1982.

———. *Trials of Authorship: Anterior Forms and Poetic Reconstruction from Wyatt to Shakespeare.* Berkeley and Los Angeles: University of California Press, 1990.

Dane, Peter. "The Figure of the Pinnace in 'Aire and Angels.' " *Southern Review: Literary and Interdisciplinary Essays* 12 (1979): 195–208.

Day, Gary. "Looking at Women: Notes toward a Theory of Porn." *Perspectives on Pornography: Sexuality in Film and Literature.* Ed. Day and Clive Bloom. New York: St. Martin's, 1988. 83–100.

De Lauretis, Teresa. *Technologies of Gender: Essays on Theory, Film, and Fiction.* Bloomington: Indiana University Press, 1987.

Deleuze, Gilles. *Masochism: An Interpretation of Coldness and Cruelty.* Trans. Jean McNeil. New York: George Braziller, 1971.

de Man, Paul. *Allegories of Reading: Figural Language in Rousseau, Nietzche, Rilke, and Proust.* New Haven: Yale University Press, 1979.

Docherty, Thomas. *John Donne, Undone.* London and New York: Methuen, 1986.

Dollimore, Jonathan. *Radical Tragedy: Religion, Ideology and Power in the Drama of Shakespeare and His Contemporaries.* Chicago: University of Chicago Press, 1984.

Donne, John. *The Poems of John Donne.* 2 vols. Ed. H. J. C. Grierson. Oxford: Clarendon Press, 1912.

———. *The Elegies and the Songs and Sonnets.* Ed. Helen Gardner. Oxford: Clarendon Press, 1965.

———. *John Donne: The Anniversaries.* Ed. Frank Manley. Baltimore: Johns Hopkins University Press, 1965.

———. *The Satires, Epigrams, and Verse Letters.* Ed. W. Milgate. Oxford: Clarendon Press, 1967.

———. *The Complete Poetry of John Donne.* Ed. John T. Shawcross. New York: Anchor Books, 1967.

———. *Letters to Severall Persons of Honour (1651).* Ed. M. Thomas Hester. Delmar, NY: Scolar, 1977.

————. *The Epithalamions, Anniversaries, and Epicedes.* Ed. W, Milgate. Oxford: Clarendon Press, 1978.

————. *The Songs and Sonets of John Donne.* Ed. Theodore Redpath. New York: St Martin's, 1983.

————. *John Donne.* Ed. John Carey. The Oxford Authors. New York: Oxford University Press, 1990.

Eagleton, Terry. *Criticism and Ideology: A Study in Marxist Literary Theory.* 1976; London: New Left Books, 1978.

————. *Literary Theory: An Introduction.* Minneapolis: University of Minnesota Press, 1983.

————. *The Ideology of the Aesthetic.* Cambridge, MA: Basil Blackwell, 1990.

————. *Ideology: An Introduction.* New York: Verso, 1991.

Easthope, Antony. *Literary into Cultural Studies.* London and New York: Routledge, 1991.

Eddy, Yvonne Shikany, and Daniel P. Jaeckle. "Donne's 'Satyre I': The Influence of Persius's 'Satire III.'" *SEL* 21 (1981): 111–22.

Elliott, Emory. "The Narrative and Allusive Unity of Donne's Satyres." *Journal of English and Germanic Philology* 75 (1976): 106–16.

Elliott, Robert C. *The Power of Satire: Magic, Ritual, Art.* Princeton: Princeton University Press, 1960.

Empson, William. "Donne the Space Man." *Kenyon Review* 19 (1957): 337–99.

————. "Donne in the New Edition." *Critical Quarterly* 8 (1966): 255–80.

————. "Rescuing Donne." *Just So Much Honor: Essays Commemorating the Four-Hundredth Anniversary of the Birth of John Donne.* Ed. Peter Amadeus Fiore. University Park: Pennsylvania State University Press, 1972. 95–148.

Erickson, Peter. *Patriarchal Structures in Shakespeare's Drama.* Berkeley: University of California Press, 1985.

————. *Rewriting Shakespeare, Rewriting Ourselves.* Berkeley and Los Angeles: University of California Press, 1991.

Erskine-Hill, Howard. "Courtiers out of Horace." *John Donne: Essays in Celebration.* Ed. A. J. Smith. London: Methuen, 1972. 273–307.

Felperin, Howard. "Canonical Texts and Non-Canonical Interpretations: The Neohistoricist Rereading of Donne." *Southern Review* 18 (1985): 235–50.

————. *The Uses of the Canon: Elizabethan Literature and Contemporary Theory.* Oxford: Clarendon Press, 1990.

Fenichel, Otto. "The Symbolic Equation: Girl = Phallus." *Psychoanalytic Quarterly* 18(1949): 303–24.

Ferguson, Margaret. "Nashe's *The Unfortunate Traveller*: The 'Newes of the Maker' Game." *ELR* 11 (1981): 165–82.

————. *Trials of Desire: Renaissance Defenses of Poetry.* New Haven: Yale University Press, 1983.

Ferry, Anne. *The "Inward" Language: Sonnets of Wyatt, Sidney, Shakespeare and Donne.* Chicago: University of Chicago Press, 1983.

Finkelpearl, Philip J. *John Marston of the Middle Temple.* Cambridge: Harvard University Press, 1969.

Findlay, Heather. "Dyke Porn 101: How to Enjoy (and Defend) Your Porn." *On Our Backs* 10 (1993): 14–43.

Fineman, Joel. *Shakespeare's Perjured Eye: The Invention of Poetic Subjectivity in the Sonnets.* Berkeley and Los Angeles: University of California Press, 1986.

————. "Shakespeare's 'Perjur'd Eye.'" *Representing the English Renaissance.* Ed. Stephen Greenblatt. Berkeley: University of California Press, 1988. 135–62.

————. "Shakespeare's Ear." *Representations* 28 (1989): 6–13.

———. *The Subjectivity Effect in Western Literary Tradition: Essays towards the Release of Shakespeare's Will*. Cambridge, MA: MIT Press, 1991.

Fish, Stanley. *The Living Temple: George Herbert and Catechizing*. Berkeley: University of California Press, 1979.

———. "Masculine Persuasive Force: Donne and Verbal Power." *Soliciting Interpretation: Literary Theory and Seventeenth-Century English Poetry*. Ed. Elizabeth D. Harvey and Katherine Eisaman Maus. Chicago: University of Chicago Press, 1990. 223–52.

Flynn, Dennis. "Donne and the Ancient Catholic Nobility." *ELR* 19 (autumn 1989): 305–23.

———. "Donne and a Female Coterie." *LIT: Literature, Interpretation, Theory* 1(1989): 127–36.

———. *Donne and the Ancient Catholic Nobility*. Bloomington and Indianapolis: Indiana University Press, 1995.

Foucault, Michel. *Language, Counter-Memory, and Practice*. Ed. Donald Bouchard. Ithaca: Cornell University Press, 1977.

———. *The History of Sexuality, Volume 1: An Introduction*. Trans. Robert Hurley. New York: Vintage, 1980.

———. *Power/Knowledge. Selected Interviews and Other Writings, 1972–1977*. Ed. Colin Gordon. New York: Pantheon, 1980.

Freccero, Carla. "The Other and the Same: The Image of the Hermaphrodite in Rabelais." *Rewriting the Renaissance: The Discourses of Sexual Difference in Early Modern Europe*. Ed. Margaret Ferguson, Maureen Quilligan, and Nancy Vickers. Chicago: University of Chicago Press, 1986. 145–58.

French, A. L. "The Psychopathology of the 'Holy Sonnets.'" *Critical Review* 13 (1970): 111–24.

Freud, Sigmund. "Three Essays on Sexuality." *The Standard Edition of the Complete Psychological Works of Sigmund Freud*. Vol. 7. Ed. James Strachey. London: Hogarth Press, 1981. 125–243.

———. "On Narcissism: An Introduction." *The Standard Edition of the Complete Psychological Works of Sigmund Freud*. Vol. 14. Ed. James Strachey. London: Hogarth Press, 1981. 73–102.

———. "Mourning and Melancholia." *The Standard Edition of the Complete Psychological Works of Sigmund Freud*. Vol. 14. Ed. James Strachey. London: Hogarth Press, 1981. 243–58.

———. "A Child Is Being Beaten." *The Standard Edition of the Complete Psychological Works of Sigmund Freud*. Vol. 17. Ed. James Strachey. London: Hogarth Press, 1981. 175–204.

———. "The Economic Problem of Masochism." *The Standard Edition of the Complete Psychological Works of Sigmund Freud*. Vol. 19. Ed. James Strachey. London: Hogarth Press, 1981. 157–70.

Fuller, Thomas. *The History of the Worthies of England*. London, 1662.

Gadamer, Hans-Georg. *Truth and Method*. Trans. William Glen-Doepel. New York: Crossroad, 1975.

Gallop, Jane. *The Daughter's Seduction: Feminism and Psychoanalysis*. Ithaca: Cornell University Press, 1982.

———. *Thinking through the Body*. New York: Columbia University Press, 1988.

Gardner, Helen. *The Business of Criticism*. Oxford: Clarendon Press, 1959.

Gilman, Ernest. *Iconoclasm and Poetry in the English Reformation: Down Went Dagon*. Chicago: University of Chicago Press, 1986.

———. " 'To adore, or scorne an image': Donne and the Iconoclastic Controversy." *John Donne Journal* 5 (1986): 62–100.

Goldberg, Jonathan. *James I and the Politics of Literature: Jonson, Shakespeare, Donne and Their Contemporaries*. Baltimore: Johns Hopkins University Press, 1983.

——— *Sodometries: Renaissance Texts, Modern Sexualities*. Stanford: Stanford University Press, 1992.

Gouge, William. *Of Domesticall Duties.* London, 1622.

Greenblatt, Stephen. "Invisible Bulletts: Renaissance Authority and Its Subversion." *Glyph* 8 (1981): 40–61.

———. "Psychoanalysis and Renaissance Culture." *Literary Theory/Renaissance Texts.* Ed. Patricia Parker and David Quint. Baltimore: Johns Hopkins University Press, 1986. 210–24.

———. *Renaissance Self-Fashioning: From More to Shakespeare.* Chicago: University of Chicago Press, 1981.

———. *Shakespearean Negotiations: The Circulation of Social Energy in Renaissance England.* Berkeley and Los Angeles: University of California Press, 1988.

Greene, Thomas M. "The Poetics of Discovery: A Reading of Donne's Elegy 19." *Yale Journal of Criticism* 2 (1989): 129–43.

Grosz, Elizabeth. *Jacques Lacan: A Feminist Introduction.* London and New York: Routledge, 1990.

———. "The Body of Signification." *Abjection, Melancholia, and Love: The Work of Julia Kristeva.* Ed. John Fletcher and Andrew Benjamin. New York: Routledge, 1990. 80–103.

Guibbory, Achsah. " 'Oh, Let Mee Not Serve So': The Politics of Love in Donne's Elegies." *ELH* 57 (1990): 811–33.

Haigh, Christopher. "From Monopoly to Minority: Catholicism in Early Modern England." *Transactions of the Royal Historical Society.* 5th Ser. 31 (1981): 129–47.

———. "The Continuity of Catholicism in the English Reformation." *Past and Present* 93 (1981): 37–69.

Hall, Joseph. *The Works of Joseph Hall.* London, 1647.

———. *Susurrium cum Deo. Soliloquies, or Holy Self-Conferences of the Devout Soul.* London, 1651.

Hall, Stuart. "Signification, Representation, Ideology: Althusser and the Post-Structuralist Debates." *Critical Studies in Mass Communication* 2 (June 1985): 91–114.

Hanson, Elizabeth. "Torture and Truth in Renaissance England." *Representations* 34 (1991): 53–84.

Hardin, Richard F. " 'Ritual' in Recent Criticism: The Elusive Sense of Community." *PMLA* 98 (1983): 846–62.

Harth, Erica. *Ideology and Culture in Seventeenth-Century France.* Ithaca: Cornell University Press, 1983.

Harvey, Elizabeth D. "Ventriloquizing Sappho: Ovid, Donne, and the Erotics of the Feminine Voice." *Criticism* 31 (1989): 115–38.

———. *Ventriloquized Voices: Feminist Theory and Renaissance Texts.* New York: Routledge, 1992.

Haskin, Dayton. "New Historical Contexts for Appraising the Donne Revival from A. B. Grosart to Charles Eliot Norton." *ELH* 56 (1989): 869–95.

———. "A History of Donne's 'Canonization' from Izaak Walton to Cleanth Brooks." *Journal of English and Germanic Philology* 92 (1993): 17–36.

Helgerson, Richard. *The Elizabethan Prodigals.* Berkeley: University of California Press, 1977.

———. *Self-Crowned Laureates: Spenser, Jonson, Milton and the Literary System.* Berkeley and Los Angeles: University of California Press, 1983.

Henderson, Katherine Usher, and Barbara F. McManus, eds. *Half Humankind: Contexts and Texts of the Controversy about Women in England, 1540–1640.* Urbana: University of Illinois Press, 1985.

Henderson, Lisa. "Lesbian Pornography: Cultural Transgression and Sexual Demystification." *New Lesbian Criticism: Literary and Cultural Readings.* Ed. Sally Munt. New York: Columbia University Press, 1992. 173–91.

Hester, M. Thomas. " 'Zeal' as Satire: The Decorum of Donne's Satyres." *Genre* 10 (1977): 173–94.

————. *Kind Pitty and Brave Scorn: John Donne's Satyres.* Durham, NC: Duke University Press, 1982.

Hill, Christopher. "The Problem of Authority." *Collected Essays of Christopher Hill. Vol. 2: Religion and Politics in Seventeenth-Century England.* Amherst: University of Massachusetts Press, 1986. 37–50.

Hodge, Robert. *Literature as Discourse: Textual Strategies in English and History.* Baltimore: Johns Hopkins University Press, 1990.

Hodge, Robert, and Gunther Kress. *Social Semiotics.* Ithaca: Cornell University Press, 1988.

Hodges, Devon. *Renaissance Fictions of Anatomy.* Amherst: University of Massachusetts Press, 1985.

Holmes, Peter. *Resistance and Compromise: The Political Thought of the Elizabethan Catholics.* Cambridge: Cambridge University Press, 1982.

Holstun, James. " 'Will You Rent Our Ancient Love Asunder?': Lesbian Elegy in Donne, Marvell, and Milton." *ELH* 54 (1988): 835–67.

————. "Ranting at the New Historicism." *ELR* (spring 1990): 189–225.

Hooker, Richard. *Of the Laws of Ecclesiastical Polity. The Folger Edition of the Works of Richard Hooker.* 2 vols. Ed. W. Speed Hill. Cambridge, MA: Harvard University Press, 1977.

Hulse, Clark. "Stella's Wit: Penelope Rich as Reader of Sidney's Sonnets." *Rewriting the Renaissance: The Discourses of Sexual Difference in Early Modern Europe.* Ed. Margaret W. Ferguson, Maureen Quilligan, and Nancy J. Vickers. Chicago: University of Chicago Press, 1986. 272–86.

Hunt, Clay. *Donne's Poetry: Essays in Literary Analysis.* New Haven: Yale University Press, 1954.

Hurstfield, Joel. *Freedom, Corruption and Government in Elizabethan England.* London: Jonathan Cape, 1973.

Irigaray, Luce. *Speculum of the Other Woman.* Trans. Gillian C. Gill. Ithaca: Cornell University Press, 1985.

Jameson, Frederic. *The Political Unconscious: Narrative as a Socially Symbolic Act.* Ithaca: Cornell University Press, 1981.

Janelle, Pierre. *Robert Southwell the Writer.* London: Sheed and Ward, 1935.

Johnson, Richard. "What Is Cultural Studies Anyway?" *Social Text* 6 (1987): 38–80.

Jones, Ann Rosalind. "Surprising Fame: Renaissance Gender Ideologies and Women's Lyric." *The Poetics of Gender.* Ed. Nancy K. Miller. New York: Columbia University Press, 1986. 74–95.

Jones, Ann Rosalind, and Peter Stallybrass. "The Politics of *Astrophil and Stella.*" *SEL* 24 (winter 1984): 51–68.

Jonson, Ben. *Works.* 11 vols. Ed. C. H. Herford and Percy Simpson. Oxford: Clarendon Press, 1925.

Jordan, Constance. *Renaissance Feminism: Literary Texts and Political Models.* Ithaca: Cornell University Press, 1990.

Kahn, Victoria. *Rhetoric, Prudence, and Skepticism in the Renaissance.* Ithaca: Cornell University Press, 1985.

————. "Habermas, Machiavelli, and the Humanist Critique of Ideology." *PMLA* 105 (May 1990): 464–76.

Kaufmann, U. Milo. *The Pilgrim's Progress and Traditions in Puritan Meditation.* New Haven: Yale University Press, 1966.

Kelly (-Gadol), Joan. *Women, History and Theory: The Essays of Joan Kelly.* Chicago: University of Chicago Press, 1984.

Kelly, Kathleen. "Conversion of the Reader in Donne's 'Anatomy of the World.' " *The Eagle and the Dove: Reassessing John Donne.* Ed. Claude J. Summers and Ted-Larry Pebworth. Columbia: University of Missouri Press, 1986. 147–56.

Kerrigan, William. "The Fearful Accommodations of John Donne." *ELR* 4 (1974): 337–63.

————. "The Articulation of the Ego in the English Renaissance." *The Literary Freud: Mechanisms of Defense and the Poetic Will.* Ed. Joseph H. Smith, M.D. New Haven: Yale University Press, 1980. 261–306.

————. *The Sacred Complex: On the Psychogenesis of Paradise Lost.* Cambridge: Harvard University Press, 1983.

Kerrigan, William, and Gordon Braden. *The Idea of the Renaissance.* Baltimore: Johns Hopkins University Press, 1989.

King, John. *English Reformation Literature: The Tudor Origins of the Protestant Tradition.* Princeton: Princeton University Press, 1982.

King, Margaret L. "The Death of the Child Valerio Marcello: Paternal Mourning in Renaissance Venice." *Renaissance Rereadings: Intertext and Context.* Ed. Maryanne Cline Horowitz, Anne J. Cruz, and Wendy A. Furman. Urbana: University of Illinois Press, 1988. 205–24.

————. *Women of the Renaissance.* Chicago: University of Chicago Press, 1991.

Kingdon, Robert M., ed. *The Execution of Justice in England by William Cecil and A True, Sincere, and Modest Defense of English Catholics by William Allen.* Ithaca: Cornell University Press, 1965.

Kofman, Sarah. *The Enigma of Woman: Woman in Freud's Writings.* Trans. Catherine Porter. Ithaca: Cornell University Press, 1985.

Kramer, Lloyd S. "Literature, Criticism, and Historical Imagination: The Literary Challenge of Hayden White and Dominick LaCapra." *The New Cultural History.* Ed. Lynn Hunt. Berkeley and Los Angeles: University of California Press, 1989. 97–130.

Kristeva, Julia. *The Powers of Horror: An Essay on Abjection.* Trans. Leon S. Roudiez. New York: Columbia University Press, 1982.

————. *Revolution in Poetic Language.* Trans. Margaret Waller. New York: Columbia University Press, 1984.

————. *The Kristeva Reader.* Ed. Toril Moi. New York: Columbia University Press, 1986.

————. *Tales of Love.* Trans. Leon S. Roudiez. New York: Columbia University Press, 1987.

Kuhn, Annette. *The Power of the Image: Essays on Representation and Sexuality.* London: Routledge, 1985.

Lacan, Jacques. *Ecrits: A Selection.* Trans. Alan Sheridan. New York: Norton, 1977.

————. *The Four Fundamental Concepts of Psycho-Analysis.* Ed. Jacques-Alain Miller. Trans. Alan Sheridan. New York: Norton, 1981.

————. *The Seminar of Jacques Lacan. Book I: Freud's Papers on Technique.* Ed. Jacques-Alain Miller. New York: Norton, 1988. 1953–54.

LaCapra, Dominick. *Rethinking Intellectual History: Texts, Contexts, Language.* Ithaca: Cornell University Press, 1983.

————. *History and Criticism.* Ithaca: Cornell University Press, 1985.

Laqueur, Thomas. *Making Sex: Body and Gender from the Greeks to Freud.* Cambridge: Harvard University Press, 1990.

Larraine, Jorge. *Marxism and Ideology.* New York: Humanities Press, 1983.

Lauritsen, John R. "Donne's *Satyres*: The Drama of Self-Discovery." *SEL* 16 (1976): 117–30.

Lechte, John. "Art, Love, and Melancholy in the Work of Julia Kristeva." *Abjection, Melancholia and Love: The Work of Julia Kristeva.* Ed. John Fletcher and Andrew Benjamin. New York: Routledge, 1990. 24–41.

Lein, Clayton. "Theme and Structure in Donne's Satire II." *Comparative Literature* 32 (1980): 130–50.

Lemaire, Anika. *Jacques Lacan.* Trans. David Macey. New York: Routledge, 1977.

Lentricchia, Frank. "Foucault's Legacy: A New Historicism?" *The New Historicism.* Ed. H. Aram Veeser. London and New York: Routledge, 1989. 231–42.

Lewalski, Barbara Keifer. *Donne's* Anniversaries *and the Poetry of Praise: The Creation of a Symbolic Mode.* Princeton: Princeton University Press, 1973.

214

——. *Protestant Poetics and the Seventeenth-Century Religious Lyric.* Princeton: Princeton University Press, 1979.

——. *Writing Women in Jacobean England.* Cambridge, MA: Harvard University Press, 1993.

Liu, Alan. "The Power of Formalism: The New Historicism." *ELH* 56 (1989): 721–71.

——. "Local Transcendence: Cultural Criticism, Postmodernism, and the Romanticism of Detail." *Representations* 32 (fall 1990): 75–113.

Low, Anthony. "Donne and the New Historicism." *John Donne Journal* 7 (1988): 125–31.

——. "Love and Science: Cultural Change in Donne's *Songs and Sonnets.*" *Studies in the Literary Imagination* 22 (1989): 5–16.

——. *The Reinvention of Love: Poetry, Politics, and Culture from Sidney to Milton.* Cambridge: Cambridge University Press, 1993.

Lyotard, Jean-Francois. "Fiscourse Digure: The Utopia behind the Scenes of the Phantasy." Trans. Mary Lydon. *Theatre Journal* 35 (1983): 333–57.

MacCaffrey, Wallace T. *Queen Elizabeth and the Making of Policy, 1572–1588.* Princeton: Princeton University Press, 1981.

Macherey, Pierre. *A Theory of Literary Production.* Trans. Geoffrey Wall. London: Routledge, 1978.

Maclean, Ian. *The Renaissance Notion of Woman.* Cambridge: Cambridge University Press, 1980.

Malloch, A. E. "Techniques and Function in Renaissance Paradox." *Studies in Philology* 53 (1956): 191–203.

Mann, Lindsay A. "The Typology of Woman in Donne's Anniversaries." *Renaissance and Reformation* 11 (1987): 337–50.

Marrotti, Arthur F. "John Donne and the Rewards of Patronage." *Patronage in the Renaissance.* Ed. Guy Fitch Lytle and Stephen Orgel. Princeton: Princeton University Press, 1981. 207–34.

——. " 'Love is not love': Elizabethan Sonnet Sequences and the Social Order." *ELH* 49 (1982): 396–428.

——. *John Donne: Coterie Poet.* Madison: University of Wisconsin Press, 1986.

——. "John Donne, Author." *Journal of Medieval and Renaissance Studies* 19 (spring 1989): 69–82.

——. "Shakespeare's Sonnets as Literary Property." *Soliciting Interpretation: Literary Theory and Seventeenth-Century English Poetry.* Ed. Elizabeth D. Harvey and Katherine Eisaman Maus. Chicago: University of Chicago Press, 1990. 143–73.

Martz, Louis. *The Poetry of Meditation: A Study in English Religious Literature of the Seventeenth Century.* Rev. ed. New Haven: Yale University Press, 1962.

——. *The Paradise Within: Studies in Vaughan, Traherne, and Milton.* New Haven: Yale University Press, 1964.

Marx, Karl. *The German Ideology. The Marx-Engels Reader.* Ed. Robert C. Tucker. 2d ed. New York: Norton, 1978.

Maus, Katherine Eisaman. "Proof and Consequences: Inwardness and Its Exposure in the English Renaissance." *Representations* 34 (spring 1991): 29–52.

——. *Inwardness and Theater in the English Renaissance.* Chicago: University of Chicago Press, 1995.

Maus, Katherine Eisaman, and Elizabeth D. Harvey. "Introduction." *Soliciting Interpretation: Literary Theory and Seventeenth-Century English Poetry.* Ed. Harvey and Maus. Chicago: University of Chicago Press, 1990. ix–xxii.

McCanles, Michael. "Paradox in Donne." *Studies in the Renaissance* 13 (1966): 266–87.

Miller, David Lee. "The Death of the Modern: Gender and Desire in Marlowe's 'Hero and Leander.' " *South Atlantic Quarterly* 88 (1989): 757–87.

Miner, Earl. *The Metaphysical Mode from Donne to Cowley.* Princeton: Princeton University Press, 1969.

215

Mitchell, Juliet. "Introduction I." *Feminine Sexuality: Jacques Lacan and the Ecole Freudienne.* Ed. Mitchell and Jaqueline Rose. New York: Norton, 1982. 1–26.

Montrose, Louis Adrian. *"A Midsummer Night's Dream* and the Shaping Fantasies of Elizabethan Culture: Gender, Power, Form." *Rewriting the Renaissance: The Discourses of Sexual Difference in Early Modern Europe.* Ed. Margaret W. Ferguson, Maureen Quilligan, and Nancy Vickers. Chicago: University of Chicago Press, 1986. 65–87.

———. "The Elizabethan Subject and the Spenserian Text." *Literary Theory/Renaissance Texts.* Ed. Patricia Parker and David Quint. Baltimore: Johns Hopkins University Press, 1986. 303–40.

———. "Professing the Renaissance: The Poetics and Politics of Culture." *The New Historicism.* Ed. H. Aram Veeser. London and New York: Routledge, 1989. 15–36.

Mueller, Janel. "Women among the Metaphysicals: A Case, Mostly, of Being Donne For." *Modern Philology* 87 (1989): 37–48.

———. "Troping Utopia: Donne's Brief for Lesbianism." *Sexuality and Gender in Early Modern Europe: Institutions, Texts, Images.* Cambridge: Cambridge University Press, 1993. 182–207.

Mullaney, Steven. "Lying Like Truth: Riddle, Representation, and Treason in Renaissance England." *ELH* 47 (1980): 32–47.

———. *The Place of the Stage: License, Play, and Power in Renaissance England.* Chicago: University of Chicago Press, 1988.

Newton, Richard C. "Donne the Satirist." *Texas Studies in Literature and Language* 16 (1974): 427–45.

Nicholson, Marjorie Hope. *The Breaking of the Circle: Studies in the Effect of the "New Science" upon Seventeenth-Century Poetry.* Rev. ed. New York: Columbia University Press, 1960.

Norbrook, David. "The Monarch of Wit and the Republic of Letters: Donne's Politics." *Soliciting Interpretation: Literary Theory and Seventeenth-Century English Poetry.* Ed. Elizabeth D. Harvey and Katherine Eisaman Maus. Chicago: University of Chicago Press, 1990. 3–36.

Novarr, David. *The Disinterred Muse: Donne's Texts and Contexts.* Ithaca: Cornell University Press, 1980.

Nyquist, Mary. "The Father's Word/Satan's Wrath." *PMLA* 100 (1985): 187–202.

———. "Fallen Differences, Phallogocentric Discourses: Losing Paradise Lost to History." *Post-Structuralism and the Question of History.* Ed. Derek Attridge, Geoff Bennington, and Robert Young. Cambridge: Cambridge University Press, 1987. 212–43.

Parker, Patricia. "Suspended Instruments: Lyric and Power in the Bower of Bliss." *Cannibals, Witches, and Divorce: Estranging the Renaissance.* Ed. Marjorie Garber. Baltimore: Johns Hopkins University Press, 1987. 21–39.

Patterson, Annabel. "Talking about Power." *John Donne Journal* 2 (1983): 91–106.

———. *Censorship and Interpretation: The Conditions of Writing and Reading in Early Modern England.* Madison: University of Wisconsin Press, 1984.

———. "All Donne." *Soliciting Interpretation: Literary Theory and Seventeenth-Century English Poetry.* Ed. Elizabeth D. Harvey and Katherine Eisaman Maus. Chicago: University of Chicago Press, 1990. 37–67.

Pechter, Edward. "The New Historicism and Its Discontents: Politicizing Renaissance Drama." *PMLA* 102 (1987): 292–303.

Pecora, Vincent. "The Limits of Local Knowledge." *The New Historicism.* Ed. H. Aram Veeser. London and New York: Routledge, 1989. 243–76.

Persons, Robert ("R. Doleman"). *A Conference about the Next Succession to the Crown of England.* 1594.

———. *A Temperate Ward-word to the Turbulent and Seditious Wach-word of Sir Francis Hastings.* 1599.

Phillips, John. *The Reformation of Images: Destruction of Art in England, 1535–1660.* Berkeley and Los Angeles: University of California Press, 1973.

Prest, Wilfred R. *The Inns of Court under Elizabeth I and the Early Stuarts, 1590–1640.* Totowa, NJ: Rowman & Littlefield, 1972.

Pritchard, Arnold. *Catholic Loyalism in Elizabethan England.* Chapel Hill: University of North Carolina Press, 1979.

Quint, David. *Origin and Originality in Renaissance Literature: Versions of the Source.* New Haven: Yale University Press, 1983.

Rajan, Tilottama. " 'Nothing Sooner Broke': Donne's Songs and Sonets as Self-Consuming Artifact." *ELH* 49 (1982): 805–28.

Rambuss, Richard. "Pleasure and Devotion: The Body of Jesus and Seventeenth-Century Religious Lyric." *Queering the Renaissance.* Ed. Jonathan Goldberg. Durham and London: Duke University Press, 1994. 253–79.

Read, Conyers. *Lord Burghley and Queen Elizabeth.* New York: Knopf, 1960.

Reik, Theodor. *Masochism in Sex and Society.* Trans. Margaret H. Beigel and Gertrud M. Kurth. New York: Grove Press, 1962.

Ricks, Christopher. "Donne after Love." *Literature and the Body: Essays on Populations and Persons.* Ed. Elaine Scarry. Baltimore: Johns Hopkins University Press, 1988. 33–69.

Roberts, John R. "John Donne's Poetry: An Assessment of Modern Criticism." *John Donne Journal* 1 (1982): 55–67.

Rodowick, D. N. *The Difficulty of Difference: Psychoanalysis, Sexual Difference, and Film Theory.* New York: Routledge, 1991.

Roof, Judith. *A Lure of Knowledge: Lesbian Sexuality and Theory.* New York: Columbia University Press, 1991.

Rose, Jacqueline. "Introduction II." *Feminine Sexuality: Jacques Lacan and the Ecole Freudienne.* Ed. Juliet Mitchell and Rose. New York: Norton, 1982. 27–57.

Rose, Mary Beth. *Expense of Spirit: Love and Sexuality in English Renaissance Drama.* Ithaca: Cornell University Press, 1988.

Rosten, Murray. *The Soul of Wit.* Oxford: Clarendon Press, 1974.

Ruffo-Fiore, Sylvia. "Donne's 'Parody' of the Petrarchan Lady." *Comparative Literature Studies* 9 (1972): 392–406.

Sanders, Wilbur. *John Donne's Poetry.* Cambridge: Cambridge University Press, 1971.

Schiesari, Juliana. *The Gendering of Melancholia: Feminism. Psychoanalysis, and the Symbolics of Loss in Renaissance Literature.* Ithaca and London: Cornell University Press, 1992.

Schwartz, Jerome. "Aspects of Androgyny in the Renaissance." *Human Sexuality in the Middle Ages and the Renaissance.* Ed. D. Radcliffe-Umstead. Pittsburgh: Center for Medieval and Renaissance Studies, University of Pittsburgh, 1978. 121–31.

Scodel, Joshua. "The Medium Is the Message: Donne's 'Satire 3,' 'To Sir Henry Wotton ("Sir, more then kisses"),' and the Ideologies of the Mean." *Modern Philology* 90 (1993): 479–511.

Sedgwick, Eve Kosofsky. *Between Men: English Literature and Male Homosocial Desire.* New York: Columbia University Press, 1985.

Shawcross, John T. " 'All Attest His Writs Canonical': The Texts, Meaning and Evaluation of Donne's Satires." *Just So Much Honor: Essays Commemmorating the Four-Hundredth Anniversary of the Birth of John Donne.* Ed. Peter A. Fiore. University Park: Pennsylvania State University Press, 1972. 245–72.

Shuger, Debora Kuller. *Habits of Thought in the English Renaissance: Religion, Politics, and the Dominant Culture.* Berkeley and Los Angeles: University of California Press, 1990.

Sicherman, Carol Marks. "The Mocking Voices of Donne and Marvell." *Bucknell Review* 17 (1969). 32–46.

Silberman, Lauren. "Mythographic Transformations of Ovid's Hermaphrodite." *Sixteenth-Century Journal* 19 (1988): 643–52.

Silverman, Kaja. *The Subject of Semiotics.* New York: Oxford University Press, 1983.

———. "Masochism and Male Subjectivity." *Camera Obscura* 17 (1988): 31–68.

———. *Male Subjectivity at the Margins.* New York: Routledge, 1992.

Simpson, David. *The Academic Postmodern and the Rule of Literature: A Report on Half-Knowledge.* Chicago: University of Chicago Press, 1995.

Simpson, Evelyn. *A Study of the Prose Works of John Donne.* Oxford: Clarendon Press, 1948.

Sinfield, Alan. "Power and Ideology: An Outline Theory and Sidney's Arcadia." *ELH* 52 (1985): 259–77.

———. *Faultlines: Cultural Materialism and the Politics of Dissident Reading.* Berkeley: University of California Press, 1992.

Smith, Lacy Baldwin. *Treason in Tudor England: Politics and Paranoia.* Princeton: Princeton University Press, 1986.

Smith, Paul. *Discerning the Subject.* Minneapolis: University of Minnesota Press, 1983.

Southall, Raymond. *Literature and the Rise of Capitalism: Critical Essays Mainly on the Sixteenth and Seventeenth Centuries.* London: Lawrence and Wishart, 1973.

Southwell, Robert. *An Humble Supplication to Her Maiestie.* Ed. R. C. Bald. Cambridge: Cambridge University Press, 1953.

Stachniewski, John. "John Donne: The Despair of the 'Holy Sonnets.' " *ELH* 48 (1981): 677–705.

Stein, Arnold. *John Donne's Lyrics: The Eloquence of Action.* Minneapolis: University of Minnesota Press, 1962.

Stone, Lawrence. *The Crisis of the Aristocracy 1558–1641.* Oxford: Clarendon Press, 1965.

———. *The Family, Sex, and Marriage in England, 1500–1800.* New York: Harper and Row, 1977.

Strier, Richard. "John Donne Awry and Squint: The 'Holy Sonnets.' " *Modern Philology* 86 (1989): 357–84.

———. *Resistant Structures: Particularity, Radicalism, and Renaissance Texts.* Berkeley and Los Angeles: University of California Press, 1995.

———. "The Root and Branch Petition and the Grand Remonstrance: From Diagnosis to Operation." *The Theatrical City: Culture, Theatre, and Literature in London, 1576–1649.* Ed. David L. Smith, Richard Strier, and David Bevington. Cambridge: Cambridge University Press, 1995. 224–44.

Tayler, Edward. *Donne's Idea of a Woman: Structure and Meaning in* The Anniversaries. New York: Columbia University Press, 1991.

Teager, Florence S. "Patronage of Joseph Hall and John Donne." *Philological Quarterly* 15 (1936): 408–12.

Thomas, Brook. "The New Historicism and Other Old-Fashioned Topics." *The New Historicism.* Ed. H. Aram Veeser. London and New York: Routledge, 1989. 182–203.

Tourney, Leonard. "Joseph Hall and the Anniversaries." *Papers on Language and Literature* 13 (1977): 25–34.

Traub, Valerie. "Jewels, Statues, and Corpses: Containment of Female Erotic Power in Shakespeare's Plays." *Shakespeare Studies* 20 (1988): 215–38.

———. "The (In)significance of 'Lesbian' Desire in Early Modern England." *Erotic Politics: Desire on the Renaissance Stage.* Ed. Susan Zimmerman. New York: Routledge, 1992. 150–69.

———. *Desire and Anxiety: Circulations of Sexuality in Shakespearean Drama.* New York: Routledge, 1992.

Turner, James Grantham. *One Flesh: Paradisal Marriage and Sexual Relations in the Age of Milton.* Oxford: Oxford University Press, 1987.

Turner, Victor. *The Ritual Process: Structure and Anti-Structure.* Ithaca: Cornell University Press, 1969.

———. "Comments and Conclusions." *The Reversible World: Symbolic Inversion in Art and Society.* Ed. Barbara Babcock. Ithaca: Cornell University Press, 1978. 276–96.

Vickers, Nancy J. "Diana Described: Scattered Woman and Scattered Rhyme." *Writing and Sexual Difference.* Ed. Elizabeth Abel. Chicago: University of Chicago Press, 1982. 95–109.

Waddington, Raymond. " 'All in All': Shakespeare, Milton, Donne, and the Soul-in-Body Topos." *ELR* 20 (1990): 40–68.

Weeks, Jeffery. *Sexuality and Its Discontents: Meanings, Myths and Modern Sexualities.* London: Routledge, 1985.

Weimann, Robert. "Discourse, Ideology and the Crisis of Authority in Post-Reformation England." *The Yearbook of Research in English and American Literature.* Vol. 5. Berlin, New York: De Gruyter, 1987. 109–40.

———. " 'Bifold Authority' in Reformation Discourse: Authorization, Representation, and Early Modern 'Meaning.' " *Historical Criticism and the Challenge of Theory.* Ed Jane L. Smarr. Urbana: University of Illinois Press, 1993. 167–82.

———. *Authority and Representation in Early Modern Discourse.* Ed. David Hillman. Baltimore: Johns Hopkins University Press, 1996.

Weiner, Carol Z. "The Beleaguered Isle: A Study of Elizabethan and Early Jacobean Anti-Catholicism." *Past and Present* 51 (May 1971): 27–62.

West, Robert H. *Milton and the Angels.* Athens, GA: University of Georgia Press, 1955.

Whately, William. *A Bride-Bush.* London, 1619.

Whigham, Frank. "The Rhetoric of Elizabethan Suitors' Letters." *PMLA* 96 (1981): 864–82.

———. *Ambition and Privilege: The Social Tropes of Elizabethan Courtesy Theory.* Berkeley and Los Angeles: University of California Press, 1984.

Whittier, Gayle. "The Sublime Androgyne Motif in Three Shakespearean Works." *Journal of Medieval and Renaissance Studies* 19 (1989): 185–210.

Wiggins, Peter De Sa. " 'Aire and Angels': Incarnations of Love." *ELR* 12 (1982): 87–101.

Williams, Linda. "Power, Pleasure, and Perversion: Sadomasochistic Film Pornography." *Representations* 27 (summer 1989): 37–65.

———. *Hard Core: Power, Pleasure, and the "Frenzy of the Visible."* Berkeley: University of California Press, 1989.

Wilson, Luke. "William Harvey's Prelectiones: The Performance of the Body in the Renaissance Theater of Anatomy." *Representations* 17 (1987): 62–95.

Woodbridge, Linda. *Woman and the English Renaissance: Literature and the Nature of Womankind, 1540–1620.* Urbana: University of Illinois Press, 1984.

Žižek, Slavoj. *The Sublime Object of Ideology.* New York and London: Verso, 1989.

———. *Enjoy Your Symptom! Jacques Lacan in Hollywood and Out.* New York: Routledge, 1992.

Index

Abjection, 123, 195n49

Adams, Parveen, 155

Agamben, Giorgio, 125

"Aire and Angels," 68, 75–82, 130; criticism of, 75–76; critique of Neoplatonism in, 78–79; inversion in, 84; master signifier in, 193n30; search for sexual identity in, 76, 78, 81, 82, 184n104; ship metaphor in, 80–81

Allen, Cardinal: *A True, Sincere and Modest Defense of English Catholics,* 140

Allen, Don Cameron, 80

Althusser, Louis: concept of interpellation, 15, 135, 155; subject of power, 21

Altman, Joel: *The Praise of Folly,* 67

"An Anatomy of the World" (First Anniversary), 109, 112, 131, 194n39; abjection in, 123; argument of, 117; baptismal conceit in, 120–21; Idea of a woman in, 110, 129–30; masculine subject position of, 129; naming as means of constructing subject in, 118–19; notion that orgasm shortens life in, 129; original sin analogy in, 118; as poem of process, 122–23; reader as a major concern of, 116

Androgyny, in "The Canonization," 91–92

Anger, Jane, 84

Anniversaries: abjection in, 123; critical readings of, 107–9, 113; Donne's explanations of his purpose in, 110, 111;

Donne's Idea of a Woman in, 109, 110, 130, 131–33, 193n30; and father-daughter relationship, 126–27; Hall's prefatory poems to, 109, 114–16; importance of desire in interpreting, 109; masculine subject-position of, 125–27, 129, 131–33; and narcissism, 124, 125, 126–27, 130; as poems about representation, 112–13, 121–22; as poems of process, 122–24, 131; as production of aesthetic ideology, 114, 121; as product of culture of patronage, 126; psychoanalytic approach to, 124; reading subject of, 111. *See also* "An Anatomy of the World"; "The Progres of the Soule"

Archpriest (Appellant) Controversy, 141–42

Aries, Philippe, 115

Aristophanes: *Symposium,* 104

Aristotelian mimesis, 98

Autoeroticism, in "Sapho to Philaenis," 72

Babcock, Barbara, 58

Bald, R. C., 142; *Donne and the Drurys,* 126; *Humble Supplication to Her Maiestie* (Ed.), 44; *John Donne: A Life,* 12, 26, 126

Bancroft, Richard, 45, 176n78

Baptism, 120

Barthes, Roland, 178n14

Bateson, Gregory, 26

"Batter my heart," 21, 147, 152–65; masochism in, 159–64; meaning of chastity